I Know What
Prayer
Can Do

CORDELL MAY THORPE

◆ FriesenPress

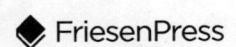

Suite 300 - 990 Fort St
Victoria, BC, V8V 3K2
Canada

www.friesenpress.com

Copyright © 2018 by Cordell May Thorpe
First Edition — 2018

All rights reserved.

No part of this publication may be reproduced in any form, or by any means, electronic or mechanical, including photocopying, recording, or any information browsing, storage, or retrieval system, without permission in writing from FriesenPress.

ISBN
978-1-5255-1443-2 (Hardcover)
978-1-5255-1444-9 (Paperback)
978-1-5255-1445-6 (eBook)

1. RELIGION, CHRISTIAN LIFE, SPIRITUAL WARFARE

Distributed to the trade by The Ingram Book Company

I Know What
Prayer
Can Do

Table of Contents

Preface: It Is Not over until It Is over — ix

Introduction: Aunt Charlotte's Philosophy of Prayer — xviii

1. The Indispensable Weapon of Prayer — 1
2. The Prayer Empowered Church: Part A — 26
3. The Prayer-Empowered Church: Part B — 39
4. The Prayer-Empowered Church: Part C — 67
5. The Key Ingredients of an Effective Prayer — 80
6. The Authority of the Name of Jesus — 100
7. The Efficacy and Uniqueness of the Blood of Jesus: Part A — 106
8. The Efficacy and Uniqueness of the Blood of Jesus: Part B — 113
9. Agonizing in Gethsemane — 123
10. Not by Might, nor by Power, but by the Spirit of the Lord of Host — 127

11.	Praying in the Spirit	148
12.	Praying in Tongues and Interpretation	156
13.	Praying According to His Will, His Plans, and His Purpose	163
14.	Coupling Fasting with Prayer: Part A	171
15.	Coupling Fasting with Prayer: Part B	177
16.	Coupling Fasting with Prayer: Part C	187
17.	Coupling Fasting with Prayer: Part D	193
18.	Coupling Fasting with Prayer: Part E	205
19.	With Jesus in the School of Prayer	208
20.	Dissecting the Lord's Prayer: Part A	214
21.	Dissecting the Lord's Prayer: Part B	219
22.	Dissecting the Lord's Prayer: Part C	225
23.	Dissecting the Lord's Prayer: Part D	229
24.	Dissecting the Lord's Prayer: Part E	232
25.	Dissecting the Lord's Prayer: Part F	238
26.	The Characteristics of Demons and the Error of Satanic Consultation	240

27.	Demonic Possession	247
28.	Praying for a Revival Revolution	250
29.	An Eternal Perspective in a Temporal World	264
30.	Wait with Joyful Hope and Expectation	284
31.	Desperate Situations Call for Desperate Actions	296
32.	The Unfailing, Unlimited Power of Prayer	306

Dedication	325
Acknowledgements	326
Disclaimer	330
About the Author	331

Preface
It Is Not over until It Is over

One of the happiest days of my life was the day I began nursing school. Becoming a nurse had been my dream since childhood.

I vividly recall one Sunday when I went to church late. I sat in the back seat. I was eight years old. It was the first day of regional convention, and it was also harvest time. The ripe fruits and produce that bedecked the sanctuary filled the atmosphere with their pleasant aroma. A vibrant female evangelist, about twenty years old, sat on the other side of the room in the front.

Evangelist Graham, the keynote speaker, was an elderly man. Due to left hip surgery, he walked with a limp. During the morning service, he asked the pastor's wife for a ripe banana. When he received it, he called the vibrant young woman on the other side of the room to come forth. He gave her one portion of banana and commissioned her to feed the sheep. He called me to the front. He gave me the other portion of banana and commissioned me to feed the lambs. This was a declaration concerning my prophetic destiny. Though young, I understood the meaning. God was entrusting into my hands the ministry of feeding the flock—especially the younger generation. I received it.

At the end of the service, the evangelist took me aside with my mother and gave me this prophecy: "You are going to become a nurse, little girl … but!" He looked at me very compassionately and then told me to run along and play, because he wanted to speak to my mother privately.

He never explained to me what the "but" meant, but I'm certain he told my mother. Some years passed, and, as he prophesied, I entered nursing school. First semester came and went, and I passed with flying colours. I looked forward to second semester, because it was Labour and Delivery—my specialty.

The first night of the semester, I finished my homework then snuggled in bed. Suddenly, I felt something like a wave of electricity pass through my body. It was so powerful, I shivered and shook violently. It almost knocked me unconscious. I thought I was having a convulsion. An apparition in the form of a slim man entered my room and stood before me. I saw only from his waist down. He was wearing silvery-grey trousers with a black belt. I wasn't in a trance or having a dream. Whatever was happening was real, and it was happening very fast.

I recovered enough strength to sit up in bed. I rebuked this headless figuration and commanded it to leave. I prayed and lay down again. Within minutes, I felt that same wave of electricity coming upon my body again. I felt numb. Within a flash, I felt four cold fingers touch me at the nape of my neck on the left side, just below the hairline. Three swift blows followed in the same spot.

I jumped out of bed, rebuked that thing, and cursed it in the name of Jesus. "Get out of my room!" I thundered. I went into a season of prayer, but the semester in which I should have done the very best turned out to be the semester in which I did the worst. I never failed a subject or a course, but I didn't pass with the distinctions I was accustomed to.

Third semester came. It was pediatrics—my second specialty. First night of the semester, the same thing began to happen again. A strong wave of electric current came upon me. It was stronger than the one that hit me first semester. Cold fingers touched me in the same spot, but before the blows could be struck, I jumped out of bed. I cursed that foul spirit and sent it back to the sender. I reversed the order. I commanded it, in the name of Jesus Christ, never to come to my home again. I called upon the Lord to cover every exposed aspect of my being and the home with his blood. I anointed my head with oil and prayed over myself.

I claimed, in the name of Jesus, that the rest of my studies would be without untoward incidents.

I was taking my prophetic destiny to the next level. By the power of the Almighty, I would accomplish it. The devil has limited power; therefore, he must back up and back off. The spirits of hindrance and bondage must be eliminated and destroyed by the power of Almighty God.

Third semester flowed as smoothly as a sweet lullaby. Fourth and fifth semesters came and went without trouble. I attained academic success. During summer vacation after fifth semester, I met a man in the spirit world, and here is what he said to me:

"So you have finished fifth semester. You don't get it, do you? No matter what you do, you will never be a nurse. I've been sent to mess with your head. I asked God to allow me to touch your head, but God said that he would not permit me to do this. I am come to seek your permission to come into your head. Ha-ha ha-a-a-a!"

The laugh was sinister. The devil wanted to get into my head, but I was under divine, comprehensive covering and protection.

It was one of the most troubling spirit encounters I'd had up to that time. I cursed the devil and his minions in the name of Jesus: "You are a lying, foul spirit from hell. Take this message back to your dispatcher: I will become a nurse, in the name of Jesus. God decreed it, and I received it."

I engaged myself in a season of fasting and prayer. At the same time, I began an internship at the first hospital and did exceptionally well. When I was at the second hospital and had only three and a half weeks left to finish the program, I received a most devastating letter. It read:

"Cordell, we regret to inform you that we have to pull you from internship, because six months ago you failed the mock exam by two points. You have been an excellent student. The reports from your preceptors at the clinical sites attest that your performance is outstanding.

"Your in-class ratings are great, and you have passed all courses and exams, but the rule states that you must first pass the mock exam before you begin internship.

"Our thoughts are that if you cannot pass the mock test, you will not pass the College of Nurses' exam. We allowed you to begin internship because we thought you would have passed the mock. We are so sorry. The good news is that you can restart the semester in September."

My preceptor found me in the clean utilities room, limp and dumbstruck. When I came to myself, I bid her goodbye. Her name was Elizabeth, and she said this to me:

"Cordell, this is not natural. A devil from hell has tampered with your exam. I perceive in my spirit that you passed. I'll be praying for you."

She brushed her tears aside. "Thanks, Elizabeth."

I left the hospital forlorn and wondering about what just happened. I went home that February evening with my head pounding, and my hopes devastated.

What does a child of God do when all hope seems to be lost? Do you throw in the towel and quit? Not by a long shot. Every now and then bad things happen to faithful people. When they do, don't shrivel up and die. That's what the enemy wants. You need to handle adversity successfully. Nothing in the life of the righteous surprises God. The Lord knows about these things before they happen.

God knows about our past—he was there. God knows about our present—he is here in it. God knows about our future—he is already there. Certain things must happen so that we can learn to trust God totally. Folks need to understand that every bed of roses has its thorns.

Some things must happen so that we can discover our dependence upon God. If everything comes easily, we might become proud, careless, and neglectful. The one who has never known hardships will never learn to be empathetic towards others who are experiencing adversities.

Hear this reality: some things must die before they can live so that God can get the glory.

Had I not been tested, I would not have a testimony. It's not possible for anybody to have a "TEST-i-mony" in the absence of "test." Testimonies come through testing. There is no message without a "mess." If God allows it to happen to you, he will get you out of it.

I sat on my couch daily, crying out to God. I was embarrassed and depressed. My entire body was in pain. I was too ashamed to tell anyone, because everybody expected me to pass. The Cordell who helped everybody to pass should not fail.

I tried to focus on God, but those ill words of my childhood flooded my mind and made it hard to concentrate on the power of God to deliver. I heard a mocking lyricist singing loudly in my ears: "A child like you will never amount to anything in life. You will only go this far and turn back."

How do I turn the voice off? I went to the seventh-floor balcony and looked over. A voice said, "Jump, and it will be over. You won't have to face anybody, the shame, or the pain." I covered my ears.

Another voice said, "You cannot jump. Remember that your mother told you she wanted to hear a good report. What will happen to her when she hears this news? She will die."

Yet another voice said, "Shame will be brought upon your family if you jump."

Then a still, small voice said, "The children of God do not commit suicide; they seek the Lord in prayer. Satan, the blood of Jesus is against you. Take your suicide order back to hell."

I was alone at home and depressed, but I didn't jump. I went inside and closed the balcony door. I regained my composure when I remembered that Jesus is the answer. He has the antidote for every situation. I prayed in between the tears of frustration.

My brother, Winston, called me from overseas a week later. I told him my plight.

"My sister," he said, "only one semester to go. You cannot quit."

I remained at home for the next seven months. It was February, and the next class wouldn't begin until September. I went back and finished my program.

December came, and it was time for graduation. The Holy Spirit spoke to me, saying, "Your prize is waiting, but you will not be taking it home." The Lord chose not to tell me why I wouldn't receive my prize.

At the graduation ceremony, all the happy graduates were seated alphabetically. Everyone was jubilant as they received their prize. The atmosphere buzzed with laughter. The successful students poised as cameras flashed. It was my turn. I marched forward with ardent hope and anticipation. My prize was indeed there ... but alas! I would not be taking it home. Why?

My name was spelled Oordell Thorpe instead of Cordell Thorpe. Of all the 320 graduates, I was the only one who went home without the prize. No family beside me, no friends... but God.

This wasn't normal. I maintained my composure as I received the decorated piece of garbage. "We're so sorry; we'll correct it," they said. I received the corrected document three months later.

The letter kills! One letter killed my spirit and left me in the doldrums. I was tired of explaining setbacks to everybody. I was belligerent against the devil. The giant was down, but not decapitated.

A Christian coming back from a setback can be very dangerous in the spirit realm. During the process, you have learned some war strategies. You have discovered the modus operandi of the enemy; therefore, when the giant shows up, you know that in order to conquer him, you must aim for the head.

"He teacheth my hands to war, so that a bow of steel is broken by mine arms ... I have pursued mine enemies, and overtaken them: neither did I turn again till they were consumed. I have wounded them that they were not able to rise: they are fallen under my feet. For thou hast girded me with strength unto the battle: thou hast subdued under me those that revolted against me. Thou hast also given me the necks of mine enemies; that I might destroy them that hate me" (Psalm 18:34, 37–40).

It was time to write my licensing exam. I wrote it with many other graduates on a Tuesday. The results were due to arrive in the mail the following Wednesday. Many jubilant graduates were calling me to report their success. I checked the mail Wednesday, Thursday, and Friday morning, but my results were delayed.

This was too much. I threw my hands up in the air and screamed loudly. I wept, and then I went down on my face before the Lord and inquired concerning this predicament. The Lord informed me that I'd passed my licensing exam but wouldn't receive my results, because there were problems with my codes. I had no idea what codes the Lord was talking about.

At 3:00 p.m. on Friday afternoon, I received a call from the College of Nurses of Ontario, telling me that I had passed my exam, but there were some discrepancies with my postal code; therefore, they couldn't mail my results.

"The devil is a stinking liar," I said aloud.

How could there be discrepancies when I'd lived at the same address for over twelve years? By the time I received my results, I felt no excitement.

I cried unto God, because I perceived that a spirit of bondage was sent to hold me captive and to prevent me from accomplishing my divinely ordained appointments and assignments. This cycle had to be destroyed by the power of Almighty God. The anointing has the capacity to destroy the yoke. The enemy was determined that I wouldn't fulfill my prophetic destiny, but I had the power of determination. I was going to be all that God said I'd be. God was, and still is, in control.

There is power in prophecy. If you are determined to succeed, you will succeed.

If Jesus says yes, nobody can say no. Never let yesterday's failures bankrupt today's or tomorrow's efforts.

The graveyard is filled with the epitaphs of people with potential. They could have revolutionized the world, but they succumbed to failure, or they procrastinated until time ran out. I have said unto failure, "Be not proud, for as long as there is breath in my body, I am going to draw my sword and fight." I refuse to go to my grave with unfulfilled potential. I refuse to wander in the wilderness when God says to go and possess the land.

"I returned, and saw under the sun, that the race is not to the swift, nor the battle to the strong, neither yet bread to the wise, nor yet riches to men of understanding, nor yet favour to men of skill; but time and chance happen to them all" (Ecclesiastes 9:11).

I received my nursing credentials despite the war. The curse of stagnation must die. I looked to the Lord, and continue to look to the Lord, who has the power to reverse all satanic orders. I cried unto the Lord, who is my strong tower: "In my distress I called upon the LORD, and cried to my God: and he did hear my voice out of his temple, and my cry did enter into his ears" (2 Samuel 22:7).

"When the wicked, even mine enemies and my foes, came upon me to eat up my flesh, they stumbled and fell. Though an host should encamp against me, my heart shall not fear: thou war should rise against me, in this will I be confident … For in the time of trouble he shall hide me in his pavilion: in the secret of his tabernacle shall he hide me; he shall set me up upon a rock" (Psalm 27:2–3, 5).

I know what prayer can do. I prayed, and God delivered. I prayed, and God placed a "cease order" on that war. Life's circumstances and challenges drove me to my knees. I have experienced the power of God through prayer and fasting. I have learned how to stand on the promises of God. I know that God is not a puppet. He does not act when we pull the strings. He comes to our rescue because of his love for us. Be encouraged in your situations, because God has not forgotten you. Do not commit suicide. It is not over until it is over.

The Word of God is still a viable document. The Holy Bible is still the most powerful apologetic on earth. You can pray the promises of God and then stand still and see him perform his Word. God will honour his words. They shall not return to him unaccomplished. As Isaiah said, when you walk through the water, God will be with you. You will not be drowned. When you are thrown into the fire, you will not be burned (Isaiah 43:2). The children of God are created for his glory. God is under divine obligation to protect those who are in covenant relationship with him.

Prayer

Most holy Father in heaven, I thank you for hearing our humble cry. I thank you because your Word says that before I call, you answer. I just come to honour your most high and majestic name.

In the name of Jesus, I pray against that spirit of suicide. I speak this word into the atmosphere: I shall not die, but live, and declare the works of the LORD. My death is a sovereign choice of God. I will live out the number of my ordained days.

Spirit of depression, I bind you in the name of Jesus. I cast you out in the name of Jesus. You shall not take up residence in the temple of the Lord.

Spirit of failure and bankruptcy, I rebuke you in the name of Jesus. I command you in the name of Jesus to pick up your weapons and run, for Christ has given us the victory over you.

Spirit of shame, embarrassment, and low self-esteem, I curse you in the name of Jesus. Go in the name of Jesus from the lives of the children of God.

Lord, I thank you for relieving your people of the wounds that have been inflicted upon them, even from childhood. I reverse the satanic orders in the name of Jesus.

I thank you, Lord, for bringing to pass that which you have spoken over the lives of your people. It shall be as you have decreed it.

Thanks, Lord, for answering prayers. Amen.

Introduction
Aunt Charlotte's Philosophy of Prayer

It was always a delight to visit Aunt Charlotte during summer vacations. She lived on a settlement in the mountainous regions of St James, south east of Montego Bay in the sunny island of Jamaica, West Indies. Her house was situated on the hillside. It gave me great pleasure to sit on the front or back verandah and gaze at the picturesque panoramic wonder below. It was most splendid during the night seasons.

The city and villages below were set aglow with the brilliance of the yellow, green, amber, and red lights. The moon shed forth its slanted beams on the dew-drenched forest at night. The glittering silver rays seemed to have a special kind of attraction for the banana trees. When those banana leaves, wet with rain or dew, began to shimmy and shake in the night wind, they appeared like dancing figurines. The tall trees, silhouetted against the extensive landscape, looked ghostlike during the night.

Aunt Charlotte rented one portion of her estate to a family of five: Mr. Ainsley and his wife, Miss Sitzah, and their three children—Joy-Anna, Bri-Anna and Babzie-Anna. Auntie never had biological children, but she adopted her family's children and treated them as her own. She never ceased to express and show her love for me.

Aunt Charlotte was a devoted worshipper of God, and a disciplined prayer warrior. Every evening at nine o'clock she started prayer meeting.

Children are taught in school to clasp their hands and close their eyes when they pray, and that's what we did at home also. As we sat in prayer one evening, Aunt Charlotte interrupted the song, "I Am Thine, O Lord," and asked sternly, "Children, when you pray, what posture should you take?"

We had no clue what "posture" meant. Bri-Anna, the second youngest and boldest child, said emphatically, "Auntie, we take the goats to pasture, we don't take pasture when we pray, Mam."

Auntie sensed our ignorance and chuckled gutturally. She rephrased the question. "What should you do when you pray?"

Not knowing what to say, we replied in chorus, "We clasp our hands and close our eyes."

She hissed lovingly. "Watch me!" We fixed our eyes on her.

Aunt Charlotte always had a revelation from on high. She demonstrated as she shared her philosophy on prayer: "I discovered that if you intend to receive something from God, you do not clasp your hands as we have been taught. Clasped hands will never get filled," she said with emphasis. "If you expect to receive from God, you need to lift your arms high and turn your hands with the front side up. Shape it like a bucket or dish." She demonstrated as she spoke. "As you pray, God will fill your bucket to the brim. From the time I started to do this, God has never ceased to supply my needs. This is how you pray!"

Wow! What a revelation! Of course, at that age it meant nothing. But if Auntie said it, we believed it. It's an interesting thought for people who do pray with expectancy. As Aunt Charlotte said, if you position your hands with the front side up, you will receive a bucket-full of blessings from God.

Auntie was zealous about her religious beliefs, and she said it like she understood it. If you expect to receive from God, you must place yourself in the proper position. You must have your spiritual eyes and ears open to what God is showing and saying. If you close your ears to what God is saying, you won't be able to hear the inaudible. If your spiritual eyes are closed, you won't be able to see the invisible. If your mind is closed, you won't be able to understand, interpret, and process the impossible.

Spiritual deafness and blindness are two of the Christian's biggest problems. God is always speaking, but we aren't hearing; he is always showing, but we aren't seeing. The elements around us testify that God is always speaking: "The heavens declare the glory of God; and the firmament sheweth his handiwork. Day unto day uttereth speech, and night unto night sheweth knowledge" (Psalm 19:1–2).

Legislating periods of corporate prayer sessions, where folks can come and make decrees and declarations, are good. Like our Father in heaven, we have the power to speak things into being. The world in which we live was activated by the word from God's mouth. God spoke into the atmosphere, and the elements obeyed his voice. We are authorized to speak as oracles of God: "Death and life are in the power of the tongue" (Proverbs 18:21a).

The tongue is efficacious in the building up or tearing down of strongholds. It lends notable contributions to life and death. It has a boomerang effect: Speak death, death will be the result; speak life, and life will spring forth. Speak death to satanic bombardments, and by faith see them crash. Our God can do above and beyond what we can ask of him.

Inasmuch as God has given us power, we need to be reminded again that God is not a puppet. Staging an emotional show with the intent of outshining and excelling over others will not work. The effectual, fervent prayer of the righteous avails much, but the Lord closes his ears to the prayers that are filled with intellectual gibberish and dictates. When we pray, especially publicly, we don't pray to impress the audience; we pray so that our prayers will enter the throne room of God.

Aunt Charlotte had no education beyond grade five, but she was brilliant and excellent. When she prayed, she received answers from God. I learned from Aunt Charlotte that excellence is progressive. I shouldn't strive to excel so that I can be better than my contemporaries. I am growing in excellence when I have reviewed life and have done better today than I did yesterday. The biggest room in any life or business is always "the room for improvement."

Prayers that produce results do so not because they are loud and expulsive, but because they are birthed out of sincere and humble hearts, and they align with the will of God. More results are manifested when prayer is prayed with the accompaniment of fasting and faith (2 Corinthians 5:7).

You are wasting valuable time if you approach the mercy seat of God with an attitude of unbelief. When you pray, you must exercise faith in the One to whom you are offering prayers. As the writer of Hebrews says: "He who comes to the Father must believe that he is; and that he is a rewarder of those who diligently seek him" (Hebrew 11:6).

God delegated authority and dominion rule to man. God never gave the devil power over his heritage. Man gave the devil power when, in disobedience, he ate of that which was forbidden. Man failed God, but God has made provision for our redemption; therefore, we can stand upon our feet like the champions of champions and fight with all our might. We are destined to win.

As Aunt Charlotte said, if you position your hands with the front side up, you will receive a bucket-full of blessings from God. She explained it in the best way that she could.

I can personally testify that prayer has the power to change things. God is still able to deliver and to keep that which you have entrusted unto him against that day. The possibilities of prayer are numerous. The bottom line is that if you come to God expecting nothing, you might receive just that. Do you believe God? If you believe God, then this should be the driving force behind your coming to him. Your faith in God should motivate you to take on a posture of prayer. When you exercise your faith in God and surrender your will to him, you will experience the supernatural.

The supernatural manifestations of God in the past give us hope for the future. The God of yesterday is the same God of today, and he will be the same forever. If God did that then, he can do it again, if he pleases.

Faith and works go together like hands and gloves. Faith that does not demand action is dead. Everyone who has hope in God behaves likewise. A driver expecting to go places doesn't just sit in the car—he puts the key in the ignition and turns it on. Then he puts the car in drive, places his foot on the gas pedal, and presses down. He then begins to move into his destiny.

God is still able.

The Chains of Insanity Broken

It was 9:00 on a Wednesday morning when my telephone rang.

"Hello!"

The caller was fifteen-year-old Mary. She was sobbing hysterically at the other end of the line.

"Mummy says to come quickly. My sister, Angelia, has gone insane and is acting crazy."

I summoned a few intercessors and together we went to the home. When we arrived, I could smell the pungent stench of urine and defecation. An evil spirit had entered and taken possession of the body of twenty-one-year-old Angelia. She punched everyone who came close to her and doused them with her excrement. Whenever the spirit came upon her, she'd go wild and operate in the strength and power of many men. Everybody stayed afar off and dared not venture near her.

The family explained that this had happened to Angelia before. It was a recurring cycle. No doctor had been able to fully diagnose or treat her therapeutically. She refused to take any medications. This cycle had to be broken, and it could only be done by the power of Almighty God.

I found Angelia lying on the bed in a back room. A bedpan filled with foul smelling fecal matter and urine sat on the floor, and she was grunting like a wild boar. I'd never met her before, but looking at her, I could see that something wasn't right. Her mother said that each time Angelia came out of the bedroom, she came with more power. The mother, her husband, and an uncle were sitting on the front porch, trembling like leaves caught in a hurricane. Other neighbours were standing in the front yard. Angelia had just finished dousing them before I arrived. They tried to restrain her, but to no avail. No man could tame her.

We entered her bedroom, and she glared at us with flaming eyes. She looked spaced-out. She repositioned herself from the belly to the left side.

"Angelia!" I called.

She didn't answer; she just glared at me and grunted. I opened my sword and read from the Gospel according to Mark 1:1–13. Then I expounded on the selected verses and placed great emphasis on the fate of demons. They are not to be tolerated or entertained; they should be discerned and exorcised.

Marva, her mother, looked on without saying a word.

"Angelia!" I called again. "Come forth! I need to speak with you."

She opened her mouth, and the voice of a man came out. The voice sounded like her Uncle Abdel, who was on the porch, soaked with urine and human excrement. That foul spirit was impersonating Abdel.

"Shut up!" I commanded. "I do not want to speak to you. I want to speak with Angelia."

The man spoke again, and the grunting continued.

"What is your name?" I asked.

"Abdel." Then he quickly changed his mind. "Abdul."

Twin spirits had entered the room and possessed the body of Angelia, which was why she was so extremely strong. Abdel behaved like a manic spirit of insanity; and was the aggressor. He moved Angelia to operate in the strength she did. Abdul was a dumb, depressive spirit and uttered not a word.

I've worked in the psychiatric department long enough to be able to differentiate between the two personalities. Manic depression, or bipolar disorder, is a serious mental condition that affects the victim's mood and behaviour. During the manic episodes, the person displays a high level of energy; in the depressive phase, the person becomes lethargic, apathetic, and tearful.

One of the prayer warriors said to the demons, "Abdel or Abdul, whoever you are, you are coming out of her in the name of Jesus." The rest of us agreed. "Both of you are coming out of her." We interceded on behalf of Angelia. We commanded the twin spirits to take a permanent leave of absence from her body. It was hard labour, but God heard and broke the hold that those twin demons had on her that morning.

At the end of the battle, I asked the girl on the bed for her name.

"Angelia," she answered in her own voice. Her eyes were their normal dark brown colour, and she wasn't grunting anymore.

Angelia was freed by the power of Almighty God. She took a shower and changed her smelly clothes. She had something to eat. We left her in a right frame of mind with her family. Last report I received, she was still free. Glory to God in the highest! Hallelujah! Amen!

The Spirits of the Fish and the Bear Destroyed

I was the keynote speaker at an eight-day convention at a certain church. During the testimony service on the Sunday night, a strange thing happened. As the congregation sang, a young man began to scratch himself vigorously while simultaneously chattering like a monkey. He also began to speak rapidly in what seemed like an Oriental dialect: "Mi-mi-mi-mi; ching chong; ching chong." He repeated this about three times. In my spirit, I felt that these words were profane, obscene, and derogatory. A foul, vulgar, abusive, and obnoxious spirit was operating through him.

The spirit was quickly silenced, but as the music continued, a young woman on the opposite side of the room stood up and began to dance.

She moved her hands and body in a swimming motion. This girl was possessed with the spirit of a fish. She and the young man had come with one of the visiting churches.

Some of you are probably acquainted with Walt Disney's 1989 animated musical fantasy film, The Little Mermaid. According to the Merriam-Webster Dictionary, a mermaid is an imaginary or mythological aquatic creature having the head and body of a woman, but from the waist downwards, she has a fish's tail instead of legs.

Stepping outside, I learned from a brother that this young woman had been behaving like a fish for over a month. She was so out of control that every time she came to any body of water, she dove in and splashed about like a fish. Everybody feared that one day she would drown. A rivulet flowed close to the church. With the strong smell of water, the aquatic spirit manifested in the testimony service that night. Those spirits came to taunt and annoy me.

I found myself in an arena of conflict. The war was on. I became very aggressive and militant in the spirit. The saints of God echoed a battle cry, and in the name of Jesus, those spirits were shut down and expulsed. They fled from the scene, and the service progressed to the finish. The Holy Spirit detained us until about 11:45 p.m.

I pause momentarily to insert that in order for demonic spirits to stay out, the one delivered must renounce every affiliation with them. No accommodation should be made for their re-entry. Some spirits are very obstinate. They believe that they have territorial rights and will fight to maintain their position; therefore, you need to live your life in alignment with the Word of God. You must learn how to wage war against the enemy. Do not give way for the devil to use your body as an instrument of sin. Also, you must keep the blooded banner raised high at all times. The devil and his minions are terrified of the blood of Jesus:

"When the unclean spirit is gone out of a man, he walketh through dry places, seeking rest, and findeth none. Then he saith, I will return into my house from whence I came out; and when he is come, he findeth it empty, swept, and garnished. Then goeth he, and taketh with himself seven other spirits more wicked than himself, and they enter in and dwell there: and the last state of that man is worse than the first. Even so shall it be also unto this wicked generation" (Matthew 12:43-45).

When church dismissed, we tarried and greeted each other. The Holy Spirit gave me a word: "Do not turn your back on that young lady. She is about to come at you with vengeance." He was speaking about the same young woman who was possessed with the spirit of the fish.

Suddenly, I felt a wind like a cyclone pushing towards me. The girl was expeditiously advancing towards me with her two hands raised in the air. Her hands looked like the paws of a bear. She exuded a guttural grunt just like a grizzly bear. Everybody looked on in frightful silence. The fish girl was also possessed by the spirit of a bear

The bear and the fish spirits co-existed together in the same body, but the bear remained dormant while the fish was dealt with. The bear is not a marine animal. It's a land mammal, but it's comfortable around water. Now that the spirit of the fish was gone, the bear surfaced.

Let me interrupt myself to share that the devil has a way of showing up at church and in the presence of the Lord. Demons will barefacedly show up in the worship service and pretend to be worshippers. We could be in for a rude awakening if we're unable to discern what we're up against.

One of my family members related a story to me that made my hair stand on end. One Tuesday morning, during an equipping and prayer conference at her church, a man entered the sanctuary and shut them down. He brandished a gun and told everybody to keep quiet and not even pray. He had them lean against the wall and then robbed them at gunpoint. She said that she and the other congregants were very scared. I imagine they were!

By the grace of God, nobody was killed. They lost their valuables, but their lives were spared. One would think that the church would be safe, but to the contrary. Some folks don't seem to have a fear of God anymore. Nobody knows what is going to happen next.

Coming back to the young woman…I turned to face her and encountered two large, glaring, glowing, yellow eyes staring at me. Everyone, including her pastor, stood in silence. A showdown was about to happen. My battle cry rang out in the midnight hour. I called out, "Jesus! Help!" I didn't even have to speak another word, because the host of heaven descended and took charge. The girl came within arm's length of me, and I looked deeply and crossly into those yellow eyes. The paws disappeared like fog at sunrise human hands returned and fell limply at her sides. The grunting stopped, the demons fled, and she stood trembling.

When asked what happened to her, she replied, "I don't know. All I remember is that a voice said, "it is midnight," and I became a different person."

God delivered me from those satanic spirits that Sunday night. He rendered them powerless against me. I give him praise and glory. The devil lost again.

Your life must be saturated with prayer. You must remain under the blood of Jesus. You must be fired up with the Holy Ghost. You cannot afford to wait until you are in the wake of fierce battles before you learn to pray. You must learn to invest prayers in the prayer bank. They will work for you at those times when you cannot pray. I know the potentiality of prayer.

Verdict—Not Guilty

I was conducting a missionary service in a certain place. The altar being opened, a couple came forward for special prayer. Before they opened their mouths, God sent them a word: "The enemies you see today you will not see ever again. The giant that is over your head is under God's feet."

After the prophetic utterance, they voiced their request. Brother Maury had a case in court. He was accused of a crime he did not commit. He'd been nowhere near the scene, yet two witnesses solemnly swore that they saw him do it and drive away. What does a brother do when he comes up against convincing liars? He prays. This was a serious charge. If it stuck, this brother would have to serve time in jail and pay an enormous fine.

Weeping bitterly, the man said to me, "The next court date is tomorrow, and this will be my eleventh appearance to answer for the same crime I did not commit. They've also moved the trial to the next precinct miles from home." He held onto his wife, and they wept bitterly.

"My brother," I said, "did you not just receive a word that the giant that is over your head is under God's feet? And that the enemies whom you see today, you shall see them no more again forever?"

"Yes," he replied.

"Hear what the Holy Spirit is saying unto you: Do not be concerned about the power of man, but fear me. The enemies that are coming against you will cease after tomorrow. It is a fixed fight. God will fight for you. Tomorrow, when you get there, hold your peace. Stop crying. Open your mouth and begin to give thanks. Your tears are out of season. It is time to rejoice."

The congregation joined me in a hell-shaking, chain-breaking prayer for Brother Maury. We telephoned central headquarters in heaven. We dialled the Father in the name of Jesus. We could feel the power of the Holy Spirit moving in that sanctuary that morning. The current of the Holy Ghost permeated the room. Brother Maury must triumph over the enemy if he is innocent. We interceded for Brother Maury.

"Father, we come to you in the name of Jesus. Thank you for deliverance and the victory. Lord, stop the mouths of the lion and the bear that are coming up against our brother to devour him. We command confusion in the demonic realm. Let them not remember their assignment tomorrow, Lord. Cancel every assignment against your son. We are shouting the praises now for what you have already done and for what you are about to do. Decapitate the giant once again. Let truth and justice prevail. Father, let the enemy that seeks the hurt of the innocent be ashamed. Thank you, Father, in the name of Jesus."

We prayed according to the promise of God over that brother and his family. We cried unto God. He heard us out of heaven, his dwelling place. This brother's situation was about to be changed by the power of the great God of heaven. He needed to put on his dancing shoes, because God was about to make him dance.

At 3:00 p.m. the next evening, the telephone rang.

"Hello!"

There was rejoicing on the other end of the line. I began to rejoice also. The witnesses went to court and perjured themselves. Under stern interrogation, they withdrew their former testimony. They confessed that they'd lied. That brother never had to speak a word. The Lord spoke for him. God stopped the mouths of the lion and the bear. Brother Maury was forever free. Eleven times in court for the same alleged crime, and it was over forever, as God had said.

Lying witnesses held this brother captive over a crime he did not commit. He and his family had become like prisoners of war (POW); they were subjected to mental torture and torment, but God had mercy. Criminal justice demanded a prison sentence and a fine, but grace and mercy came and opened the prison bars and set the captives free. Prayer changed things.

Once you're a child of God, you will be persecuted and accused falsely. Jesus encourages us to rejoice and be very happy. The major incentive of demonic oppression is to bring you down and keep you down. The accuser of the brethren will erect strongholds in your life and use them to bombard you. Do not become discouraged. God has a plan. If he allows you to get into it, he will get you out of it.

Many people are enchained by the spirit of oppression. They need the bondage-breaking, chain-breaking prayer of the saints of God. Some of the displayed behaviours that we see in certain people might be cries for help.

"No weapon that is formed against thee shall prosper; and every tongue that shall rise against thee in judgment thou shall condemn. This is the heritage of the servants of the LORD, and their righteousness is of me, says the LORD" (Isaiah 54:17).

We need to learn to lift our faith, even when the storm clouds are hanging low before us. Mental anguish and emotional pain can be very overwhelming, but hold on to God's unchanging hands. Do not give up; do not back down; stand your ground. Your champion and tag team partner is on the way. Do not lose your praise; your nightmare is over. There is a light at the end of your tunnel.

"For I know the thoughts that I think toward you, saith the LORD, thoughts of peace, and not of evil, to give you an expected end. Then shall ye call upon me, and ye shall go and pray unto me, and I will hearken unto you. And ye shall seek me, and find me, when ye shall search for me with all your heart. And I will be found of you, saith the LORD: and I will turn away your captivity, and I will gather you from all the nations, and from all the places whither I have driven you, saith the LORD; and I will bring you again into the place whence I caused you to be carried away captive" (Jeremiah 29:11–14).

The devil has a weird sense of humour. He's like the cat that catches a mouse and toys with it before the kill. The cat has fun as it viciously tortures the unfortunate mouse. The cat just knocks the mouse about then sits and watches. The mouse tries to run, but as it makes a move, the cat knocks it over with its paw again. It eventually kills the mouse. It doesn't eat the flesh, but leaves it there to rot and stink.

What seems like a funny joke to you might prove deadly for others. The devil will back you into a tight spot. Unless you get divine intervention, you will not get out. You need to learn how to wield your offensive and defensive weapons of warfare against him.

"Is any among you afflicted? Let him pray. Is any merry? Let him sing psalms. Is any sick among you? Let him call for the elders of the church; and let them pray over him, anointing him with oil in the name of the Lord: And the prayer of faith shall save the sick, and the Lord shall raise him up; and if he have committed sins, they shall be forgiven him" (James 5:13–15).

There is enough power in the name of Jesus to pulverize every chain. There is deliverance in the name of Jesus. Jesus can break every shackle. I decree and declare this day that those chains must fall. You are loosed by the power of Almighty God.

Chapter 1
The Indispensable Weapon of Prayer

Dictionary.com defines prayer as a spiritual communion engaged with God. It is a devout petition to God or an object of worship, supplication, thanksgiving, and adoration.

Like the Son and the Holy Spirit, the Christian involves himself in a two-way interactive communication with the Father in heaven. Every chapter in the history of faithful men and women of God amplified intercessory prayer. Intercessory prayer has always been a prominent feature of their daily walk with God. Both the Old and New Testament bear record that the saints of God were prayer-driven. Those who succeeded to the utmost were those whose lives and ministries were saturated with prayer.

It's impossible to be a servant of God without prayer, because our adversary, the devil, is always standing by to harass and challenge us. The goal of the saint's prayer should always be for the glory of God. Anyone who expects to become intimate with God must pray. Anyone who has a relationship with God will have a burning desire to pray. When you are in love, you want to communicate regularly with the one you love.

Prayer works in the same manner as the gospel message. In the closet, one speaks with God only. But when one prays publicly, one is not only speaking to God, but to a larger audience. Many people respond positively to the prayers of the saints. There has never been a revival revolution anywhere around the globe, in any era, that didn't commence with prayer.

Had it not been for the sincere intercessory and strategic prayers of the saints, I would not have lived past my first birthday. Elijah prayed, and the Zarephath woman's son received life again (1 Kings 17:19–24). Elisha prayed, and the Shunamite woman's son was revived (2 Kings 4:18–36). Peter went down to Joppa and prayed the prayer of faith over Tabitha (Dorcas), who had been declared dead. The woman was delivered from the clutches of death. She opened her eyes and sat up. Many people believed in the Lord because of this miracle (Acts 9:36–43).

In prayer, we speak to the spiritually dead and let them know that Jesus Christ is not only the giver of life, but also the sustainer of life. He has power to bring back to life that which is dead or dying. The spiritually dead hear the gospel of prayer and respond, not only by receiving life, but by living in the liberty wherewith Christ had made them free.

Believe when you pray, and you will conquer the unconquerable, ascend the insurmountable, and navigate the impenetrable (James 5:16b).

Rehearsal Matters

As an educator, I teach my students well. One of the things I foster is excellence. The Ministry of Colleges and Universities has set a certain standard that must be maintained. I adhere to the curriculum meticulously, and I enhance my teaching and lecturing skills by continuing education. I introduce guest speakers from various relevant fields, and I incorporate interesting educational extracurricular activities. I facilitate student-centred learning. I do for students above and beyond what is expected of me. Every student in my class is treated equally. One of the things I do is pray over my students and pronounces the blessings of the Lord upon them, especially before an exam. Every now and then I would deliberately withhold prayer to see if they would request it. Every time I did this, somebody would remind me that I hadn't prayed.

Ninety per cent of my students usually do exceptionally well by scoring between 90–100% on a given module (the passing grade is 70%). Nine per cent score between 80–90%. The remaining one percent scores between 70–80%. I seldom have a class in which more than one person fails a grade or a module. Oftentimes the ones who didn't do great, or failed, would ask me this question: "Why did I not do well?" Or they might say, "I am disappointed with myself."

The first questions I'd ask them were, did you study your notes and reviews? Did you do the practice exercises I gave you? Did you utilize all the resources that are available to you? Why do you think you failed? The anticipated answer always was: "I honestly didn't study," or "I didn't study as I know I should."

I share this to introduce a point. You cannot expect to perform with excellence at the recital if you haven't been actively involved in the pre-recital drills or the rehearsals. What you do after the lecture is very important. I've learned that the person who reviews his notes within twenty-four hours after the lecture is more likely to remember what has been learned than those who waited until just before the exam to review. A student will not pass any exam if he does not study and retain what was studied. It's not enough to study; but it's enough to retain that which was studied. The test will determine how much a person has retained.

A child of God who doesn't pray cannot expect to be victorious. One can only extract from the bank account what he has deposited. One is headed for prison if he tries to withdraw from the bank machine money that is not there; neither can one expect to gain interest on an account that has zero principal.

The effectual, fervent prayer warrior doesn't beat the air with repetitious gibberish. He doesn't surf the Internet and copy the empty jargons of every so-called prophet and prophetesses. He prays, from the heart, an intense, passionate, and fervent Holy Ghost-soaked prayer. He prays intelligently and specifically. He prays according to the will of the Father.

The Apostle Paul and his contemporary, Silas, found themselves under maximum security in the Philippians jail. They could have spent the time lamenting on their calamity, but they chose not to. They considered it more beneficial and more edifying to worship God in singing and praying. It matters how you react to your confinement. If Paul and Silas were not fully charged with the dynamite of the Holy Ghost, they would not be able to conduct a worship service in an atmosphere charged with the presence of the devil and his agents.

After the reception of many stripes in their bodies, they should have been in excruciating pain and mental anguish, but God gave them the power and strength to triumph over the prevailing situation. At a time when they should have been in lamentation and bitter weeping, they were singing and praising God, for his mercy endures forever (Acts 16:25–28).

You Cannot Tap into the Power Unless You Are Plugged into the Power Source

The effectual, fervent prayer will not necessarily flow from the lips of those who are mentally efficient or intellectually proficient. It will proceed from the mouths of those who are spiritually rooted and grounded in God. God reserves the right to use whom he will.

In my time, I have seen many people with capabilities sitting idly down. They sit in stagnancy with their multiplicity of abilities; they are never willing or available to invest in the lives of others. All around us you can see many disabled capable stuck in the cul-de-sacs of time, having numerous abilities but no availability. Like Moab, they have settled on their "lees" (Jeremiah 48:11). "Settled on its lees" is wine-making lingo. In order to extract the delectability of wine, it must be poured from vessel to vessel during the fermenting stage to eliminate the dregs.

"Prayer warriors" walk in the spirit and have a divine connection with the empowering source—our Lord Jesus Christ and the Holy Ghost. They don't just pray occasionally when needs precipitate it, but they pray without ceasing. They don't have to prepare themselves to pray when a crisis is in progress, because they are already prayed up. They are always plugged into the source.

Follow me in this mental demonstration: Picture yourself standing beside the ironing board, ready to iron your wrinkled garment. Now place the iron on the fabric and move it in any direction you choose. After a few minutes of doing this, the garment remains wrinkled. What might be the problem? Have you found the problem? I did.

The iron wasn't plugged into the electrical socket. You've wasted so much effort trying to iron your garment with an iron that wasn't plugged into the electrical outlet. This iron will never do the work it was built to do, because it has no connection with the source behind its power.

Now plug the cord into the electrical outlet and set the gauge on the right temperature for that fabric. Begin to iron. Look! All the wrinkles are gone. What made the difference? The right connection! The iron is plugged into the right source with the right voltage. You can only acquire the intended results when you are connected to the right source.

A person who is out of fellowship with the Holy Spirit and the Saviour is automatically out of fellowship with the Father. Achan's disconnection from God caused the army of Israel to suffer defeat at the hands of the few people of Ai, but when the breach was mended, Israel won the battle (Joshua 7 and 8).

Prayer Stopped the Funeral

For many years, I've been engaged in the ministry of prayer. I've discovered that next to the Word of God and faith, prayer is the most powerful and energy-generating weapon in my spiritual arsenal.

Being in healthcare, I've stood many times at the bedside of those who were pronounced clinically dead or given the prognosis of having only a few days or hours to live. I remember the shifts I had on the palliative floor of a certain hospital. There was a gentleman, who having discovered that I was a minister of the gospel of Jesus Christ, asked me to pray for him one Sunday morning. He had end-stage lung cancer. He'd given up on life and had stopped eating three days prior. He confided in me that he believed in the efficacy of prayer, but his son and daughter-in-law did not believe; therefore, they wouldn't pray with him or call his clergyman. He was a sad but sober man. He was so physically weak that he could no longer sit up in the bedside armchair. His voice had been reduced to a whisper. He gasped for breath as he asked me to pray for him.

I finished his care and propped him up in bed.

"Mr. Robertson," I said, "in order for you to triumph over this sickness, you must agree with me as I pray."

He whispered, "I will agree with you."

I interceded that Sunday morning on the behalf of Mr. Robertson. He agreed with me and prayed—as much as his lungs allowed him at that moment. We sent forth an S.O.S. up to heaven and asked God to reverse the death order. We thanked God and began the victory shout. That brother, who was given just days to live, received strength. God, the upper taker, stopped the undertaker that morning. God stopped the funeral.

Mr. Robertson got out of bed, sat up in his chair, and ate a hearty breakfast—the first in days. His son and daughter-in-law were shocked to see the change in him. They took their dad for a walk, and while walking they learned the source behind his victory. The family, who was busy making funeral arrangements, returned to give God the glory for delivering their dad. God alone gets the glory. It is God who yielded the increase. We prayed believing, and God delivered.

The dunamis of God is inexhaustible. Dunamis is a Greek word meaning, might, power or marvelous works. (Strong's Concordance) You cannot deplete heaven's storehouse. Nothing can short-fuse the power of God. In God, there is no such thing as a power shortage. There is no such thing as a power cut to save energy. The holy transmitter distributes power proportionately to the receiver. God releases higher voltage when it is needed, and decreases the current as he reckons it fit. When the Holy Spirit is in operation in the life of the believer, there can be no short circuit. God gives his servants power for the hour, and the authority to exercise that power.

Sister Malley

After speaking to Sister Malley, I learned that she had a problem from which she greatly desired to be liberated. In her genealogical background, there is a practice in which the spirits of dead ancestors are sought out and entertained. For example, if the dead family member loved rice or coffee, rice and coffee would be incorporated into family celebrations and feasts. They would sprinkle or scatter a portion of the drink and meal on the ground outside the meeting place. The present generation was commanded to inform the next generation of this familial practice. This ritual was to be performed any time there was a marriage, a new birth, or the christening of a baby. Anyone who broke that promise suffered certain physical and/or mental ailments. Sister Malley believed that she would be tormented, even unto death, if she did not carry through with those practices.

Sister Malley decided not to continue those practices when she became a Christian. She planned not to pass them on to her children. When she got married, she decided not to give in to this generational ritual. She had her first child and decided that she was not going to do what was ancestrally expected. Her child became sick unto death. Having heard the story, I told her that she needed to break that cycle, and she could only do that by the power of Almighty God. She could not serve two gods. She must either choose the God of heaven, or the god of the world.

She refused to remain a prisoner of ancestral beliefs, indulgences, and practices. She had to bring herself to the place where she believed that the dead have no power over her or her young child. As a Christian, she is indwelled by the Holy Ghost. She chose the God of heaven. She believed his Word and acted upon it.

Intercessory prayer was made to deliver her. It was a battle, but that sentence was destroyed by the power of Almighty God. She and her household were forever free from that generational indulgence and trap. She stopped those practices, and it went well with her, her firstborn, and subsequent births. The next generation was free, because she dared to trust the God of heaven to deliver her from something that began long before she was born. To God be all the glory. He is a spell-breaker. No one needs to remain bound by traditional, generational, or cultural traps. You can be freed by the power of the Most High God of heaven.

The preaching of the gospel impacts the heart of man, but the effectual, fervent prayer that the saint utters touches the heart of God. Prayers saturated with the Holy Ghost will be effective. The prayer that is saturated with the glorious presence of divine providence and with the power of the Holy Ghost will quicken that which is dead, whether physically or spiritually.

And he said unto me, Son of man, can these bones live? And I answered, O Lord God, thou knowest. Again he said unto me, Prophesy upon these bones, and say unto them, O ye dry bones, hear the word of the LORD. Thus saith the Lord God unto these bones; Behold, I will cause breath to enter into you, and ye shall live: And I will lay sinews upon you, and will bring up flesh upon you, and cover you with skin, and put breath in you, and ye shall live; and ye shall know that I am the LORD. So I prophesied as I was commanded: and as I prophesied, there was a noise, and behold a shaking, and the bones came together, bone to his bone. And when I beheld, lo, the sinews and the flesh came up upon them, and the skin covered them above: but there was no breath in them (Ezekiel 37:3–8, emphasis added).

The first thing that caught my attention in the above passage is the fact that God commanded Ezekiel to prophesy upon the dry bones (v. 4) as opposed to prophesy to them (v.12). That which is dead cannot hear. It would be a waste of time and breath to prophesy to that which is dead, whether spiritually or clinically. He had to first prophesy upon them. After they experienced revival, Ezekiel could prophesy to them.

The second thing I observed is that the bones' first response was to make a noise and shake, and then they came together. Sinews, flesh, and skin covered them, but there was no breath in them. The bones were making a noise; they had a noticeable shake; they had flesh, sinews, and skin, but they were still not functional, because they were devoid of the life that can only be produced by the breath of God.

Then said he unto me, Prophesy unto the wind, prophesy, son of man, and say to the wind, Thus saith the Lord God; Come from the four winds, O breath, and breathe upon these slain, that they may live. So I prophesied as he commanded me, and the breath came into them, and they lived, and stood up upon their feet, an exceeding great army. (Ezekiel 37:9–10)

After the four winds came and breathed upon them, they lived and stood upon their feet, an exceeding great army.

Mother Tomei

Mother Tomei would become gravely ill at the same time every year, but the condition wasn't caused by a medical deviation. Her condition seemed to be precipitated by something occurring in the spiritual realm. Somewhere in the ancestral line lay a ritual that Mother Tomei believed was affecting her health.

Her family never washed dishes overnight, because they believed that the spirits of their dead ancestors would come looking for food. On a specific day each year, they would congregate at the family's burial site and have a day-long feast and dance on the behalf of the dead. The food that they offered to the dead was cooked without salt and garlic.

Mother Tomei and her family truly believed that engagement in this ritual would stop one from getting sick. They had become slaves to what they had sold themselves to. They indulged themselves in this yearly ritual instead of seeking the Lord.

Eventually, Mother Tomei became a Christian and placed her life into the hands of God. It was another year, and she was very ill. Whatever was affecting her was very strong and stubborn. On a Thursday evening, a group of intercessors gathered at her house for a deliverance prayer meeting. During the service, the pastor's wife went down on her knees, lifted the bed sheets, pointed under the bed, and prayed. When she arose from her knees, she was dumb and could not speak a word. She was attacked and inflicted with dumbness. Instead of one battle, there were now two battles—one to clear Mother Tomei, and another to clear the pastor's wife.

It took the prayer and intercessory team three days and three nights of round the clock warfare prayer and fasting to clear the pastor's wife of the dumb spirit. Mother Tomei had to renounce every affiliation with the ancestral rituals and the obsession with the spirits of the dead. Although she was saved, she was still struggling with the idea of feasting at the cemetery and leaving dishes with scraps of food in the kitchen overnight. She had to understand that she wasn't betraying her ancestors by not continuing these practices. God is not a God of the dead, but a God of the living, for all live unto him (Luke 20:38). She had to trust God totally for her and her family's deliverance.

God must be the only object of our worship. One can remember dead relatives, but the worshipping of the dead by the Christian is unorthodox. The worship of spirits is an aberration from biblical norms. It is incongruous with the Word of God. The Lord God is a jealous God. Scriptures teach that there is only one true and living God, and he only should we worship. The God of heaven must be the only God of our lives.

Mother Tomei came to the understanding that she cannot serve light and darkness, God and the devil; neither could she continue to hold dear a pagan belief and practice while clinging to the Word of God. That is called spiritual or religious syncretism. There can be no blending of the works of the Spirit of God and the works of the flesh. There can be no association or mingling with God and the devil. One is either serving God or serving the devil. Light and darkness are diametrically opposed to each other.

Mother Tomei was a victim of ancestral beliefs and customs. This woman of age could only be set free from the powers of darkness and from self-imprisonment by taking heed to the Word of God and through prayer and intercession and fasting. Intercessory prayer was made to God continually on her behalf, but she had to believe God and desire to break free. She needed to liberate her mind from the warped and twisted thinking that the dead have power over her mind, body, and health (Job 14:12–14; Psalm 115:17, 146:3–4; Ecclesiastes 9:4–6; Isaiah 38:18–19). Mother Tomei believed God and was totally delivered.

Strongholds were set against those sisters before they were born. They needed to understand biblical truths about the dead. To begin, the worship of the dead is idolatry. The faculties of the living are at work; therefore, they can hope and grasp opportunities to do things. Ecclesiastes 9:4–6 says that the dead have no knowledge of anything. They are cut off from active duties; their time has expired, and they are finished. Their memories are only kept alive by the progenies and people who had loved and adored them.

Lazarus knew nothing until Jesus Christ woke him up in John 11:11–14. As I told these sisters, the feeding of the dead is not possible, because at death all faculties are shut down for good. The dead have no appetite for food. They cannot participate in anything under the sun. All their abilities perish when they die. I have been in the business of health care for twenty-five years. I have bagged and labelled the dead. When a person is dead, he is dead. Only God can bring him back. And if God has not brought him back from the dead to the land of the living, he remains dead.

One will become a slave to what he has given power to, as I said before. The devil had no power on earth until Adam and Eve gave it to him. God gave man dominion over all created orders on earth. The devil became strong when man gave him dominion over their lives. No spirit, besides the Holy Spirit, can dominate a mind that has renounced it.

Christians do not intermingle with the dead. Jesus asked the woman on resurrection morning: "Why seek ye the living among the dead?" (Luke 24:5b) As the apostle Paul asserts: This I say then, Walk in the Spirit, and ye shall not fulfill the lust of the flesh. (Galatians 5:16) Although we are walking in the flesh, we do not war in the flesh. Our battles are waged in the regions of the heavens, where the war between good and evil, light and darkness, is hot. God will never send you to fight with the evil one unless he has prepared and armored you.

Sister Malley and Mother Tomei had been ensnared in a generational trap and stronghold, but prayer and the mercies of God set them free. God has the power to break generational curses and strongholds.

Pseudocyesis

Pseudocyesis is a medical condition in which a woman (or even a man) believes that she is pregnant. The woman exhibits many or all the symptoms of pregnancy—with the exception of the fetus. The false symptoms trick the body over a period of a few weeks to a few years into believing it is pregnant. The person gains weight but will never give birth, because there's no baby.

A Christian who is disconnected from the vine cannot reproduce. He or she will suffer from spiritual pseudocyesis—feeling pregnant and looking pregnant, but giving birth to nothing. There is movement in the spiritual womb, but there is no baby.

The person of prayer is always pregnant with possibilities. He or she is active in the ministry of deliverance. Many times, like the Israelites of the Diaspora, we surrender in the prevailing storms of life. God assured the children of Judah and Jerusalem that they would be exiled for a period of seventy years; therefore, the Babylonian insurgents could only hold them captive for that long. They had the chance of a better future, but they had to believe God. They had to pray and seek his face.

By the rivers of Babylon, there we sat down, yea, we wept, when we remembered Zion. We hanged our harps upon the willows in the midst thereof. For there they that carried us away captive required of us a song; and they that wasted us required of us mirth, saying, Sing us one of the songs of Zion. How shall we sing the LORD's song in a strange land? (Psalm 137:1–4)

As per the song above, we see that they had lost faith in God. They were famous for their musical talents. Their captors demanded that they entertain them with their gift of music. They decided not to sing the songs of Zion in a foreign land.

David was a nostalgic and exuberant worshipper. He led the people of Israel into one theocratic nation. He sang and danced before the people of God when he brought the Ark of the Testimony back to Jerusalem (2 Samuel 6:14–17). He worshipped God despite the predicament.

There are times when God might not answer our prayers quickly. He might delay answering them, or he might not answer them at all. God's reasons for not answering our prayers are always valid. God is not Santa Claus.

God has a way of keeping us in certain places or situations because he wants us to be the change in that atmosphere. Jesus came to Bethany and reclined at the table of Simon, the leper. A woman broke her alabaster box of precious ointment and poured it on Jesus' head. The ointment was to prepare Jesus for burial (Mark 14:8). After the alabaster box was broken, the atmosphere changed. It was infused with the fragrance of the perfume (John 12:3). The behaviour of this woman was not considered orthodox; therefore, it brought her stern criticism and rebuke from the clergy. They couldn't discern that she was chosen of God to change the atmosphere.

Could the exiles of the Southern Kingdom of Judah cause a shift in the satanic atmosphere of Babylon by singing and praising God? The Babylonians might have been mocking them and their God when they asked them to sing, but you and I know that prayer can stop the mouths of the lions. It happened for Daniel. In despite the royal edict, he prayed as he was accustomed. The lions had no power over him, because God sent guardian angels to stop their mouths. God can turn what the enemy meant for bad into good. He did it for Joseph in Egypt.

The people of God should always seize the opportunity to make a difference in the world around them. They can accomplish this through prayer and worship of Jehovah. Extraordinary, supernatural, unconventional signs and wonders happen when people of prayer break forth in prayer and praise.

Prevailing circumstances cannot silence a person of prayer. Jonah cried out from the belly of the whale (Jonah 2:1–10; Matthew 12:38–41). Elijah found himself in Zarephath of Zidon, the place where the heart of Baalism beat loudest, but he made a difference in the widow's life. Satan has set up his emissaries and battlefields everywhere. Be prepared to stand your ground and pray wherever you are. How oft we or our loved ones are stuck at the gate or in the land of what the doctors diagnose as a terminal illness? How many times has God descended and reversed the orders?

The children of Judah and Jerusalem suffered from spiritual pseudocyesis. For seventy years, they were seemingly pregnant with something, but gave birth to nothing. They shook and made noise, as Ezekiel envisioned, but they were stuck in the valley of despair. Until God sent the four winds from heaven and filled them, they were alive, yet dead. They produced nothing.

Every now and then our prayers can become like mere noises, producing nothing. I have gone to a few prayer meetings where I felt as if I was in the cemetery—the prayers were dead. At times, we come across some pews that are filled to capacity with dressed-up corpses. There's a lot of noise and a lot of shaking, but no power. Nothing much is going on. Folks walk out the same way they come in.

It's sad when the prayer meeting becomes like a social club. Folks are entertained, but not delivered. The ego is pampered, but the soul isn't edified. The spiritual digestive systems are filled, but not satisfied. If one has no personal relationship with God, he will become dry, empty, and dead. We have pregnancy potential, but if there's a lack of intimacy with the Father, we'll produce nothing.

The Brood Parasites

A few girls lived down the street from Aunt Charlotte. She labelled them "brood parasites." A brood parasite is an organism that relies on other organisms to raise their young. It deposits its eggs in the nest of the host. The parasitic bird, fish, or insect is relieved of building its own nest, incubating its own eggs, or foraging for its own young. Strangely, the parasite's eggs go unnoticed by the host because of the close resemblance of the eggs. The parasite will sometimes shove the host's eggs from the nest. The greatest danger of brood parasitism is that the offspring of the host parent dies from want of nourishment. The young imposter, which is usually larger, survives at the expense of the host and her young ones.

Aunt Charlotte explained that these girls were like brood parasites because they'd just have babies and dump them to be raised by their parents and grandparents. Once the children were grown, the parents took credit for the success of the children they never reared.

God desires each person to work on the gifts or talents he's been granted. Every talent has the potential to yield increase. It's imperative that each person guards what God has deposited in him. Aunt Charlotte's words still echo in my ears, even though she said them years ago.

One of the essential keys in the productivity and survival of a Christian in this present age is his affinity to abide in Christ or in the position God has placed him. Earlier we identified the negativities of the children of Judah while in captivity. Now let us look at some of the positive things. Even though they were in a place of hopelessness and despair, they had potential for change and growth. God's strategic move brought them back together as one organized body. God infused them with life and transformed the old mindset. Formerly they said, "Our bones are dried, and our hope is lost" (Ezekiel 37:11b). They hung up their harps and refused to sing the songs of Zion. Now they are standing up and behaving like a valiant army (Ezekiel 37:10).

Until we are permeated with the power of the Holy Ghost, we will remain noisy, rattling bones. We need a life-transforming word from Jehovah. Jesus spoke to his subjects as one having authority and not as the scribes (Matthew 7:29). You move mountains not because of your verbosity, not because you can speak a given language with polished roundness, and certainly not because you are superior to all else. You articulate prayers and solicit answers from God when you pray according to his will and command.

Some prayers minister to the psyche but not to the heart. They fill the atmosphere, but they do not impregnate the soul. Prayers uttered under the anointing of the Holy Ghost will penetrate the stony heart of man and feed his famished soul. Praying under the anointing brings healing to the sick, resurrection to the spiritually dead, and national and global revival revolution.

An Essential Life-Line

The American Heritage Dictionary defines a life-line as: an anchored line thrown as a support to someone who is falling or drowning; a means or route by which necessary supplies are transported; or one that is regarded as a source of salvation in a crisis.

The Merriam-Webster Dictionary's summation of a life-line is that it is used to keep contact with a person in a dangerous or potentially dangerous situation; it is something regarded as indispensable for the maintaining or protection of life; it is a system providing all or some of the necessary items for maintaining the life or health of an injured person.

The Free Dictionary describes the life-line as: a vital line of access or communication; or something which provides help or support that is needed for success or survival.

A long time ago while I was praying, this dropped into my spirit: prayer operates like an umbilical cord or a life-line that allows the believer to stay spiritually alert and divinely connected with the throne room of heaven.

A fetus will not survive if the umbilical cord disconnects from the placenta, and neither will the believer who is severed from divine connection with God survive. I have worked in labour and delivery and have coached mothers in labour. The first thing doctors do when a baby is born is ensure that he's breathing normally. Soon the umbilical cord is cut, separating him from his mother.

The obstetrician or the midwife checks the umbilical cord for the following features: two arteries, one vein, and any other peculiarities. The two arteries convey deoxygenated blood and waste products away from the baby to the placenta. The vein takes oxygenated blood and nutrients to the baby. The umbilical cord is lengthy, allowing the baby freedom of movement within the uterine cavity. Every now and then the baby gets entangled in its cord, or the cord wraps itself around the neck and strangles the baby. This is a very serious situation and a medical emergency in the natural realm.

Once outside the womb, a baby no longer needs an umbilical cord. The umbilical cord has served its purpose within the womb and is no longer relevant in the life of the growing child. The interdependence and the bond between it and the newborn must be severed and discontinued; however, the navel remains as a tell-tale mark for life. Everybody knows that this person was once connected to somebody.

Unlike the temporal umbilical cord or life-line, prayer will always be a relevant discipline throughout the life of a Christian. It remains constant. The umbilical cord has three vessels, as cited.

The Bible says that there are three who bear record in heaven: The Father, the Son and the Holy Spirit (1 John 5:7). The Father is omnipotent, omniscient, and omnipresent. He is the supreme ruler and has total control over everything and everyone in heaven and in earth.

Jesus Christ, the living Word, washes us and redeems us with his precious blood. Therefore, we can boldly approach the mercy seat. We aren't endowed with the spirit of a coward or a weakling, but the spirit of love and soberness. We are quickened by the Holy Spirit, who also bears record in heaven that we are the children of God; fear will be expelled when the Holy Spirit enters.

There are three who bear record on earth: The Holy Ghost, the water, and the blood (1 John 5:8). When the believer prays unto the Father, who bears record in heaven, the prayer passes through the blood of Jesus

Christ and is breathed upon by the Holy Spirit. We receive answers according to the tender mercies of God, and because the Son and the Spirit make intercession for us.

Whereas a baby will survive outside the womb without the umbilical cord, a Christian's spiritual life will not survive without that continued spiritual attachment to the Father through prayer and adherence to the Word.

As mentioned earlier, no electrical instrument will generate power to do the work it was designed to do unless plugged into a power outlet. Likewise, no Christian can expect to operate in the fullness of his or her potential unless he or she remains plugged into the source—the Holy Spirit.

The Holy Spirit is known for his prolificity. Under the prolific operations of the Holy Spirit, the Christian produces fruit.

A person who is controlled by the Holy Spirit will never be barren. He or she will always be producing and giving birth to things that will be beneficial to the Kingdom of God.

The world needs to know that the devil is the prince of the air and the world of darkness, but he is not the king. No prince is ever king while the king lives and reigns. God is the supreme monarch of heaven and earth.

The hour is coming, and now is, when the dead shall hear the voice of the Son of God: and they that hear shall live. For as the Father hath life in himself; so hath he given to the Son to have life in himself; And hath given him authority to execute judgment also, because he is the Son of man (John 5:25–27).

Prayer is the essential element. Like the umbilical cord, it serves as the life-line of the believer. Pray without ceasing, and you shall live.

A Fighter Escort and a Dynamic Weapon

Prayer is such a dynamic weapon that it creates shifts in the elements around us. A person of prayer is a person of authority. The elements must obey those who are in covenant relationship with God, and those unto whom he has given his exousia. Exousia is a Greek word meaning power or authority.

To become disconnected from God in this dark and dismal wilderness will be fatal. Ravenous beasts wait to devour he who is disconnected from his maker.

I'm an avid watcher of wildlife documentaries. I've noticed that many animals fall prey to the predators either because they are sick and physically weak, they become separated from the group, or they are very young and have not yet learned the maneuvers that will help them survive in the wild.

Unity is strength. The enemy likes nothing better than to separate a person from the back-up source or fighter escort.

A fighter escort is a fighter plane equipped to accompany other planes (especially bombers, on missions) as a protection against air attacks.

The Holy Spirit is not a gofer, and neither is he the local, regional, or international errand boy. He is a co-essential member of the Trinity. He gives us clearance as a fighter escort.

Jesus Christ preceded the three Hebrew men, Meshach, Shadrach, and Abednego, into the fire. The Holy Spirit enters the battlefield ahead of us. He has the battlefield under surveillance and knows the enemy's modus operandi. Whether we are caught up in the fight, the battle, or the war, the Holy Ghost is right beside us, giving us the support, strength, and perseverance needed to conquer the foe.

In days of antiquity, the Holy Spirit of God revealed to King Jehoshaphat the location of the enemies (2 Chronicles 20:16). As a result, he was not taken unawares. The king and his army were well informed ahead of time. To be forewarned is to be forearmed.

Christians need to seek God for the spirit of discernment so that they can spot the enemy coming. In this way, they will not be caught off guard.

We shouldn't only pray when we are in desperate situations. We should pray before the adverse occurs. Prayer is not just another spiritual discipline, but the discipline of disciplines.

He who prays must have a personal faith in God. Faith and prayer are interdependent principles. Without faith, it is impossible to be a witness to certain manifestations in the Spirit.

Our God is able, and those who come to him must believe that he is able and will perform that which he says he will do. As Aunt Charlotte said:

"If you intend to receive something from God, you do not clasp your hands. Clasped hands will never get filled. If you expect to receive from God, you need to lift your arms high, turn your hands front side up, and make a cusp. Your hands become like a bucket. As you pray, God will fill your bucket to the brim."

The first doctrinal teaching of the church is that it is a place of prayer. Jesus showed his disgust by overturning the tables of the moneychangers in the temple of Jerusalem. He made a scourge and whipped them and chased them out.

Why? They desecrated the house of God when they used it as a place of merchandising, stealing, and robbery instead of a house of prayer for all nations. Jesus identifies the house of God by her standards—a place of prayer for all nations. We commit a horrible crime when we refrain from having corporate prayer in the house of God.

Each year, auditors visit the healthcare and educational systems where I work. They carefully examine all the accounts; accounting records' vouchers; and income, expenditure, and balance sheets. They scrutinize patients' files and students' files to see if the proposed standards are being adhered to correctly. They look for accuracy in documentation; they check immunizations and CPIC (Canadian Police Information Centre) records. This is only a fraction of what might be checked.

When the Lord makes a check on the church, I believe that the first thing he looks at isn't the number of sermons preached in a month, or how eloquently they were presented. His first check isn't even how many people were added to the church. The Lord's first and urgent priority when he enters the sanctuary called by his name isn't how many people got baptized with the Holy Ghost and fire within the year, or the sophisticated way in which the worshippers express themselves.

The first thing that the Master examines when he enters the sanctuary is the record of prayer. When Jesus comes into town, he doesn't visit the casino on the other side of the street, or the body rub parlour yonder, or the pub or the club within proximity.

When Jesus rode, triumphantly into Jerusalem over two thousand years ago, the first place he visited was the temple (Matthew 21:12–13).

In writing to his protégé, Timothy, Paul shared his thoughts on the priorities of the church.

I exhort therefore, that, first of all, supplications, prayers, intercessions, and giving of thanks, be made for all men; For kings, and for all that are in authority; that we may lead a quiet and peaceable life in all godliness and honesty ... I will therefore that men pray everywhere, lifting up holy hands, without wrath and doubting. (1Timothy 2:1-2, 8, emphasis added)

When you enter his presence lifting holy hands, you show that you are surrendering your will to his will.

The prayers of the saints are like sweet smelling perfume in the nostrils of the Father. The lifting up of holy hands is indicative of reverential respect, honour, and praise.

Show me a prayer-less person, and I will show you a powerless person.

I believe in my spirit that in these last days, God is raising up a generation of people who will be militant in prayer and supplication.

God isn't looking for more prestigious executives or people with greater degrees of business acumen. He's not looking for people with accolades. God is looking for men and women, boys and girls, who are totally sold out to him. God is looking for faithful people who will place prayer at the top of the agenda.

God is looking for individuals who will storm the forces of hell with passionate prayer and intercession. There are some satanic strongholds that will only be moved by the dynamite of prayers. These are the days when the people of God must pick up the battering ram of prayer and advance with eager haste upon the satanic ramparts and demolish them.

God is raising up a generation who will rise above the many barriers that bombard and restrict. They will rise above the noise of philosophy and the din of political correctness. They will execute righteous judgment according to the will of God.

Prayer Is Not Just an Emergency Kit

Prayer is not a first aid kit that one pulls from the cabinet when an emergency or crisis arises. It's not a magical wand that one waves during times of trouble; neither is it a "genie lamp" one rubs to make a magical genie pop up. Let's be careful to not use God as an instrument of our convenience. He cannot be manipulated into acting out of our desperation. God answers prayers in his own time and on his own terms.

Yes, his ears are aware of the cries of his people. The Lord, through his meritorious atonement, has given us access to the throne of grace. We can come boldly and receive according to his will. Prayer is not an alternative; it is the first and essential choice. The angels that sinned were not given this privilege. They are forever lost. But we, humans, have access to God's throne of grace through prayer.

Jesus Christ has torn down the middle wall of partition. His blood is on our souls; therefore, when we come to the Father in his name, the Father does not see us, but the atoning blood of the Lamb that was slain before the foundation of the world and manifested at the cross of Calvary.

He who has an active private prayer life will be able to operate boldly in public.

Praying before an audience can be very scary and intimidating; but if you have practiced in private, you will not be afraid when the occasion calls for you to pray in public. Every successful tradesman will test his wares before he presents them to the public.

In 2 Timothy 2:15 God says, "Study to shew thyself approved unto God, a workman that needeth not to be ashamed, rightly dividing the word of truth."

An active prayer life is a consistent prayer life. Consistency in the closet will give you boldness in public.

In his sermon on the mount, Jesus told his disciples, "But thou, when you prayest, enter into thy closet, and when thou hast shut thy door, pray to thy Father which is in secret; and thy Father which seeth in secret shall reward thee openly" (Matthew 6:6).

We need to pray under the anointing of the Holy Ghost. The Holy Spirit is our paraclete (advocate). He knows the areas of our lives where we need help the most. He is acquainted with our infirmities; therefore, he will step in and help us: "Likewise the Spirit also helpeth our infirmities: for we know not what we should pray for as we ought: but the Spirit itself maketh intercession for us with groaning which cannot be uttered" (Romans 8:26).

The Holy Spirit refreshes us and imparts life into our prayers. He matures us over time so that we don't become stagnant, but we move from one dimension of the Spirit to the next. He moves us from deeper depths to higher heights. The Holy Ghost adds fire to our prayer. He destroys the yoke of bondage and breaks the spirits of oppression and depression so that they don't destroy us.

He who prays under the power of the Holy Ghost has confidence that what he has bound on earth is paralleled in heaven, and what he has loosed on earth is loosed in heaven. It's not possible for the prayer warrior to stand in this evil day and generation and recover territories unless he is drunk on the Holy Spirit. David pursued, overtook, and recovered all that the enemies had taken. The same God who was with David is with us today (1 Samuel 30:8).

In the arena of conflict, there is always defensive and offensive warfare. In defensive warfare, you protect yourself against the wiles or attacks of the wicked one. In offensive warfare, you are the aggressor. It is you who has staged an attack upon the enemy. You attack before you are attacked. You inflict blows on the enemy and deploy spiritual missiles geared to destroy his strongholds.

The Christian's offensive tactics place the devil and his minions on the defensive. By faith, we wield our spiritual weapons and are determined not to miss the target. He is outnumbered by the enemy, but he knows that by faith, he can conquer all. The weapon of prayer is more dangerous than America's patriot missile systems.

The coward takes no territory, because he attempts no venture. He remains spiritually impoverished, because he is not proactive. The coward is in the army, but not necessarily a part of the army. It is the militant prayer warrior who will conquer territories for God.

Chapter 2
The Prayer Empowered Church: Part A

Creating an Atmosphere of Prayer in the Local Church

My first car was a 1998 Ford Contour that I received as a gift. The power the engine exuded amazed me. I'd turn the ignition on, and this blessed car would run as smoothly as a sweet, melodious, sacred song. The body was a rich maroon, with hardly a scratch, and it was devoid of rust. It was powerful. It was kicking.

Within four years, it became troublesome. Right in the middle of the highway, the engine light would appear, the car would become very sluggish, and then slowly shut down. I'd have to switch to the right lane quickly so that I could pull onto the shoulder. Many times, while I waited for a red light to change, the car decided that it wasn't going to move—it shut down. The mechanic did an overhaul and reported to me that the engine was deteriorating, and it would no longer drive efficiently.

In addition to all this, the brakes failed three times. One night while travelling home from church in heavy traffic, the brakes failed as I neared the traffic lights that had just turned red. I was headed for a crash, but the angel of the Lord appeared as a brilliant light before me and diverted every other vehicle elsewhere. I was brought through the red light safely.

On another occasion, I was driving downhill with a biker in front of me. As the light was changing from amber to red, the Holy Spirit told me to get out from behind the biker. As I did, the brakes failed. The angel of the Lord brought me safely again through the red lights.

The third attempt on my life came when I was about to pass over a raised manhole. The car began to swerve out of control, even though it was a very dry, sunny day. God prevented an accident by allowing every other vehicle beside and in front of me to move out of the way. A stop at the mechanic shop revealed that not only were the engine and brakes failing, but the gas tank was sweating gas.

"Do you mean it's leaking gas?" I asked the mechanic.

"It would have been better if it was leaking gas," he explained, "but it's not. It's sweating gas. The least spark and you'll be blown away."

Then I remembered the raised manhole. God swerved the car away from it so that there wouldn't be any sparks. Had I driven over that manhole, there would have been a spark, because the bottom of the car likely would have touched it. The Lord stopped the plans of the enemy to blow me to smithereens. I prayed over the car, but prayer didn't repair it, so I sent it to the scrap yard. It was time for a new car.

Even though the car was exquisite within and without, it could no longer handle the work it was designed for, or commanded to do. The engine—the most important aspect of the car— was dying.

A church, a leader, or a Christian without an active prayer life will soon shut down. I believe that evangelism fills the church with people; however, prayer drives the predators out so that they do not nest and reproduce in the church.

A car with a dead or diseased engine won't go anywhere. A church, a spiritual leader, or a Christian devoid of a prayer life will indeed die spiritually.

When the engine of the church, prayer, dies, what's next?

It's a blessing to know that when we die spiritually, we don't have to end up in the graveyard; we can seek the face of God, and he will revive us. If we don't feel as close to him as we used to, let it be known that he did not leave us … we left him. We will always find the Lord right where we left him. God is waiting for us to return. He wants to send us revival fire.

Today the children of God delight in chasing after signs, but that is incongruous with scriptures. Signs should follow them that believe. If the people of God would humble themselves and devote themselves to prayer and intercession, they would see more signs, wonders, and miracles manifested (Mark 16:17–18).

As an itinerant evangelist, I move around. Many churches mourn over the decline of participation in corporate prayer. People seem to be more inclined towards the supper room than the upper room. There is a clarion call to rebuild the altar of prayer in our individual lives and in the churches.

The Fire Should Ever Be Burning

How can we expect to see miraculous manifestations if our prayer altars are dead, or the fire is dead? The fire of God should always be burning upon the altar. It should never go out. Under the old covenant, the law of the burnt offering dictated that the priest had a duty to keep the fire always burning upon the altar (Leviticus 1:1–17, 6:8–13). God lit this fire himself (Leviticus 9:23–24). Under the new covenant of grace, the burnt offering is obsolete; therefore, we don't need to keep a literal fire burning on the altar, neither are we required to offer burnt offerings unto God: "For our God is a consuming fire" (Hebrews 12:29).

It's not unusual for the awesome presence of God in the sanctuary to be described as fire. He appeared as fire at the burning bush (Exodus

3:2), and his glory and fire came down when the tabernacle was reared up (Exodus 40:34–38; Numbers 9:14–15). This fiery presence lit the way and guided the children of Israel (Numbers 9:17–23). In Ezekiel's vision, God appeared as fire (Ezekiel 1:4).

The ministers of the Lord are made a flame of fire (Hebrews 1:7). The Word of God was like unto fire in Jeremiah's bones (Jeremiah 20:9). King David felt the infusion of the fire of God as he mused (Psalm 39:3–4).

Wherever there was a sacrifice to God, there was fire.

And David built there an altar unto the LORD, and offered burnt offerings and peace offerings, and called upon the LORD; and he answered him from heaven by fire upon the altar of burnt offering (1 Chronicles 21:26).

Aaron used burning coals of fire to burn incense before the Lord in the holy of holies. The incense sent its fragrance towards heaven. The golden altar of incense was symbolic of the prayers of the saints. The burning coals came from the brazen altar upon which the sacrificial Lamb was slain.

We cannot experience the fire of God until we have gone to the brazen altar upon which the Saviour was slain.

The fire of God will always be upon committed Christians.

"I beseech you therefore, brethren, by the mercies of God, that ye present your bodies a living sacrifice, holy, acceptable unto God, which is your reasonable service. And be not conformed to this world: but be ye transformed by the renewing of your mind, that ye may prove what is that good, and acceptable, and perfect, will of God" (Romans 12:1–2, emphasis added).

Believers in Jesus Christ are summoned to offer their bodies as "living sacrifices" unto God. This is a daily offering; therefore, every believer who remains steadfast in the Lord is surrounded and engulfed by the divine promise of the Father: the inextinguishable fire of the Holy Spirit.

John the Baptist prophesied that when Jesus came, he would baptize his people with the Holy Ghost and with fire (Matthew 3:11). The Holy

Spirit appeared as cloven tongues of fire when he filled the believers on the Day of Pentecost. Through the enablement of the Holy Ghost, they all began to speak in unknown tongues (Acts 2:1–4).

As fire, the presence of the Holy Ghost can be felt moving amongst the people of God. As he moves and operates, he sanctifies that which is offered unto God. He manifests himself in signs and wonders.

Our bodies are the temple of the living God, in which the Holy Spirit dwells. (2 Corinthians 5:1, 6:16) The men on their way to Emmaus confessed that their hearts burned within them as the risen Saviour walked with them and expounded the scriptures unto them (Luke 24:32). The burning presence of the Holy Ghost purifies us of all impurities. He purges our system of the sinful dross in the same manner that the silversmith refines precious metals (Titus 2:14:1 Corinthians 6:11; 2 Thessalonians 2:13; 1 Peter 1:2).

Do not allow the fire to die. If I don't have a personal prayer life, I won't have an interest in corporate prayer. Prayer is the most intense and intimate act that a Christian movement can ever be involved in, because it is communication with the one and only wise, holy God. As a child, I learned to pray unto God.

As living sacrifices, we offer up Holy Ghost-saturated prayer unto God. When the saints offer their bodies unto the Lord, he responds by answering their petitions.

My mother, a pastor, never ceased to pray. Every morning and night she entered a time of prayer. Every Sunday morning there was pre-service prayer in the church. By the time the messenger was ready to deliver the Word, the service was already consumed with the flames of Holy Ghost fire. It was a great joy to hurry to church on Sunday evenings for pre-service prayer at 6:00 p.m. In those days, Christians loved prayer meetings.

The Holy Ghost would infiltrate the sanctuary, and sometimes the prayer meeting would continue for the rest of the service. I remember the altar workers having to lift people bodily from the floor to bring them out at the end of the service. The language of prayer was simple, so nobody felt intimidated when they were beckoned to pray.

I see a trend in Christendom today—everybody wants to imitate everybody else. I can always go online and adopt a prayer from one of those who calls himself a warfare prayer warrior. People need to know that they don't have to be eloquent in speech or grammar when approaching the Father. They just need to enter the throne of God with reverential fear and respect. The Master didn't bid us to come with our eloquence. He bid us to approach boldly. If you stutter like Moses, God will hear. Jeremiah said he was a child and could not speak, but God used him. God doesn't care about our polished verbosity or our loquacity. God is looking for vessels he can use for his glory.

God wants to hear prayers that emanate from hearts filled with gratitude, humility, and submissiveness. Our heavenly Father wants to hear prayers that originate in the depth of the spirit. Blind Bartimaeus' prayer was short, concise, and precise: "Jesus, thou Son of David, have mercy on me" (Mark 10:47b). This simple prayer touched the heart of the Master insomuch that he stood still and commanded that Bartimaeus be called. Even those who forbade him not to trouble the Master changed their attitudes and became compassionate. Jesus delivered him out of the world of darkness.

Luke 18:9–14 tells the story of the Pharisee and the publican, or tax collector, who went to the temple to pray. The Pharisee thought that because he kept the Law of Moses meticulously, he would gain audience with God ... not by a long shot. His legalistic approach did not earn him favour with God. God was not impressed by his show of piety. Piety without a heart of compassion for people is offensive to God, because he is love.

The publican, on the other hand, was a despised person. He had a bad reputation amongst the citizens of the country, because he was a tax collector. Tax collectors were considered traitors and thieves, because they used treachery to extract money from the citizens by charging them more money than was owed; at the end of the day, they pocketed the excess.

In thirty words, the Pharisee bragged about his pious acts. What the Pharisee needed to understand is that only a sincere prayer can effectuate forgiveness of sins to the seeking soul.

The publican stood afar off, smote his breast and cried, "God be merciful to me a sinner." In seven words, the publican confessed that he was an unworthy sinner and asked for God's mercy. He called out to God to save him. The publican went to his house justified rather than the other (Luke 18:10–14). In this passage, "justified" is synonymous with "righteousness." Justification is a legal declaration establishing that somebody is righteous. The high courts of heaven looked down and granted this penitent sinner pardon. Then God purged his record so that it appeared as if he had not committed a crime.

If we aren't careful, we can become pharisaic and enter the throne of mercy with puffed up hearts and inflated egos.

In prayer, we decrease and God increases. The will of man becomes irrelevant when standing in the always-relevant will of God. Prayer is a humbling experience, because man must place himself and his intellect in the lowest place and give precedence to the Holy Trinity. God promises in 2 Chronicles 7:14 that if man will, he will.

We are not worthy to stand in the presence of the Holy Father. The sin of Adam and Eve left us with a crimson stain, but the blood of Jesus Christ set us free from the penalty of the Law.

Righteousness is now imputed into our account because of the meritorious work of Jesus. A sinner can receive forgiveness of sins by praying and confessing his sins unto God. Many folks choose to be part of prayer networks online or over the telephone. There's nothing wrong with this, but we are cautioned not to neglect the assembling of ourselves together for corporate prayer. We need to get excited when we hear the word "prayer."

To cultivate an atmosphere of prayer in the local church, the people need to understand the essentiality of prayer. We need to re-erect the broken-down prayer altar and ask God to rekindle holy fire around and upon that altar. Whenever there is a downpour, there will be an outpouring.

The barometer of any Christian's spiritual life, growth, and endurance in this apostate world is prayer. A barometer is a device that measures atmospheric pressure, or it can be a measuring system that shows the extent, amount, quantity, or degree of something. When Elijah prayed on Mount Carmel, the fire came down from heaven and consumed the offering and licked up the water. After that prayer, he was so full of the power of God that he outraced the chariot of King Ahab (1 Kings 18:41–46).

The church is not without strength, because she was born in the fire of Pentecost.

"But ye shall receive power, after that the Holy Ghost is come upon you: and ye shall be witnesses unto me both in Jerusalem, and in all Judaea, and in Samaria, and unto the uttermost part of the earth" (Acts 1:8).

The body of Christ has suffered from growing pains since the ascension of Jesus, but spiritual growth and expansion comes from growing pains. Shortly after the descent of the Holy Spirit on the day of Pentecost, the body of Christ experienced a growth explosion. The infant Jerusalem church came under the attack of the enemy, and its members were scattered abroad. Everywhere they went, revival broke out, and the church grew daily.

It seems that corporately and individually, Christians grow when they are under persecution or undergoing great affliction. Why? Persecution seems to bring people together, and most folks will pray when trouble comes.

United in Prayer

The church of God is at a strategic point in her life. She is on the verge of takeoff, and the most critical point of any airplane flight is either the takeoff or the landing. The church must keep the prayer banner high, because we are in desperate times. Jesus found it necessary to pray, and before he left, he taught his disciples to pray. The pressure on the church to backslide or enter gross compromise is intensifying. She needs to discipline herself to pray fervently again.

The ministry of prayer has been and will always be a wonder-working spiritual discipline in which Christians are privileged to participate. God sends down his love in a vertical way; now we must allow our love to permeate the world around us in a perpendicular way. Without the love of God reigning in our hearts, we won't pray fervently for the world around us ... and the world needs prayer.

Was Christ not paying us a high compliment when he endorsed us as salt and light?

"Ye are the salt of the earth: but if the salt has lost its savour, wherewith shall it be salted? It is henceforth good for nothing, but to be cast out, and to be trodden under foot of men. Ye are the light of the world. A city that is set on an hill cannot be hid. Neither do men light a candle, and put it under a bushel, but on a candlestick; and it gives light unto all that are in the house. Let your light so shine before men, that they may see your good works, and glorify your Father which is in heaven" (Matthew 5:13–16).

Salt touches dead things and stops the putrefactive process. Like salt, prayer changes things. You are the change that God wants to see in society.

The early church discovered that the key to successful Christian living was dining on a daily diet of the Word of God and prayer, coupled with fasting. The first century believers surrounded themselves and the church with consistent prayer. They had seen the martyrdom of Stephen in Acts chapter 7; therefore, when Peter was incarcerated by the wicked, the church came together in prayer (Acts 1:13–14, 12:5, 11).

When the devil comes to town, he comes with an agenda. When he sends his minions out, he has a specific subject and a specific territory or geographic location in mind. Several people bearing the name Herod are mentioned in the Bible, but the Herod of significance in Acts 12 was Agrippa I, the grandson of Herod the Great. Herod Agrippa was a tyrant—a dangerous man. He executed his vicious acts against the church by mercilessly executing high profile leaders in the body of Christ. He slaughtered James, Zebedee's son, with the sword.

James, as well as Peter and John, were close companions of Jesus. They'd gone places with Jesus and had spiritual experiences with him more than any other disciple. On the Mount of Transfiguration, they experienced the glory of God. They were chosen to be watchmen with Jesus as he prayed in the Garden of Gethsemane, and were eyewitnesses in the room when Jesus brought back Jairus' twelve-year-old daughter from the dead. James was epitomized as a spiritual giant.

God is famous for sending the church a word of consolation when she is under fierce persecution (John 16:33).

Prided by the overwhelming response of the Jews, Agrippa apprehended and placed under maximum confinement the most visible and vocal icon in the Christian movement—Peter. He dared not execute Peter, because one of the dictates of Jewish law is that such should not occur during the season of the Passover, or Feast of Unleavened Bread.

The devil is a tactician, but God is a strategist.

God allowed Peter to be taken into custody at a most strategic and historical time of the year. The Feast of Unleavened Bread is very sacred to the Jewish people.

Peter was delivered to four quaternions, or squads, of soldiers. Time was divided into four military watches, and each watch lasted three hours. A soldier served for three hours, rested for nine hours, and then served again. A soldier must be alert and attentive always while on duty, so rest was necessary. Peter was shackled with two chains and placed between two guards. Other guards kept watch at the door of the prison. (Acts 12:1-12) Herod probably took extra precautions because he knew that this apostle had been supernaturally delivered from prison once before by the all-powerful, all-mighty God of heaven and earth.

Peter and the church were operating under the power of almighty God. The power of God is a one-of-a-kind power that has the capacity to open prison doors, pulverize chains, and cause earthquakes in diverse places. God doesn't need to employ camera tricks or special effects; neither does he need gimmicks or a stuntman. God knows when to slow down the process, and he knows when to expedite. He is strategic.

Herod Agrippa had likely heard how God had been using Peter as a mighty catalyst in his kingdom. God used Peter as a conduit to spread the gospel of the kingdom after the descent of the Holy Spirit on the day of Pentecost. Three thousand souls were saved and added to the church that day alone. God instrumentally used Peter and John in the healing of the lame man at the Gate Beautiful.

Herod probably heard how Peter boldly spoke to the council at Jerusalem; after prayer, the place shook. He would know of the fate of Ananias and Sapphira (Acts 5:1–11). High on the anointing of the Holy Spirit, Peter discerned that this couple had jointly planned to lie about the returns gained for the property sold. Ananias and Sapphira died because of their error.

Having known the power of God, Agrippa set forth to challenge God. He heeded not the fact that security guards, high walls, and prison bars couldn't survive under the chastening hand of El Shaddai. While Peter was kept in prison, the church assembled together and prayed on his behalf. According to Leviticus 23:6, the Feast of Unleavened Bread lasted seven days. The Lord allowed the church seven days and nights of ceaseless praying. The brethren called upon the name of the Lord. They aimed at a specific target.

The days of the feast of Passover passed. Peter was awaiting the verdict, but he didn't seem concerned about the terrors of the next day. While Herod waited for the day to dawn to bring him before the people, the man of God slept comfortably between the two guards. The odds were against Peter, but the church had been travailing in prayer for six days. Tension was mounting. In scriptural numerology, six is symbolic of man. Seven is God's number of perfection. Man had done his time; God was about to step in.

While Peter slept, an angel of the Lord came into the prison cell with a shining light. The angel shook Peter and told him to get up. Peter got up, and his chains fell off. The angel told Peter to dress and then took him into the streets and departed. Peter thought he was having a vision, but he soon realized he wasn't dreaming. He'd been delivered from the hands of Herod.

Peter's release from prison came as a shock, even to the brethren who were tarrying for his victory. He knocked on the door of Mary's house, where prayer was being made. Peter was indeed outside—delivered by the power of Almighty God.

The world doesn't need more weapons of mass destruction. The world needs Jesus and more people of prayer. The devil has charged his minions with the office of seeking, stealing, killing, and devouring individuals, families, cities, countries, and nations. Prayer will win the unregenerate to God, turn the backslider from the paths of destruction, restore unity in the house of God, and strengthen the weak.

Throughout history, the devout men and women who influenced the world spiritually were men and women devoted to prayer and seeking the face of God. Every powerful leader who conquered the enemy was a person of prayer. He or she sought God before entering combatant warfare with the enemy.

Herod Agrippa, who killed James and caused pain to come to others, died a terrible death. God dealt him a fatal blow. He was eaten by maggots and he died. One who lived by the sword died by the sword. The Word of God multiplied, and souls were saved. (Acts 12:20–25)

God still works miracles and saves souls by the blood of the Lamb. The battering ram of prayer is still active and powerful. It still pummels the enemy and brings down the strongholds of Satan. It is no mistake that the house of God is a place of prayer.

I reiterate, if you don't have an active private prayer life, it's not possible to have a successful public prayer life.

Chapter 3
The Prayer-Empowered Church: Part B

Initiating and Maintaining a Prayer Ministry in the Local Church

The Prayer Pastor or Coordinator

One of the biggest problems in the church and in the lives of individual Christians is the lack of consistency in our ministry of prayer. You've been praying, but you haven't organized and set in motion a prayer ministry in the church. You cannot have an effective prayer ministry without a designated leader or coordinator. Any movement or organization without significant headship or leadership will evolve into a monster: "In those days there was no king in Israel: every man did that which was right in his own eyes" (Judges 21:25).

The generations that followed Joshua and his contemporaries failed because there was no significant leader to reinforce the statutes of God. Leadership kept dying, and after each death, everything went into a tailspin. Everything and everyone took a downward spiral until they hit rock bottom and ended up in sin and idolatry.

Leadership seemed to have ended in a vacuum (Judges 2:6–23).

One would think that the book of Judges would have been an astounding sequel to the book of Joshua, but as the scripture above states, every man did that which was right in his own eyes.

One has to search diligently in order to find committed people today. Some folks operate on the principles of "feel good." I will do it or be a part of it if it makes me feel good.

The church needs to seek God in prayer and fasting before she chooses people to lead in significant roles. A candidate might be able to pray, but that doesn't mean that he is ready to give significant leadership to the ministry of prayer, or to any other ministry. A person might be able to pray a polished, awe-inspiring prayer, but that doesn't mean that he's ready to take on the challenges of leadership of a congregation. On the other hand, a person might not be able to pray fire down from heaven, but that person is committed and can be taught. Every leader has the capacity to learn and grow.

No great person or leader became great or excellent overnight. Greatness, excellence, and effectiveness are progressive entities. Before you appoint a prayer pastor or coordinator, you must first seek God.

The prayer pastor or coordinator should be responsible for arranging prayer sessions in the local church and designating individuals to facilitate prayer meetings in private homes or the communities beyond the four walls.

It's not the expository preaching, the sanctimonious appeal, the wonderful singing, the beautiful cathedral, or the high-calibre people attending that give a local church credence. What gives the local church credence is the way in which she practices what she preaches by serving the community. The church's attitude prints a more lasting impression upon the minds of the people than her preaching. People are more apt to join the fellowship of the local church that is visibly involved in community activities. The church should model Christ, and Jesus had a prosperous and effective outreach ministry. The first century church also had an effective and prosperous outreach ministry.

The church evangelizes the world. She baptizes the new converts. She educates and equips the evangelized interns, and then she sets them forth to serve their communities with excellence. The church is not the physical edifice where we congregate for worship services. The church is within you; therefore, everywhere you go, you bring the church.

When we expect visitors, we hurriedly clean up the church building and premises, but the believer—the true church—must remain in a state of constant readiness, because we don't know the minute or the hour when the Son of Man will put in his appearance.

God chooses different people to lead in specified areas of ministry. If God chooses the eagle, then use the eagle. If he chooses the raven, then use the raven to the glory of God. Every choice of God is a sovereign choice.

In 1 Kings 17:3–6, God sent Elijah to hide by a brook. He also commanded the ravens to feed him. Elijah had a choice. He could have abhorred and refused the ministry of the ravens, because the raven is considered a ceremonially unclean bird (Leviticus 11:13–15). Had he done that, he would not only be impeding and tampering with the ministry of the ravens, but he also would have impeded and opposed his own ministry and the work God wanted to do in that region. His ministry was effective because of his willingness to do the work of the Father according to his will.

In 1 Samuel 6:10–12, we see the Ark of the Testimony on a cart drawn by two milking cows. The Philistines captured the ark when they won the victory over the children of Israel; but, God had not appointed cows and carts to carry the Ark of the Testimony.

In 2 Samuel 6:1–7, we learn that King David attempted to bring the Ark of the Testimony back to Jerusalem. He committed a great error when he placed it on an oxen-drawn cart. David imitated the Philistines—the world system. The oxen stumbled, and Uzza died when he tried to steady the ark. God had appointed and consecrated the Levites to bear the ark, with the staves thereon, upon their shoulders when in transition (Numbers 4:15; 1 Chronicles 15:14–15). God always anoints before he appoints.

How often have we abused, abandoned, forsaken, and rejected the supernatural works of God because we didn't like his choice. Every member of the body serves a purpose. The body will never function optimally if I chose to inflict a damaging blow to the head, or to any other member of the body. The body is hurting because some of the faculties are maimed. Spiritual paralysis is one of the prevailing conditions of the era. The Great Physician is here. We need to seek him for healing.

Elijah came to a place where he had no choice but to receive the ministry of the ravens. The supernatural power of God cannot be manifested in an atmosphere of resentment of the sovereign choices of God. God will not manifest his presence amongst a people who have set their hearts on selectivity according to their own fleshly appetites and desires.

Here is another scenario. Elijah was at the place of divine appointment, yet the brook dried up. Next, he was instructed of God to go to Zarephath of Zidon. God had commanded a widow there to sustain him. Again, Elijah had a choice: obey the will of God, or die. He could rehearse to God what God already knew. God knew that Zarephath of Zidon was the home of Etbaal, Jezebel's father. God already knew that the heart of Baalism beat strongest in this region. In that patriarchal society, it was unusual for a woman, especially a widow, to sustain a man.

There is nothing that Elijah could tell God that he didn't already know. God intended to use this woman for his glory. God was about to perform the supernatural in a place where Satanism was prevalent. He chose this place in which there would be a showdown between the powers of darkness and light, the forces of evil and good, and the powers of obedience and rebellion. God knew that the enemy was going to kill the widow's son, but he was going to descend and demonstrate his resurrection power.

Elijah obeyed God. He worked with the ravens and the widow and became a part of the change that God wanted in that society. He didn't question why the ravens or why the widow. He received them, without prejudice or discrimination, to the glory of God.

The person to whom God has chosen to give leadership to the ministry of prayer must show readiness, because this is demanding. The prayer leader must be in touch with the reality of time and season. Prayer is hard work and can be very draining. A prayer pastor or coordinator will soon burn out if he or she doesn't have back-up support or fighter escort. He or she is designated to enter the harshest spiritual atomic war zones; therefore, support is needed. God didn't call the prayer leader to stand alone. The entire church is expected to be actively engaged in prayer, especially those who are anointed with atomic prayer power.

As a child, I grew up in the countryside, where dogs were mainly kept outside. Almost every family had one or more dogs. You could tell whenever something fishy was going on outside during the night, because one dog up the street would begin to bark, and soon every dog in the neighbourhood would join in the chorus. If the intruder was a bandit, he or she was in for a rude awakening—being ripped apart in the wake of canine madness.

This is one time when all dogs forgot about personal conflicts and allied together to expel the perpetrator. Every householder was alerted by the persistent barking, and was therefore able to stand guard. You could always tell when the danger, or supposed danger, had passed, because the barking subsided and all was quiet again.

The prayer leader is not called to work solo. Leaders cannot do it alone. The spiritually armed soldiers need to join forces with the prayer pastor or coordinator.

Prayer Teams, Intercessory and Strategic Prayer Forces

Now that we have a prayer leader, it's time to prepare the people for prayer. Later, we can incorporate auxiliary activities such as a call centre, a drop-in centre, prayer walks, chain prayers, prayer bulletin for praise reporting and outreach, and other ministries. We can join with the world in prayer on Global Day of Prayer. We can also create a website where we can post various documents on prayer and related subjects. For now, let's focus on building the main artery of prayer in the local church. Every other ministry in the local church should make prayer a priority.

The prayer teams and strategic prayer forces are not in the local church just to pray. They are there to assist the prayer leader in developing a prayer manual and distributing pamphlets emphasizing the relevance of prayer in the advancement of the Kingdom of God.

Prayer is vital to spiritual growth and development.

The prayer manual will be subdivided into sections relating to prayer for: the church, church leadership, the governing body of the church, the country, the community, the congregation, the unsaved, the new converts, missions and missionaries, and other areas the team decides upon.

The communities adjacent to the local church need to know that they are situated next to a power-packed, Holy Ghost-empowered church that prays, and that she is available to meet their needs according to the instructions of God.

The Zarephath widow had to exercise her own faith in Jehovah to meet her needs. She had to come in obedience to the voice of the one who was hearing from God.

Elijah gave her a word:

Thus saith the LORD God of Israel, The barrel of meal shall not waste, neither shall the cruse of oil fail, until the day that the LORD sendeth rain upon the earth. And she went and did according to the saying of Elijah: and she, and he, and her house, did eat many days. And the barrel of meal wasted not, neither did the cruse of oil fail, according to the word of the LORD, which he spake by Elijah (1 Kings 17:14–16).

God was true to his promise. He did what he said he would do. The servant of the Lord was not ashamed when he acted according to the will of God. Elijah offered his service and the Word of God. People are fed up with empty words that God has not spoken.

The Necessity of a Safe Operation

Jesus never dispatched the disciples to traverse the streets alone. They travelled in companies. Think safety before you act, and be wise. This is why we formulate prayer groups or teams. When the prayer group is called, especially to a private setting, instructions need to be clear. What is the nature of the situation that we are being called into? This question needs to be answered so that the prayer force can prepare. Even if it's an emergency, the team needs to know what they are walking into.

Never knowingly walk into a situation uninformed. Choosing to meet somebody on a one-on-one basis depends on the person you're meeting, the situation, and the setting. Be accountable to somebody. Let that person know where and when you're going. Report when the session is through.

Too many times we behave as if we're invincible. Satan challenged Jesus to leap from the pinnacle of the temple, but Jesus dismissed Satan with his words. Jesus did not oblige; he did not need to play the hero. The world would eventually learn about him and who he is. His work spoke for him then, and it's still speaking today. Our mission is not to prove ourselves to be super-people before mankind. Our commission is to go into the world, teach all nations, and baptize them in the name of the Father, the Son, and the Holy Ghost. We are called to teach folks to observe all the things God commanded (Matthew 28:19–20).

The Personal Qualities and Attributes of a Prayer Team Member

The Lord qualifies people to become members of a prayer team or any ministry in the church. Those whom God has called, he will also anoint for service. A person called to give leadership to any ministry must possess certain characteristics:

- A personal relationship with God

You cannot be of God and of the devil at the same time, because you'll love the one and despise the other. You'll shun the one and cling to the other. You cannot have a one-night rendezvous with the devil while engaged to be married to the King of Glory. You cannot politick with the enemy and still claim to be a child of the Most High God.

No tree can logically bear both sweet and sour fruit at the same time; likewise, sweet and bitter water will not spring from one stream at the same time. Until you commit yourself to one master, you're not ready to be a part of a prayer team.

- A godly love for souls

A person with godly love for others will be able to pray in an unbiased manner for folks. You need to be able to look beyond the person's faults before you can minister to his needs.

The woman at the well had faults, but Jesus met her in order to minister to her. He even sent the disciples into town to buy food, because they'd probably try to hinder the meeting. Jesus chose to commence the conversation with a current issue, water, before he addressed the real issue.

It takes somebody with the agape love of God to win a sinner. God hates sin, but he loves sinners. We must have a godly attitude when we come to minister to the needs of people. If you don't love people, you're not ready to stand in the gap for them.

> ✤ The heart of a servant, humbleness, and a personal passion for the ministry whereunto you are called and made a minister

Every ministry must be geared to match the vision of the movement. A ministry usually stems from the plans God has for the house and from the vision of the house. The vision of the house and the ministry must align with the plans of God.

A ministry is as powerful as its minister. When we do ministry, we must realize that it's not our ministry, but God's ministry, or gift to the body. The ministry shouldn't be handled as a personal trophy given to decorate the walls of our minds. A ministry will become ineffective if the minister visualizes himself as intellectually superior to everybody else, or if he places himself on a pedestal, so high that nobody can reach him. A minister with such an attitude will inevitably self-destruct. As the apostle Paul reminds us: "[Ministry is] for the perfecting of the saints, for the work of the ministry, for the edifying of the body of Christ" (Ephesians 4:12).

The greatest and most powerful leader is a servant leader. The greatest leader is one who leads with a follower's heart. Your heart will be where you have laid your treasures. If you have laid your treasures in the ministry of prayer, then that is where your heart and passion will be. If you consider yourself a servant, then you will be a humble steward of the ministry of God.

> ✤ The ability to teach and be teachable

I delight to break bubbles, mainly my own. If I'm not teachable, then it's not likely that I'll be effective in teaching others. Why? I don't know everything, so I need to sit under the tutelage of somebody else, so that I might learn the valuable nuggets needed to become an asset to the ministry. If one is not an asset to a ministry, then he will become a liability. Proper training has the affinity for stopping or alleviating liabilities.

Any person who thinks that he doesn't need continuing education will be an embarrassment to himself or to the movement of which he is a part. The world around us is changing because of continuous learning, discoveries, and inventions. New technologies are being developed yearly; therefore, the church cannot sit in her little corner and be out-of-touch with the realities and developing realities of the outside world. She needs to get out of her box and educate herself so that she won't be bamboozled by people of higher learning. You cannot expect to sit with learned men and women and be able to ask and answer questions unless you take the time to study. A workman must give himself to study if he doesn't want to be ashamed.

At the age of twelve, Jesus was found in the temple amongst the doctors, both hearing them and asking them questions. Those educated men were stunned at Jesus' understanding and answers regarding the subject matter (Luke 2:46–47). Paul studied at the feet of Gamaliel (Acts 22:3). If you have something valuable to impart into my life, I'll sit at your feet and learn.

Martha's heart for hospitality was not wrong. There's always a need for hospitality. The problem with her choice was that it subtracted from her time with the Lord. The kitchen and time for feeding the body would always be there, but Jesus would not. The greatest need of the moment was to feed the soul. Martha missed that opportunity, because she was encumbered with many unnecessary things (Luke 10:40–42). As was said before, people today are more inclined towards the supper room than the upper room.

Mary chose the better part, because she sat at the feet of the only one who could feed her famished soul—Jesus. She chose the better part, because Jesus had the tools that were vital to the advancement of the Kingdom of God. The blind cannot lead the blind; they will both fall into the ditch. The learned can teach the ignorant, because he has subjected himself to learning. I must acknowledge the fact that I am ignorant of some things and need to learn them from somebody.

Nebuchadnezzar realized that Daniel and his colleagues would not serve the purpose of Babylon unless they learned the language of the Chaldeans (Daniel 1:3–5). He didn't subject his people to a mere workshop experience; instead, he gave them three years of intensive training and nourishing. He catered to their health. Nebuchadnezzar caught the vision that a healthy person will give better service; therefore, he catered to Daniel and his compatriots' good health. Poor health will engender poor service.

Some of us are under the impression that we can home-school or learn by ourselves. You can certainly do this, but remember that you did not pen the materials, nor did you write the books from which you are self-learning. You didn't invent the Internet, the computer, or the other electronic devices involved in self-learning. Somebody else did. Every time you surf the Internet or open a book, you're tapping into the resources that somebody else provided.

A member of the team must be able to teach and be teachable.

- The understanding that you are comforted to be a comforter

Too often I receive complaints from the seeker that he has been burdened by the problems of the intercessor. Intercessors need to realize that they are there for a purpose—to offer comfort to those who mourn. Some of our experiences might be edifying to some people; however, they might be a turn off to other enquirers. Let the Holy Spirit guide you so that you share only that which will be beneficial to the case at hand. If it's not to the client's advantage, don't mention it.

- Sensitivity to the leading of the Holy Spirit

When you have nothing to say, the best thing to do is say nothing. No matter how much we think we know, the Lord knows much more.

The Holy Spirit is here to guide us so that we don't speak from the depths of our emotions or from the collection of our personal beliefs and ideologies. Personal opinions might lead to false hope.

You're not part of a prayer team to give a person false hope; you're there to speak as an oracle of God. If the Holy Spirit doesn't tell you to say it, don't say it. Use wisdom in all that you say and do. Your personal opinions, even if solicited, might not be the best answer. God knows the maturity of an individual. He will communicate what needs to be communicated at the right time.

A mature Christian who is walking in the Spirit will not fulfill the lusts of the flesh; he will not speak unless the Holy Spirit advises him to do so. Always remember that you're not God; therefore, you cannot solve every problem. You don't have all the answers. Jesus is the answer; he also has the answer.

✣   An awareness of your weaknesses, limitations, and vulnerability

One of the things I learned in nursing school is that I should not take the problems of others onto myself. Many of the needs that might be brought to our attention will be bigger than we are. They might be out of the scope of our learning and practice; therefore, we must employ the knowledge and expertise of those who are specifically trained in that given area.

For example, if the situation demands prayer and counselling, don't offer counselling unless you're trained to counsel. You're not there to counsel; you're there to pray. You can point a person to available resources and options, but if you're not a credentialed counsellor, don't counsel. A doctor is trained to diagnose and treat diseases. Leave the diagnosis and treatment of the disease to the doctor.

Never try to undertake a matter for which you're unprepared. Therefore, it's important to have prior information concerning the cases you are called upon to tackle. When you work as a team, your client needs to know beforehand that you're a part of a team. There are some things that must be shared if intercession is going to be made.

It's not a sin to take a sabbatical from your duties if you're not emotionally or physically stable. After a prayer meeting, you need to be poured into. One of the biggest mistakes ministers make is to give and give until their reserve is depleted. When you pray, you release virtue, and others pull from your strength. The minister needs to be ministered to. Do not neglect your spiritual health. If you don't take care of yourself, who will?

✤ The awareness that you are under the banner of an overseer.

We know that many people cannot handle success. As soon as they get promoted, they want to do their own thing. Filled with pride, they begin to undermine the senior leader(s). They speak with condescension to those who have authority over them. You are accountable unto your overseer, because he watches over you.

Obey them that have the rule over you, and submit yourselves: for they watch for your souls, as they that must give account, that they may do it with joy, and not with grief: for that is unprofitable for you. (Hebrews 13:17)

Remember that when you go out to do service for the Lord, you're not going for yourself alone, but are representing the body of Christ. You represent your church and your overseer.

Most of all, you act as an ambassador for God.

Your overseer is accountable to God for you. If you find him in error, don't expose his nakedness in public. Speak with him privately, if possible. The prayer force watches over the local church and the people of God. You are a blessed and vital member of the prayer force, so whatever you do will either bring the ministry glory, or shame. At the end of the day, it doesn't matter who scores the winning goal. The entire team takes the prize.

✢   A reputation for being trustworthy, confidential, and available

People in dire situations will confide in pastors and people of prayer. They need ministers who are available. We are called to be fishers of men. How can I fish if I'm never at the river? As a healthcare provider and professor, I've learned and taught the importance of confidentiality when dealing with privileged information. A person reserves legal rights to his privacy; therefore, keeping confidence is one of the core duties of a healthcare provider.

A minister is a healthcare provider engaged in the office of spiritual healthcare of individuals in a covenant community setting. The minister of prayer gives spiritual healthcare to people who might have desperate needs, some of which are highly personal and sensitive. I know the importance of being specific in prayer, but if the subject matter can't be shared openly, then a person should not be coerced into doing so.

What is shared in private must remain in private unless consent to share has been attained. Most churches don't usually ask the folks they minister to in prayer for signed consent to share their information, but it's a thought to be considered. Do you share privileged information over the telephone, via email, in the marketplace, or on Facebook? Remember that these modes of communication aren't safe, neither do they guarantee confidentiality. Information can get lost in the system.

Lasting relationships form as trust develops. When trust and confidentiality are breached, relationships die.

Some years ago, I sat on a bench in a shopping mall. My back was turned to the three ladies who sat on the other side of the bench. The highlight of their conversation was the pastor's son, who was undergoing a divorce. They took no thought that I was listening and might know the people involved (which I did).

The church creates a trusting environment; however, anyone who wishes to become transparent must first know that it's not always possible to keep all information private. Certain information must be shared with the proper personnel. What do you do if a person tells you that he needs to confess a crime to you, such as murder or sexual molestation? Are these things to be covered up, or should they be reported to the authorities? There are certain circumstances in which the obligation to confidentiality can be overridden.

The prayer manual should clearly outline the legal ramifications of withholding or releasing such information from/to the authorities. You don't want to become an accessory to a crime, nor do you want to impede justice. It needs be established that certain information cannot be withheld but must be released to the proper personnel. An enquirer who is requesting prayer needs to know that the church has a legal responsibility to share or report things of a criminal nature. In this way, a person who is about to release sensitive data cannot say later that he was not informed.

The release of confidential information is a serious undertaking, and the decision to report a situation must be legally warranted and not malicious. The permissibility of breaching confidentiality must be based on proven facts or reasonable proof. Seek legal advice, seek the advice of your superior, and seek the Lord before you attempt disclosure of confidential information. Cover yourself and your church. Know your legal rights and limits, and know your client's legal rights.

Let us not be naïve in thinking that because this is church, we reserve the right to invade a person's privacy. If a person doesn't want to reveal his prayer request, let him be. The church is in the business of healing, not hurting. People will approach the prayer team for various needs. They will come on the behalf of others. Again, we need to know what to broadcast and what to keep quiet about.

The prayer ministry in the church is vital to the ministry of the Word. The preacher needs the prayers of the saints, because many times he's bombarded by the forces around him. Prayer can offer the preacher clearance. In ancient times, the Ark of the Testimony preceded the children of Israel as they went to battle. The singers would go before the army as heralds. Prayer should precede the preaching of the Word. It can set the stage for miracles.

- A good disposition and a good reputation amongst the brethren and in the community

"Wherefore, brethren, look ye out among you seven men of honest report, full of the Holy Ghost and wisdom, whom we may appoint over this business" (Acts 6:3).

"Moreover he must have a good report of them which are without; lest he fall into reproach and the snare of the devil" (1Timothy 3:7).

The person appointed to be part of the prayer ministry team must earn the respect of the people he serves. Your authenticity should not be questionable; if doubts about your integrity arise, let them be false. The person of prayer must live a life devoid of licentiousness and not lacking in legal or moral restraints, especially in matters of a sexual nature. You should display moral decency and etiquette always. You should not be one who resists constructive criticisms or loving correction: "Brethren, if a man be overtaken in a fault, ye which are spiritual, restore such an one in the spirit of meekness; considering thyself, lest thou also be tempted" (Galatians 6:1).

A prayer warrior is a peace maker and not someone who facilitates the continuation of war and strife. You are called to be a part of the solution, not a part of the problem. The prayer warrior, or anybody placed in a position of leadership, should not lack decorum. He or she should exhibit good taste and propriety in conversation and in behaviour. You should have strong will-power and uphold the holy standards of God.

The person standing in the office of prayer should be one who follows godly protocol and teaches others to comply. He should be a person of his word, and not be double-tongued or double-minded. He should not be crafty or deceptive in his business association, but be honest and always keep in mind that he is a representative of Jehovah.

- A willingness to dress in modest apparel when on the battlefield for the Lord

When we gather to pray, whether in a corporate or private setting, we should be mindful of our attire. A man or a woman in a posture of prayer or worship should not have his or her attention captivated by the sexy persona standing or kneeling next to him or her. Attention should be focused on the Lord and prayer. We should adorn ourselves appropriately so that we don't put a stumbling block in the way of our sisters and brothers. Modesty in apparel applies to both the woman and the man of God. The way I choose to garb myself will be determined by the attitude and intent of my heart: "And, behold, there met him a woman with the attire of an harlot, and subtil of heart" (Proverbs 7:10).

What is the attire of a harlot?

The chronicler of the book of Proverbs doesn't elaborate, but in my opinion, the attire of a harlot would be any manner of dressing that is sexually explicit and revealing. It is the type of garment bearing with it an undertone which might be saying to the viewer. "I am available for…"

The child of God should strive, always, to communicate the message that he wishes the listeners or viewers to see and hear. Your moral character should not be questionable. We should studiously refrain from drawing attention to ourselves. Is my choice of garments geared towards attracting and enticing my brothers to lust and consequently sin? I should attire myself as a sober saint of God.

The woman of Proverbs 7 not only dressed herself in a tell-tale fashion, but she had devised a scheme to lure the wanton man into her bedchamber. Like the spider, she spun her web to catch the unsuspecting victim. Overcome by his own lust and by the smooth and slippery speech of the seductress, he got caught. My manner of dress speaks volumes whether I mean for it to or not. Am I dressed to kill, or am I dressed to edify? Every provocatively sexy persona knows her intent.

The Lord doesn't want to see our nakedness when we come before him.

When Adam and Eve discovered their nakedness, the first thing they did was make a covering for their bodies. God changed their partial coverings of aprons, made from fig leaves, to full coverings made from the skins of animals. These coverings carried a double meaning: they needed full covering, and blood had to be shed to cover sin.

Anybody who professes to be godly will do what pleases God. Whatever we do to draw attention to ourselves and not bring glory to God is sin. We also make the Word of God of none effect. A woman should adorn herself with shamefacedness and sobriety. We don't want to do anything that will negatively affect our testimony as children of God.

Many people won't be offended by the immodest apparel donned by the unsaved, but they will be offended by what the redeemed of the Lord wear. The Christian is expected to be an example of Christ. A wise woman builds her credibility and reputation, but a foolish woman tears down herself with her own hands. The Lord also addresses the way we dress our hair, and the accessories we wear. Paul admonishes women to adorn themselves in a manner that communicates godliness with good works (1 Timothy 2:10).

The Policies and Procedures Manual

Every church should have a policies and procedures manual. The statutes of God remain constant over the ages, but the same cannot be said about society's legal climate. The church of today is not exempt from lawsuits; therefore, she must prepare herself for anything. She must take every measure to protect her members and the ministry.

As a member of healthcare community, I'm in constant contact with policies and procedures manuals. Policies are documents outlining the rules, regulations, and actions to be executed in given situations. A policies and procedures manual should clearly define the vision, mission, and expected outcome of the ministry. While policies outline rules and regulations, procedures address the way in which an action should be undertaken.

- ❊ A policies and procedures manual provides vital and relevant information about the movement or ministry. It furnishes materials for reference; it also contains records for evidence and for authentication of the ministry and the services provided. When formulating policies and procedures:

- ❊ Be short, clear, concise, and precise. Express exactly what you mean to convey to the reader. Write in such a way that the reader will not be misled into thinking that you mean something else besides what you intended.

- ❊ Do not use jargon or terminology that is not common to everybody.

- ❊ Be mindful of grammatical errors and misspelled words. These can change the meaning of the thought that is meant to be conveyed to the reader. For example: "Pray without ceasing" is not the same as "pray without season" or "prey without ceasing."

- ❊ Do not overstate or exaggerate a point. Once you have made a point, stop talking. Do not blow it out of proportion. You want to captivate the readers, not bore them to death.

- ❊ Have somebody else read and edit your documents before they are posted for the consumer's use. Two heads are better than one.

✼   Acknowledge contributors, properly identify resources gained from the Internet and other sources, enlist references, and get written permission if you wish to utilize the work of others. (Do not allow neglect or complacency to cause a good thing to be blamed.)

God saw the necessity for policies and procedures; therefore, he inspired men and women to write the volume of the book (2 Peter 1:20–21). We don't live in a perfect world. The church must have rules and regulations to guide the workers and for reference in the case of lawsuits. Here are two scenarios to ponder.

A.   Mr. Bob and Miss Meg Prayer Meeting

The prayer team was having prayer at the home of Mr. Bob and Miss Meg. Brother Bruce placed his arm around Miss Meg's shoulder as he prayed for her. As a habit, he kept squeezing her gently. At the same time, Sister Julie innocently held Mr. Bob a little too close. Her breasts rubbed against him as she ministered to him in prayer. Mr. Bob was very conscious of it and embarrassingly uncomfortable. He moved away from Sister Julie, because he thought she was making a sexual advance upon him. Sister Julie felt very bad, and the prayer was ineffective.

B.   Altar Call

People gathered at the altar for prayer at a certain church. The prayer team and altar workers got busy laying hands upon folks and praying. This is not an unusual practice in a church. Sister Mable began to pray for little Jenny, who is only five years old. Sister Mable was an exuberant worshipper and prayer warrior. She towered over little Jenny and spoke loudly into her ears. The little girl looked frightened and began to cry. Mummy came to her rescue.

At the other end of the prayer line, Pastor Pepe laid his hands on the forehead of Sister Evangelina, who is seven months pregnant. She began to fall. Up came Brother Cymbala, who quickly grabbed her around the waist and brought her to the floor. Evangelina winced.

Is anything wrong with these scenarios? Inasmuch as this is prayer, there is a way in which to touch and speak to people when we pray for them. There is a way to handle a child. There is a way to handle people who are pregnant, or people with disabilities. We don't want to injure anyone or repel anyone from ever coming to church or the altar again.

The policies and procedures manual should outline appropriate behaviour at the altar. As soon as the altar service is proclaimed, the ministers should be standing there waiting for the enquirers. The catchers and linen bearers should be in position, even if nobody comes to the altar. When ministering to a person in prayer, it's important to know what language and tones are age-appropriate. Language should be simple yet clear and intelligent; tones should be soft yet audible.

We need to understand the meaning of private space. Be conscious of your breath and spittle, which do fly at times when we speak. We need to be as professional as we are spiritual in the ministries of the church. One must be as human as he is spiritual. Jesus was both spiritual and professional; he was as human as he was divine.

Resource Personnel

Resource personnel can be used as a quick reference when the manual is not readily accessible.

This person is a part of the prayer team and an adjutant to the appointed prayer pastor or coordinator. He has firsthand knowledge of the ministry activities because of his involvement in the design and creation of the manual. He is equipped with vital tools for spiritual growth and advancement in the Kingdom of God. This person is in sync with everything going on in the ministry. He is aware of, and contributes to, the objectives, vision, and mission of the ministry. The resource person can also be engaged in the secretarial aspects of the ministry.

God also has an advisory team—God the Father, God the Son, and God the Holy Spirit. These three make up the executive board of heaven. God consulted with his board at creation:

And God said, Let us make man in our image, after our likeness: and let them have dominion over the fish of the sea, and over the fowl of the air, and over the cattle, and over all the earth, and over every creeping thing that creepeth upon the earth (Genesis 1:26, emphasis added).

God wasn't speaking to himself, but to the members of the Trinity, which included himself. Before he made man, he consulted with and involved every member of his board.

The resource personnel knows that the Holy Spirit should be the mastermind behind the rubric of Christian ministering; therefore, he continually seeks the guidance and counselling of the Holy Spirit.

Dealing with Challenges

We make a big mistake if we think that because prayer is divine communication with God, the ministry won't be challenged. The ministry of prayer will face more challenges and lack of congregational support than any other ministry in the body. The hardest battle to be won in any church ministry is the battle from within. Jesus tells us that any kingdom that is divided against itself will disintegrate. Division will eventually lead to failure (Amos 3:3).

Nothing defeats a purpose more quickly than disunity. Efforts can die quickly when there is no team spirit, whereas unity evolves into strength when team spirit and collaboration exist. Synergism is the heartbeat and breath of teamwork.

It's amazing what can be accomplished in an atmosphere of unity. If you gaze into the azure distance above us, you'll see the sun, the moon, and the stars. Every element of the galaxy is held together by gravitational attraction. God designed it so that they would work together in perfect harmony. You can see what happens when the sun and the moon work contrariwise to the way in which they should work—we have a solar/lunar eclipse, or occultation. In an eclipse, the sun or moon darkens because of its position in relation to the other and the earth.

We live in an interdependent world; somebody is always dependent upon somebody for optimal survival and success. The Father, the Son, and the Holy Spirit provide a perfect example of unity. God gave me a wonderful revelation the other day as I was playing with the word "unity." You and I are inseparable entities of unity. If "U" and "I" are removed from "unity," a devastating crisis automatically unfolds. "NTY" evolves into nothingness if "U" and "I" are not in front of and between them. But when "U" stands before "N," and "I" stands between "NT" and "Y," the equation is completed. "U" and "I" strengthen "NT" and "Y." That is unity.

Unity is the language of love, and it's the spirit needed for kingdom building. An empire-builder facilitates team spirit to draw attention to himself and his accomplishments. He employs others, but doesn't see them as equals. He spreads himself wide like Nebuchadnezzar (Daniel 4:30–34, 37), or like the banyan tree.

A kingdom-builder facilitates team spirit to bring glory to God. He doesn't think about self-aggrandization. He thinks about God and the expansion of the Kingdom of God. A kingdom-builder keeps the unity of the spirit. He not only equips others for followership, but he builds up and endorses others to become prominent leaders.

When the body of Christ faces challenges, it must come together. The law of synergy dictates that unity is strength. A three-fold cord is not quickly broken. God considers the locusts wise creatures, because they work together in bands. If you must separate from each other, do so in peace and don't hinder the ministry with contentions and strife. There came a time when even Paul had to separate from some of his ministry colleagues (Acts 15:36–40).

We won't always see eye-to-eye with each other. Not everyone will embrace the vision of the house. Circumstances will sometimes erupt, causing bitter contentions and conflicts that cannot be resolved readily. There comes a time when apartness might be the better choice. If one must separate, try to do so in peace.

Paul, Barnabas, and John Mark might have prayed over the prevailing situation, but they ended going separate ways. When contentions erupted between the herdsmen of Abram and the herdsmen of Lot, Abram came up with a solution. He suggested to Lot that the best remedy for the situation was separation (Genesis 13:8–9). Let not the angry passion of strife and contention arise amongst us, because we are children of the Most High God.

Prayer creates an atmosphere for miracles, but strife and contention interfere with the flow of the Spirit. They will eventually lead to division. God is not the author of confusion. Paul challenged the Ephesians brethren to keep the unity of the Spirit in the bond of peace.

Praise Reporting

When the Lord has done something good, the world needs to know. Nobody should tell you that you need to burst forth in praise and thanksgiving. You have received answers to prayers. God has yielded the increase. It's time for you to encourage others who are still waiting for their breakthrough: "And one of them, when he saw that he was healed, turned back, and with a loud voice glorified God, And fell down on his face at his feet, giving him thanks: and he was a Samaritan" (Luke 17:15–16).

The Lord is worthy of our thanksgiving. He is worthy to be worshipped in the beauty of holiness.

The Lord has done great things for us, whereof we are glad. Give him praise and glory.

Praise him for his grace and his mighty acts. He did not have to do what he did, but he did.

Settings for praise reporting can include:

- Testimony services

- Weekly prayer meetings

- Prayer outreach meetings and prayer through telephone connections

- Prayer vigils and chain prayer meetings

- Strategic intercessory prayer meetings

- Prayer breakfasts

- Prayer conferences and concerts of prayer meetings

- Upper room convocations where there is tarrying for things such as healing and deliverance.

- Prayer tea parties

- Other gatherings

✣ Publications, Facebook, Internet, etc.

Have a prayer request box available so that prayer requests and praise reports can be dropped off. The designated personnel will retrieve them periodically. The prayer pastor or coordinator must encourage the prayer teams and church leaders to submit whatever praise reports they must share.

Praise reporting need not be confined to the ministry of prayer. Any ministry with a praise report can seize the opportunity to let others know what the Lord is doing. When bad things happen, the world hears about it. Should the world not know when great things are happening?

A Watch and a Back-up for the Watchman

The appointed prayer warrior is also the watchman. God didn't call the watchman to stand alone. Prayer is very demanding work, and every watchman needs to be watched over. We know that the angel of the Lord encamps around those who fear him, and that God will deliver his servant (Psalm 34:7); however, the watchman needs somebody he can turn to when the need for spiritual support arises.

A prayer warrior needs somebody who is watchful in the spirit. The watchman's watchman is like an armour bearer. He is equipped with additional weapons as back-up, or reinforcements, for the commander.

Moses became physically drained during the battle with the Amalekites, so Aaron and Hur provided a stone for him to sit on. Then they held up his hands so that they wouldn't fall. In so doing, Israel won the battle against the Amalekites (Exodus 17:9–14). Physical maladies and fatigue can weaken the leader; therefore, back-up support must be set in order.

Abimelech (Judges 9:54), Saul (1 Samuel 16:21), Jonathan (1 Samuel 14:6–17), and Joab (2 Samuel 18:15) had armour bearers. Part of their responsibility was to have extra weapons ready for their leader. The watchperson finished the job of killing the enemies wounded by their masters.

We don't read about armour bearers in the New Testament; however, right after his wilderness experience, Jesus travelled to Capernaum and began to preach repentance. There he recruited disciples, but he never sent a disciple on the mission field by himself. They always travelled in company (Mark 6:7; Luke 10:1). Judas went on a mission by himself and fell into sin; he suffered the consequence.

When we come under satanic attack and spiritual pressure, we need spiritual back-up to pray us through.

"… woe to him that is alone when he falleth; for he hath not another to help him up … And if one prevails against him, two shall withstand him; and a threefold cord is not quickly broken." (Ecclesiastes 4:10, 12)

People are more apt to fall into sin and trouble when they have no mentor, or when they fail to walk in the counsel that the mentor or advisor gives them. King Saul fell into trouble because he did not heed the wise counsel of the prophet Samuel or submit to the instructions from the Lord (1 Samuel 15).

One of the biggest mistakes a prayer warrior makes is to pray for everybody else but not pray for himself. You need to surround yourself with praying people. You are a target, because you are a firing-line person. Engage yourself in regular personal prayer. We know that God will take care of you, because you are his child, but you also must take care of yourself. You'll be of no use to anyone if you burn out.

The devil and his angels know the genuine Christian and prayer warrior. If nobody else encourages you, learn to encourage yourself in the Lord. Even David encouraged himself when the people thought to stone him (1 Samuel 30:6). God has positioned you in the Spirit upon the walls and at the gates to keep watch and be on the alert for intruders. You are the one who is expected to sound the alarm so that the others can stand guard.

If the watchman sees the sword coming and doesn't warn the people, he will be guilty of the blood of anyone who gets harmed. But he is free of the blood of the people if he warns them (Ezekiel 33:6–9). You cannot be careless, because you're always in a position of offense or defense. The enemy is always on the lookout for you. He has assigned some vicious agents to keep tabs on you, but you are under the blood of Jesus.

In addition to watching over the watchman, the back-up support should know what the will of God is for the people. Like the appointed prayer warrior, the support should be able to discern the battle in the spiritual realms: "… as soon as Zion travailed, she brought forth her children" (Isaiah 66:8b). If we travail together, we shall bring forth together. When Jacob desired to receive the blessing of God, he travailed all night until the breaking of day. He said, "I will not let thee go, except thou bless me" (Genesis 32:26b).

Every now and then, the prayer team, along with the church, might have to wrestle all night long in order to bring forth. The apostle Paul also travailed for the people of God: "My little children, of whom I travail in birth again until Christ be formed in you" (Galatians 4:19).

A mother will tell you that the pangs of labour are almost unbearable, but she pushes as she travails, because she knows that at the end of the pain, a beautiful baby is coming.

We are all stewards in the vineyard of the Lord. If we build righteously upon the foundation that Christ laid, we will one day reap the blessings of the Lord (Matthew 25:21–23; 1 Corinthians 9:24).

In closing this chapter, let me say that no two leaders lead alike. A ministry is as strong as its leader. People will gravitate towards what the leader emphasizes, promotes, and practices. Remember that we have people under our tutelage. We should always lead by example. Ministries and visions are birthed when we pray and intercede.

Chapter 4
The Prayer-Empowered Church: Part C

Motivating Youth to Pray

Leaders reproduce their kind. It's true that a chain is only as strong as its weakest link. Every movement is as strong as its leader(s), and the church is no exception. The power of God manifests greatest in the church and in people whose lives are soaked with prayer. Seated at the helm of every prayer-soaked church is a leader who makes prayer a priority.

Any church assemblage without an array of younger people and youth is on the verge of extinction. Today's youth will be tomorrow's giants. If we don't engage our young people in the prayer life of the church, we'll most definitely lose them.

As I quoted earlier, Jesus spoke with the doctors in the temple. He both listened and asked questions, and he was only twelve years old. Jesus could have been gallivanting around town with his peers, but he was not. He was responsibly engaged in useful and effective conversation in the temple at Jerusalem.

Samuel was a young boy when his mother brought him to the temple to serve. He'd been a Nazarite from the womb. As a child, he was girded with a linen ephod, which was part of the priest's garments (1Samuel 2:18). I pause here to insert the importance of prenatal influence. A child might not be able to say or do anything in the womb, but it's believed that he can hear the voice of the mother and father. I believe that if a child is taught in utero about the things of God, he may be born with a spiritual inheritance or predisposition towards godliness.

Many children stray from the path of their upbringing when they grow up, but by the grace of God, the seeds sown from the womb will take root and spring up in later days. The best thing to do in this errant age is to pray and seek God for your posterity. When the spirit of rebellion enters them, do not curse or give the devil more reason to stalk and conquer them. Place them in the hands of the Almighty. God knows everything, and he will give answers accordingly.

Samuel began to do service for God while he was yet young. He gained favour both with man and with God. He grew in grace and in the knowledge and admonition of God. His light shone before men, and many came to glorify God because of his ministry. Samuel could have chosen the other route, because the influence of Eli's sons infiltrated the atmosphere in which he lived. The behaviour of the priesthood of Israel was corrupt and disgraceful. Samuel was young and vulnerable, but God kept him so that he would not backslide.

Eli the priest failed to correct his own sons, but he did an excellent job in rearing and mentoring Samuel. Is it not strange how many times we are quick to condemn others for not supervising and managing their children and homes properly, yet we become slack and permissive with our own children in our own homes? Eli did not fail to confront Hannah about her supposed drunkenness, yet he failed to discipline his own sons. He allowed them to continue with their gross immoral conduct in and around the temple. He addressed the issues concerning them, but that's as far as he went. As a priest and a father, he reserved the right to suspend or remove them from office.

Eli instructed Samuel to communicate with God (1 Samuel 3:9–10). Every person called of God should echo this sentiment: "Speak, Lord, for thy servant heareth." God is still speaking to young people today. I often exhort church leaders, parents, and guardians to speak, especially to young people, according to the words of God. Young people need to hear the older heads speaking positively and graciously about that which concerns the church and holiness. They are already under pressure from the media to sway to that which is ungodly; therefore, they need to hear those things that will nourish and uplift their spiritual man.

The Lord tells us not to undermine and despise the youth amongst us. They have a prophetic destiny. No prophet delights in being the bearer of bad news, but Samuel was given a word for Eli—and he delivered it respectfully. Eli received the word of God from Samuel, because he knew that Samuel was hearing from God (1 Samuel 3:18).

Hannah was a woman of prayer and a worshipper of God. Like the apostle Paul, she had a heart for the young. In prayerful song, she prophesied of the Messianic reign and work of Jesus Christ. Jesus catered to the young as well as to the older. The Lord gave Hannah the son she prayed for, so she made a declaration: "…I have lent him to the LORD; as long as he liveth he shall be lent to the LORD" (1 Samuel 1:28).

God has called and deployed a multitude of young people all over the world to be a voice in this age of grace. As we look at Timothy, we see that Paul tapped into the tremendous power of his youth. Paul saw in Timothy something that was worth salvaging, and he engaged Timothy in the work of ministry. Paul taught Timothy how to carry himself in society and in the church.

In this generation, we need to teach our young people how to carry themselves in the church and in the world. Teach them that adherence to the Word of God and to prayer will keep them in this blood-thirsty and perverse age.

If our young people are going to become prayer warriors, they must learn to pray. How will they learn to pray? They learn to pray when they observe adults bowing before God in prayer.

As you put your prayer teams together, be sure to involve your young protégés. Who is better able to draw other young people into the fold than young people?

Whenever we assemble in corporate weeks of prayer, the young people need to be given the opportunity to participate. The potential of the youngsters around us is amazing, but we'll never learn their true worth until we engage them. Prayer will empower the youth as much as it empowers the adult. We need to speak to our young ones in the language of prayer.

Home-schooling

The first place a child learns anything is in the home. Parents should take the initiative to share their prayer life with their children. The church should only reinforce what they learn at home. If they learn to pray at home, they'll not be stuck when they go abroad. When I was a child, my mother taught me this phrase: "Learn to dance at home before you dance abroad."

Corporate prayer meetings should be designed in such a way that the youth feel it's their prayer meeting also. Give them a chance to read the scripture, lead the devotion, give a word of exhortation, and pray. Corporate prayer meetings should provide the youth with a deeper understanding of the impact of faith on prayer. The one who prays must believe in the one to whom he is praying.

We don't just tell our youngsters to pray—we teach them why they need to pray and then demonstrate by praying and attending prayer gatherings. Most people are comfortable leaving the children at home when they go to prayer meetings, because they think children will be a hindrance. What do you leave them at home to do? In your absence, most of your children will involve themselves in all the lawless things that the multimedia has to offer. Most them will not tune in to a religious program or Bible study while you're absent from home.

It's said that when the cat's away, the mouse will play. Many parents attend prayer meeting and receive the victory but lose it as soon as they get home. Your children might be well trained, but the devourer is loitering outside your crib. His intention is to turn your home upside down in your absence and devour your posterity. We are under divine obligation to train our children, and we do this even before they are born (Proverbs 22:6).

Divine Intervention Needed

The younger generation needs to know that God is not Santa Claus; he is our sovereign Creator. He hates sin, but he loves us whether we're naughty or nice. We have done well ensuring that the next generation earns college and university degrees, and we've taught them the art of self-aggrandization. We haven't failed to supply them with the nuggets on how to be suave businessmen and corporate executives. They are keen on politics and the business of government. Healthcare is well fortified with the young and energetic. We have taught them how to apply makeup, design hairdos, and wear artificial fingernails. Our youngsters wear the most expensive brand name clothing of the era.

Most of our youngsters are marketable, because we've educated them, encouraged them, prepared them, and helped them construct the most appealing resumes. Sadly, after all of this, many of our next generation have lost interest in the church assemblage—even worse, some have lost their interest in God. They even deny the existence of God. The name of God is irritating to many of the children born and raised in the church.

It's heartrending to hear a youngster who was born and raised in the church deny the existence and power of God once he or she gets into the secular world. One would hope that a person raised in the house of God would be rooted and grounded in the Word, but it's not necessarily so.

The power of the prince of the atmosphere is very strong. He is here to devour; therefore, we need to develop young people holistically: physically, spiritually, and emotionally.

Should we be praying for God to make today like the days of Samuel? No! The era in which Samuel lived had its own challenges. Perverseness and wickedness existed. We need to pray that God will turn this generation back towards him, and that the Holy Spirit will visit us with his pulverizing power and crush the calcified hearts of humanity.

Have you noticed that many of our educational institutions and public sectors have rejected the reading of scriptures from the Holy Bible, and the praying of the Lord's Prayer in their gatherings? Is it any wonder why some of our children have turned away from the faith? We cannot leave our children to the world system. It will not lead them to Christ.

The secularists have influenced our young people to forsake the God of their fathers. In Jude 1:3–4, we read:

"Beloved, when I gave all diligence to write unto you of the common salvation, it was needful for me to write unto you, and exhort you that ye should earnestly contend for the faith which was once delivered unto the saints. For there are certain men crept in unawares, who were before of old ordained to this condemnation, ungodly men, turning the grace of our God into lasciviousness, and denying the only Lord God, and our Lord Jesus Christ."

We live in perilous times. We need to contend for the faith and teach this generation to pray. Only God knows what is going to happen next.

Let's challenge our young people to have a genuine love for God and the things of God. Let's also bring to their attention the fact that they need to love others, even as Christ has loved them and given himself as a ransom for their souls. Young people need to know that God hates sin, but he loves sinners with a passion.

Young people today are faced with unique challenges. They have needs and feelings. They have questions about their identity and sexual orientation. The church seems to be losing ground while the media is gaining. If church leaders and prayer warriors have no answers to their questions, they will go into the world to find the answers. Do you think that the world, that is so hostile towards God and holiness, will give them godly answers? No! The satanic world system loves your children—to death!

We equip our children and young people with all the latest in technological gadgets, which has served to isolate children from parents. Technological gadgets have replaced meaningful family times together. It's easier to furnish our youngsters with things today than to spend time with them. Spending time with them doesn't seem to fit our busy schedule. In some homes, parents and children are like strangers to each other. In many homes today, the children are in one section of the house, experimenting with their gadgets, while parents are on the other side doing whatever. We seem to have lost our young ones to the world of consumerism.

Is technology a bad or harmful commodity? Not necessarily. Some of what we use technology to configure might be bad, but technology itself isn't bad. The American Heritage Dictionary defines technology as the application of practical sciences to industry or commerce; the total knowledge and skills available to any human society for industry, art, science, etc. The Free Dictionary describes technology as the application of science, especially to industrial or commercial objectives.

Technology is here to help us, not to become a god. When one makes the television or the Internet an idol, and is more captivated by it than worshipping God, then a problem develops. When the creature worships the created over the Creator, he has made the created his god.

The greatest asset a parent can leave a child is a legacy of prayer and faith in God. I know that everyone must develop his own personal prayer life and faith in God, but a child is more likely to gravitate towards that which he learns from his parents than anyone else. Your life is more of a testimony to the world than is your preaching and teaching.

A child is more likely to imitate what he sees at home than what he sees abroad. David was a victorious shepherd before he ascended the royal throne of Israel. The spiritual example David had at home was probably a part of the reason why he was so strong in the spirit. If his knowledge base of God was non-existent at home, he wouldn't have had the same confidence in God. David was able to apply abroad what he learned at home; therefore, when the devourer came against his flock, he was able to stand his ground. David went from strength to strength, and the Lord of hosts did not fail to deliver him.

Grooming our young people at home is essential to their well-being abroad. It is said that environment has a way of influencing and shaping children. Yes, I know that everyone has a mind of his own and should make the right choices, but we aren't all strong. Some are weak and vulnerable. Faced with a flurry of choices, they become confused and might fall for anything and everything. The weak and vulnerable ones need our attention the most.

What we invest in the young lives around us today will not go to waste; it will come back tomorrow, either as a blessing or as a curse. People, good or bad, shape the communities around them. The communities further shape the expanse of the metropolis, and the metropolises influence the nation. Nations will have either a positive effect or a negative effect upon the world.

The growth or demise of a community, metropolis, nation, or the world is heavily affected by the deeds of the first person or the first family. One act of Adam and Eve changed the world forever, but the action of Jesus Christ changed and revolutionized the world for eternity.

If the church can change one person, she might be able to change one family. If she can change a family, she might be able to change a community. A changed community is one step towards a changed metropolis, and a changed metropolis is a step towards a changed nation. If the church can change a nation, she might be able to change and revolutionize the world. Through prayer and the intervention of the Holy Trinity, the church strives to change the world one person at a time.

Chastity in a Sex-gluttonous Age

We live in a sex-gluttonous and promiscuous age. Almost everywhere you look, you see or hear something that is sexually explicit or bears sexual innuendos. The world system teaches safe sex and the use of condoms. As a healthcare provider, I have seen too many cases of STDs or diseases caused by blood and body fluid transmission or contamination.

Our youngsters need to know that the body of Christ does not teach or uphold sexual promiscuity, adultery, or fornication. The Christian church teaches chaste living and abstinence from sexual encounters until after marriage. Sexual engagements are to occur in a conjugal relationship between a man and a woman (Genesis 2:21–25).

Our youngsters also need to be made aware of the fact that condoms can accidentally break in the act, or be deliberately punctured by a spiteful partner. Many of our youth are under the false impression that it's alright to have sex as long as they don't get pregnant, or that abortion is the best solution to an unplanned pregnancy.

I believe in my spirit that if folks are properly walked through the process of an abortion, they might make other choices. Many children never get to see the light of day because they end up in the vacuums and incinerators of the abortionists. You will never know who you just laid to rest.

Our youngsters should not have to contemplate, attempt, or commit suicide because they feel like they've been caught in a trap with an "unwanted" pregnancy. We need righteous teachers to teach young and unmarried people the truth. Truth brings clarity, and clarity might lead to a change of mind. In my opinion, no baby is an unwanted baby.

Our young people are exposed not only to premarital sexual liaisons, but to alcohol, tobacco, illegal drugs, and other forms of destructive behaviour. It's not enough to say to young people: "Thou shall not." We must be prepared to explain to them why they should not. Youngsters are more advanced in their knowledge of the world than we care to admit.

What cannot eradicate the sins of the world? Only the blood of Jesus can. What can give people the strength to remain committed to their vows? Prayer and more prayer, is the answer. There is a clarion call for the young people of this age to be transformed by the redeeming blood of the Lamb, and to be baptized with the Holy Ghost and with fire. They need to be drenched and soaked with the latter rain. What will cause this to happen? Consistent prayer will be a key factor.

I believe in my spirit that despite what is happening around the world, God is raising up a generation who will organize a campaign against the kingdom of darkness. This generation is going to move through the land with the battering ram of the Word of God and with prayer. They will be empowered by the Holy Spirit. They will not be cowards; they will not be stopped. They will level the enemy's fortifications and confuse and discomfit his garrisons.

He who has a vision for youth has a great vision. The youth ministry is not a peripheral ministry of the church; like prayer, it's a core ministry with promising prospects, potentiality, and possibilities. You cannot begin to minister to young people until you have built a relationship with them. Most members of the next generation will speak to you only if they feel they can trust you. Trust is earned through continuous relationship. This generation is easily turned off by people who dictate to them but remain inconsistent in what they say and do.

Are you youth-approachable and youth-friendly? When was the last time you embraced a youth or a youth activity? It doesn't have to be an activity in the church. It can be one in the community, one in the nation, one in the world, or, better yet, one in your own home. Many of us are quick to support those who are outside, but we give very little love or support to those who are right in our own homes.

Some years ago, I dealt with the case of a thirteen-year-old girl who was in bitter agony and conflict with her mother. I could sense the girl's cry for love and affection. Getting to the bottom of the issue, I learned that she was pining for her mother's love and approval. Mother hugged everybody but her. Mother had a kind word for everybody else, but never commended her child for anything. Mother used derogatory terminology to describe her child. Other members of the household paid her the same distasteful sentiments. The list went on and on. The mother never denied her guilt.

Food, clothing, and shelter are great, but they aren't everything. A child needs to be loved. Some people seek love in all the wrong places, because they aren't getting it at home. Charity begins at home. Nobody can leave home without himself. You always bring "you" wherever you go. It's imperative for children to have a healthy and emotionally stable upbringing to transition smoothly to the next level of growth and development.

Some children might grow up and remain unstable if divine or therapeutic intervention does not intercept. If they aren't healed, they will subject their children, or society's children, to the same abuse they endured. One can only build on the foundation one has. Can one fit a square peg into a round hole? I don't think so, but one can choose to either remain in the rut or seek help to get out. Life's setbacks and challenges can be used as launching pads to catapult us into the next dimension of life and the spirit.

Partner with a young person in prayer. Plan to encourage them according to the Word of God. The prodigal son could have chosen to remain with the pigs and live an unaccomplished life forever. Thank God, he came to himself. When he did, he made a life-changing decision. He arose from his condition and returned to his father. His father accepted him and showed him unmerited love. His son had come home, not in a casket, but alive and well (Luke 15:24).

Yes, he'd insulted his father and, according to the law, he deserved death. To demand an inheritance before the death of his father, or before the father willingly gave it, was another way of saying, "I wish you were dead, Father." What this son did was grossly insolent. Home and family life can have a great impact on children.

Many years ago, I lived next door to a sweet little three-year-old girl named Josie. One morning, Josie approached me by the elevator. She had run ahead of her parents, who were coming not too far behind. She looked me up and down and then in the eyes. She then said the most shocking thing I'd ever heard from a person of her age: "I hate blacks!" I wondered where sweet little Josie learned that.

Whoever and whatever we laud at home will probably receive the same recognition from our children. Our children learn a mighty lot from the system outside, but they learn even more in the home. It is said that we are what we eat. Children are what they learn. The former generation, the present generation, and the next generation have a lot to offer each other. We must all learn to respect diversity.

My neighbourhood is famous for its expertise in landscaping. It gives me great pleasure to drive along the road and admire the exquisitely arranged flower gardens. The colours—red, white, blue, yellow, orange, and peach, among others—stand out in flawless beauty. One cannot help but stop and take pictures. No matter what the colour or ethnicity, no matter if a child came in wedlock or out of wedlock, every child is a beautiful gift from God. Let us pray for our children, but most of all, let us teach them to pray and involve them when we gather to pray. What we invest in them today will bring great returns tomorrow.

My Prophetic Declaration over Our Children

I make this prophetic declaration today:

-Our children will be the valiant soldiers in tomorrow's covenant community of believers in Jehovah. They will sit in the higher echelons of society and over the tumultuous rumbling of ethical dilemmas, sexual perversions, moral declension, and spiritual darkness, they will echo the good news—Jesus saves.

-Nobody will be able to muzzle them, nobody will be able to blindfold them, and nobody will be able to stop their ears.

-In this world filled with religious and political propaganda, the children we have brought up in the fear of the Lord will stand up in this day and age and will win the lost at any cost. No strong man will be able to bind them; no seducing spirits will be able to seduce them; no doctrines of devils will be able to itch their ears, entice them, penetrate their hearts, and conquer their minds and thought processes; and no Judas goats will be able to lure them into the traps of destruction.

-They will be discerners like the children of Issachar.

-Our children will not be tamed by the devil or his agents. The Holy Spirit will keep them sealed, and they will maintain their sanctity. They will become the devil's worst nightmare. He shall tremble in their presence and at the mention of their names.

I seal and endorse this prophetic declaration in the name of the Father, and of the Son, and of the Holy Spirit.

Chapter 5
The Key Ingredients of an Effective Prayer

I find it especially fascinating that Jesus, the Son of God, deemed it necessary to pray. He is the second member of the Holy Trinity. Jesus had the capability to speak the word into the atmosphere and see things happen. He spoke to the wind and the waves, and they obeyed him. He spoke to demons, and they fled, yet he made prayer a priority in his life.

Jesus' faith was intrinsically strong. He arose early in the morning and pulled himself aside to pray. He taught his disciples not merely to pray, but how to pray. From my perspective, the key ingredients of prayer include, but aren't limited to, the following.

1. Recognition

In prayer, we ascribe our deepest veneration, praise, and worship unto God for who he is—the Almighty God, the Everlasting Father, and the Prince of Peace. He is sovereign. He is worthy. As Aristotle put it, God is "sommum bonum," which means, "God is the greatest, supreme, or highest good."

In adoration of God, we focus our heart, mind, soul, and spirit on him, because he is omnipotent, omniscient, and omnipresent. The God of heaven is to be worshipped from the rising of the sun to the going down thereof.

I will love thee, O LORD, my strength. The Lord is my rock, and my fortress, and my deliverer; my God, my strength, in whom I will trust; my buckler, and the horn of my salvation, and my high tower. I will call upon the LORD, who is worthy to be praised: so shall I be saved from mine enemies (Psalm 18:1–3).

God is our Father because he has legally adopted us into his family. An adopted child is entitled to the same benefits and privileges as the biologic child. As an adopted child, I have a duty and an obligation to bless the name of my Father.

My lips were made to give God praise and adoration. His name is great among the nations. He is God above all gods. I will offer myself unto him as a living sacrifice, for he is good, and his mercy endures forever.

What shall I render unto the LORD for all his benefits toward me? I will take the cup of salvation, and call upon the name of the LORD. I will pay my vows unto the LORD now in the presence of all his people (Psalm 116:12–14).

God deserves praises from the objects of his beneficence.

In prayer, we acknowledge God for all that he has been to us. When we come before God in reverential fear, we create an atmosphere for miracles. A truly humble spirit will attract divine attention. As the scripture says, God inhabits the praises of his people (Psalm 22:3). God chose to manifest himself in the context of personal or corporate worship. There is power in praise and worship.

The devil's dominion is overthrown and his chains are broken in a place where God is recognized and worshipped.

And at midnight Paul and Silas prayed, and sang praises unto God: and the prisoners heard them. And suddenly there was a great earthquake, so that the foundations of the prison were shaken: and immediately all the doors were opened, and every one's bands were loosed. (Acts 16:25–26)

In this passage, we see that these men of God were placed under maximum security for an alleged crime. They had cast the spirit of divination from a damsel. This enraged the Philippians authorities so much that Paul and Silas were beaten and jailed. Their feet were immobilized in stocks. If they urinated or defecated, they would have to sit in it and endure the pungent stench of human excrement. The entire atmosphere was one that should have caused Paul and Silas to go into the depressive mode, but they chose rather to glorify God.

At midnight, a shift came in the atmosphere. The other prisoners didn't hear Paul and Silas cursing or charging God foolishly for allowing this to happen. They heard them praying and singing praises to God. Suddenly, God sent an earthquake that violently shook the foundations of the prison and tore the doors asunder. The chains upon their feet were shattered, and every captive was freed. Praises ushered Paul and Silas into the presence and power of the Almighty. Their praises and worship charted the course right to the holy of holies, right into the throne room of God. The power of God descended and intervened in the prevailing circumstances.

God dwells in the atmosphere where he is acknowledged and worshipped. It's not our thunderous prayer that impresses God. It is not our titles, degrees, or accolades that bring us oneness with him. It is sincere worship. Sincere worship and adoration of Jehovah is an index of the heart. God has no respect or desire for lip service. He wants recognition, praise, and worship. Worship speaks of his worth-ship.

The Lord must be at centre stage when congregants come to worship him. All attention is to be upon his majesty. We do not draw attention to ourselves. The more we submit our will to him, the more closely knitted we become with him. As intimacy climaxes, the supernatural happens. Spiritual revelation and pregnancy occur.

Unpretentious worship enters the nostrils of God like the sweet-smelling aroma of incense. God is a spirit, and they that worship him must do so in spirit and in truth (John 4:24).

Habitual worship of Jehovah will become a lifestyle for the individual. The offering of grateful laudation continues even when we are tired and drained. This is what sacrifice is all about.

Satan and his agents hate God; therefore, they hate the sacrifices of praise that are offered unto God. The devil is present at every worship service, trying to shut it down by bringing confusion, tiredness, and lethargy. But the devil cannot stop a genuine worship service. Eventually, he must evacuate the premises.

God manifested his presence and power on the battleground when the children of Moab, Ammon, and Mount Seir waged war against King Jehoshaphat of the Southern Kingdom of Judah (2 Chronicles 20:21–26). Praise and worship preceded victory. God had told the king that he wouldn't have to fight in that battle. All the king had to do was get the praise and worship team together and worship.

God chose to manifest his presence in the most unique way in the context of a prison setting. By his demonstrative and authoritative power, he showed the prisoners and the wardens that he can set captives free. Chains cannot stop God. Bars cannot bombard God. God will show up when we break forth in individual or corporate worship. Prayer and the singing of praises have breakthrough power. Worship is the Christian's declaration to the world of the worthiness of Jehovah. Unpretentious praise and worship send the enemies running. When we begin to usher up praises to God the host of hell will evacuate the premises. "Whoso offereth praise glorifieth me…" (Psalm 50:23).

Trust God to show up when you call unto him.

2. Admission/Acknowledgement

The second ingredient of prayer is acknowledgement of guilt. In acknowledgement, the guilty party admits that he has sinned. He comes before God with a repentant heart and asks God for forgiveness and cleansing from the sins of omission and commission (Psalm 51:3, 32:5).

One cannot confess his sins except he first admits that he has sinned (1 John 1:8-10). If we must receive answers to our prayers, then we must ask the Lord to dip us in the cleansing flow of his blood. Only the blood of the Lamb can cleanse us of blood guiltiness.

David prayed for the hidden sins more than the open ones. Man looks on the outward and judges accordingly, but God knows the constituents of man's heart. He will expose the gross sins that have taken up residence within the recesses of the heart. God has a way of bringing into the open the skeletons of sin hidden within the closets of our minds. (Psalm 51:1–7)

God exposes sin not to embarrass an individual, but to deliver him—if he will receive what God is offering. Confession of sins opens the way for the confessor to be filled with new and better things.

No man also seweth a piece of new cloth on an old garment: else the new piece that filled it up takes away from the old, and the rent is made worse. And no man putteth new wine into old bottles: else the new wine does burst the bottles, and the wine is spilled, and the bottles will be marred: but new wine must be put into new bottles. (Mark 2:21–22)

When a person confesses his faults, repents, and changes his behaviour, he becomes like a brand-new person. As stated in Jeremiah 18, God is the Master Potter. He has a way of breaking us into pieces, and putting us through the sifting, the fire, and the shining. He reshapes us into brand-new vessels, as seem fit to him. In an appointed time, God delivers us.

Daniel Prayed for the Southern Kingdom

Daniel was a young man when he was taken captive into Babylon. According to the prophecy of Jeremiah, the captivity would last seventy years (Jeremiah 25:11–12). The seventy years captivity was precipitated by the sins and constant rebellion of the people against Jehovah (Daniel 9:2–4). Jeremiah's prophesy motivated Daniel to pray. Daniel confessed not only his sins, but the sins of the people of the Southern Kingdom of Judah.

We confess because we're sorry for the wrongs we've committed against God. God has power to destroy the body and then cast the soul into hell. Daniel placed his faith and trust in God. He believed that through human dialogue with God, things could change. God kept his word and delivered the children of Judah.

3. Appreciation

The third component of prayer is appreciation. The grateful recipient acknowledges that God is his source and provider and freely give thanks. Without God, nothing that is possible would have been possible.

How does a parent feel when he has given all he can to his children and never receives a thank you from them? I tell the folks around me that if they ever have flowers to give me, give them to me now while I'm alive and can appreciate them. Don't send any courtesy flowers to my funeral. The only thing that the dead need is burial.

Humans tend to give thanks to God only after he has done great things, but the Lord is always doing marvellous things for us. I appreciate you, Father, for all the things you have done. Even if God doesn't grant us all that we ask of him, we should still give him thanks (Psalm 63:3–6, 107:9). Grateful hearts give thanks unto God without prompting or prodding (Philippians 4:6).

Gratefulness will manifest itself in thanksgiving. It will manifest through our mouths, because our hearts are like granaries; therefore, the lips will deliver the words stored within.

The lovingkindness of God is more than life. God speaks the word, and life is sustained. He sends his words, and our diseases are healed; therefore, we must open our mouths and show him appreciation all the days of our lives. God has given us his word that before we call, he has already answered; therefore, we do not wait until we see the manifestation to give him thanks. We thank him in advance for all the things he has already done. As Meshach, Shadrach, and Abednego said, "Even if he does not deliver us, we will not bow" (Daniel 3:16–18, paraphrased). Appreciating God should come naturally to the believer.

Jesus didn't just command us to show expressions of appreciation to the Father—he modelled it himself. He enables us to articulate what he has commanded by being a doer himself. Jesus practiced what he preached and taught.

A heart of appreciation is the epitome of worship. Saying thanks attests to the fact that God is our source. Ingratitude is a punishable sin. Man needs to develop an attitude for giving thanks unto God for everything.

4. Petition/Supplication/Intercession

The fourth constituent of prayer is petition, supplication, and intercession. We go before God and petition him for specific needs, and we intercede on behalf of others. Having taken on the whole armour of God, the apostle Paul encouraged the Ephesians brethren in this manner: "Praying always with all prayer and supplication in the Spirit, and watching thereunto with all perseverance and supplication for all saints" (Ephesians 6:18).

There were times when Jesus had to make supplications unto God, even though he was 100 per cent God. We, therefore, must make supplications in the spirit, because our warfare is not against flesh and blood, but against principalities and powers, against the rulers of the darkness of this world, and against spiritual wickedness in high places. (Ephesians 6:12)

According to the Free Dictionary, supplication means: To ask for humbly or earnestly, as by praying; to make a humble entreaty or petition; to beseech. It defines intercession as: entreaty or petition to God on the behalf of another.

Supplication is a human behaviour characterized by humility and sincere appealing unto the God of heaven. There must be a relationship between the supplicant, the intercessor or the petitioner, and the God of heaven. Prayers of supplication and intercession can help us win the victory, not just over all things in general, but in specific things.

In intercession, we approach the mercy seat of God in humble askance. We don't deserve his favour; nevertheless, we ask for it in the name of Jesus. Prayers of petition and supplication are usually general prayers. You might have a multiplicity of targets. The subject matter might be personal, it might be for a specific individual, or it might be for all people in general.

Intercessory prayer is warfare prayer. The battleground is infested with guerillas of the spirit realm. Our wrestling is not against the natural forces of the earth, but against personally assigned demons. Therefore, we enter spiritual warfare with the understanding that only God can give us the victory, because he can see the unseen.

The child of God can access the hotline to God any time (Hebrew 4:16). In intercession, you deliberately choose the target(s). The arena of conflict involves a fight, a battle, and a war. An intercessor enters the battle fully armed for spiritual conflict (2 Corinthians 10:3–6). The weapons of the intercessor's warfare are uniquely different from any other weapon. They can demolish the fortresses erected against us. We are able, through God, to overcome the obstacles set to trip us. The people of God are blessed and exceptionally favoured.

An intercessor does not give up or give in. Like the woman with the issue of blood, the intercessor presses past the doubters, past the proud, past the indifferent, and past the unbelievers. The intercessor is determined to touch heaven and disarm the host of hell through the power of the Holy Spirit and the blood of Christ Jesus. An intercessor understands the need for breakthroughs; therefore, he persists (Luke 11:5–8).

God's almighty power still brings down the giants of this world. Every giant has always been under God's feet. The intercessor's mind is set not only on bringing down the enemy, but on destroying the enemy's strongholds. The intercessor fires atomic power prayer missiles into the enemy's camp, and God pulls down the fortifications, leaving the devil exposed: "Thou hast also given me the necks of mine enemies; that I might destroy them that hate me" (Psalm 18:40); "Judah, thou art he whom they brethren shall praise: thy hand shall be in the neck of thine enemies; thy father's children shall bow down before thee" (Genesis 49:8).

Interceding for Mrs. Graydon

It was Tuesday afternoon when I received a call from a concerned sister. Mrs. Graydon was gravely sick unto death. She had gone to the doctor on Monday and had grown worse. The doctor sent her home to die. He said it wasn't even necessary to admit her to the hospital. The desperate request was for the church to visit her home and pray. She wasn't from my local assembly, but she was still a child of the king and in need of our compassion and support. Having received some background information about her situation, I began to fast and pray at home. Apparently, she and her house were being attacked by evil spirits. Those tormenting spirits had taken over her home and were torturing her to death. Her problem wasn't physical, so the doctor's medicine was useless. Mrs. Graydon needed the supernatural intervention of God Almighty.

Three of us set out for Mrs. Graydon's home on Wednesday afternoon at about 2:00. We arrived and noticed that a few of the brethren from her church were visiting. They prayed outside from the porch, but didn't enter the house. As soon as we entered the premises, they gathered their belongings and hurried away. They lingered a while, deep in conversation in the driveway. Even the family members would not come near. They went to another section of the home. Mrs. Graydon was left inside alone to do battle with whatever was coming up against her.

She was sprawled like a rag doll in a brown leather recliner. The house felt like a fiery furnace, even though a large fan was operating in the far corner of the room. The atmosphere was charged with the presence of the forces of darkness. We began prayer with songs testifying of the blood of Jesus. The blood of Jesus has ultimate power to deliver. The blood of Jesus is famous for its distinctiveness to heal and to save. The infallible Word of God teaches us that Jesus saves us and makes us whole. The sick of the palsy, let down through the roof, had this testimony. We also have this testimony.

"There shall no evil befall thee, neither shall any plague come nigh thy dwelling. For he shall give his angels charge over thee, to keep thee in all thy ways. They shall bear thee up in their hands, lest thou dash thy foot against a stone" (Psalm 91:10–12).

I anointed Mrs. Graydon with oil, and we began to travail in prayer. We called upon the name of the bondage breaker. We applied the blood of the Lamb. In the spirit realm, everything took on the appearance of blood. I knew total victory was imminent. Whatever omen was stationed in that house was coming out in the name of Jesus and by the power of Almighty God. With my spirit's eyes, I looked back to Calvary and saw the atoning blood of Jesus Christ streaming down the cross to the ground. The blood of Jesus is still flowing to cover us and to grant us protection.

God the Father told the children of Israel that if they applied the blood of the sacrificial lamb to their dwellings, the destroyer would pass over them. The atoning blood of Jesus Christ makes a difference in the lives of the believers.

The Bible reminds me of that time when the king of Moab rebelled against the king of Israel. The children of Israel had no water. God instructed the people to dig ditches in the valley. God supernaturally filled the ditches with water so that his people could quench their thirst.

When the Moabites arose in the morning, the rays of the sun fell upon the water in the ditches. The water appeared as blood to the Moabites. They thought that all the kings had been slain, so they entered the Israelites' camp. It was a setup from heaven. The Israelites utterly confused and defeated the Moabites (2 Kings 3:16–25).

Mrs. Graydon was about to be revived by the water of life, and the evil spirits were about to be chased from her home by the blood of Jesus. The blood of Jesus Christ prevails every time.

Suddenly, as we continued to call unto God, a great wind passed between us and Mrs. Graydon. As if by hands, we were moved out of the way. The opened front doors banged as the wind swept through them. The wind of heaven came down in that home and banished the host of hell.

We were nowhere near the fan, so we knew that the wind came from another source. It was the power of God. Not only did a strong wind push past us, but it took the burning heat as it went. The temperature in the house dropped. Mrs. Grayson was no longer pale and ashy; she became robust and energetic. She was delivered from the spell of the evil spirits that had held her hostage for months. She and her house were delivered by the power of Almighty God. Her family members came into the room and rejoiced with us.

As we left the compound, we reflected on the events of the afternoon. Everyone commented on the great wind that passed between us as we travailed in prayer. God still answers the cries of his children.

The world is a dark place, because it has rejected the Light—Jesus Christ. The children of the Most High can access heaven's hotline any time. It's never busy, so you'll never be placed on hold. You don't have to pass through an operator to get to Jesus. Before you called, God already answered. God answers expediently the prayers that demand swift attention.

Interceding for Richardo

It was a Sunday afternoon when I was summoned to visit Richardo, who was on the verge of death from cancer of the liver. A few Holy Ghost-empowered people accompanied me. We arrived on the scene to find Richardo lying down with a bucket at his bedside. He was roasting from a high fever. He was also vomiting. Richardo was in excruciating pain and could hardly turn himself in the bed. His belly was blown up like a balloon. I could see the yellowing of his skin, even though he was of a very dark complexion.

We began prayer meeting and found ourselves in the wake of a great spiritual conflict. I discerned that there were other forces involved in Richardo's dilemma, besides cancer; however, we knew that Jesus Christ had mastery and was in total control of everything in the universe. In the name of Jesus, we aimed at the stronghold. The elevated body temperature was the first target. We stood upon the premise that God in us is greater than the evil forces that are in the world. We persisted in the battle, and the fever instantaneously broke: "And he spake a parable unto them to this end, that men ought always to pray, and not to faint" (Luke 18:1).

Even though a friend won't rise at midnight to meet your needs, God promises that he will arise when you call upon him, because he is a friend that sticks closer than a brother. The unjust might be hesitant to meet your needs, but God promises that he will avenge you of your adversary speedily. If you have faith, God will hear and answer prayer.

The fever broke, and the vomit stopped also. I encouraged Richardo to get up from that bed and go outside for a breath of fresh air. He went outside and gave God the glory. Richardo's healing was to be in stages. The Lord stopped the vomiting so that Ricardo would not become dehydrated or lose his electrolytes. He could now eat his food. Richardo needed to continue to believe God and not waver in faith. We encouraged him to visit the doctor to confirm certain things. He promised to come to prayer meeting and attend the church services the next week, but he never showed.

Richardo chose the alternatives. He forsook God and the church for the concoction of a "so-called" medicine woman. The fever and the vomiting returned. In the height of the very high fever, he asked for food. They gave it to him. As he ate the hot food, his temperature skyrocketed. He went into convulsions and passed from this life before he could get to the hospital.

Disobedience is a cyclical offense. If we wish to receive answers from God and healing of our infirmities, we must be obedient. One of the keys to total deliverance is trust in God. Every now and then, God might ask us to do things that might not fit into the normal way of doing things—but if God says it, obey it.

At the time of the conquest of Jericho, God commanded Joshua and all the men of war to do something that was quite unlike the military strategies of the day. For six days, they were to march around Jericho once each day. On the seventh day, they were to march around the city seven times. Six times they were to march around in silence. On the seventh march, the priest would make a long blast on the trumpet. The children of Israel would then make a great shout, because God had given them the city. As strange as it sounds, this is what the children of Israel, led by Joshua, did. After meticulously following the Lord's command, they witnessed the wall of Jericho fall flat to the ground. They won a great victory over that fortressed city (Joshua 6:1–27).

Sometimes God delivers instantaneously. At other times, he chooses to heal and deliver in stages. Sometimes God uses doctors and medical therapy. Whatever God chooses to do, we must not doubt or waver. He is God all by himself and will do things as he deems fit. Wait on the Lord and follow his directions.

Richardo might have lived had he not quit on God. God reveals his secrets to his servants, the prophets. The admonition to this young man was to come to prayer and start attending church.

He promised to do this, but forfeited on his promise. He chose the alternative.

Samuel pointed out the sinfulness of not praying for each other. The apostle Paul and his contemporaries followed Christ's admonition and prayed for their authority figures. Even in the wake of persecution, he interceded and prayed for them. We also need to pray for our adversaries: "But I say unto you which hear, love your enemies, do good to them which hate you, Bless them that curse you, and pray for them which despitefully use you" (Luke 6:27–28).

We live in a society that is hostile towards God and Christianity. Christians have been delegated the power and authority to speak as oracles of God. We speak as God speaks. As I quoted before, death and life are in the power of the tongue.

Abraham Interceded for Sodom and Gomorrah

The stench of the sins of the twin cities of Sodom and Gomorrah went up into the nostrils of God, so he decided to smite them with fire and brimstone. Abraham cried out to God on behalf of the people of those two cities (Genesis 18:20–21, 23–24, 26). Abraham interceded and asked God if he would spare the city if there were ten righteous therein; God said that he would not destroy it for the sake of ten righteous (Genesis 18:32).

We need to pray for our nations, stand still, and see if God will intervene and cause a shift and a change in the atmosphere. I discovered that there are several words concealed in "intercession." The two I choose to unveil are "secret" and "cession." One Greek word for "secret" is "musterion" (moos-tay'-ree-on), which according to Strong's Concordance means, "anything hidden, a mystery, or a secret."

In the New Testament, "secret" translates to mean, "The counsel of God, once hidden but now revealed in the gospel; particular truths or details of the Christian revelation; or that which can only be known through revelation from God." The other Greek word for secret is "kruptos," meaning "hidden, or secret" (Strong's Concordance).

The English word "cession" means "a giving up; the act of ceding; a yielding; surrender; relinquishment of property or rights; or a giving up of power." "Inter" is a prefix that means "among" or "between." As the prefix suggests, intercession is between you and God, or between the people of God and God. In intercessory prayer, God releases his secrets to his people (Amos 3:7).

One receives revelations from God so that he or she can instruct the one for whom intercession is made. When God speaks, the enemy must back up, back down, or back off. The enemy must surrender and release the captive.

Intercessory prayers interrupt the conference call of the devil and his minions; and, put a cease order to their plans.

In intercessory prayer, the warrior storms the forces of hell and dispossesses the enemy of the territories he is illegally occupying. Continue to pray and do not give up. God is coming to the rescue.

Interceding for Wilhamena

Wilhamena was experiencing unusual problems in her neck and throat regions. After testing, she was diagnosed with thyroid cancer. She was booked for surgery that Wednesday morning. I visited her room on the evening before surgery. She was alone.

"Wilhamena," I said, "I'm going to summon heaven on your behalf so that there will be no sign of cancer when the doctors go in. I'm also going to issue a stop order against metastasis. My God is alive; therefore, this cancer will proceed no further."

I called upon the name of the Lord and pronounced the curse of death upon the thyroid cancer and the spread of it. We believed God for a miracle. We believed that the God of heaven who did it before could do it again. If God could make a way through the Red Sea for the children of Israel, he could counteract and eradicate cancer from the body. The Egyptians sank in that which the children of Israel walked on. What was concrete or asphalt to the children of Israel was mud and mush to the enemies.

I prayed the promise over Wilhamena that evening and the morning of the surgery. I interceded on her behalf, because, like Job, I knew that Jesus Christ was still alive and well. He had never lost a battle. I heard the voice of Brother Job, but I also heard another voice. It was the voice of David crying out in the cave of Adullam for God to grant him mercy. David sought God to show him how to escape the harsh blows that life had dealt him (Psalm 57:1–2, 5, 7, 9–11, 142:1, 5, 7).

God is not slack concerning his promise.

He healed Wilhamena by his strong and mighty power. Our God reigns. He is exalted above the heathen, as his words declared.

The diseased tissues were removed during surgery, and they found no evidence of cancer in the surrounding tissues or beyond the thyroid gland. There was no need for chemotherapy. Wilhamena remains cancer free to this day.

Not only can God deliver, but he can also set free forever. Wilhamena now walks in the liberty wherewith God has made her free. God is still summum bonum—the highest good.

Interceding for Mr. Jameison

Every time God moves supernaturally, you can expect that the enemy will retaliate. It behooves us to keep our spiritual eyes and ears alert. The devil is coming back with vengeance on his mind. He will send the scavengers to try and devour your victory. Learn to drive them away, in the spirit. When the scavengers came down to devour the sacrifice that Abram laid before the Lord, he drove them away (Genesis 15:7–11).

The enemy struck Mr. Jameison, Wilhamena's husband, with multiple myeloma.

According to the American Cancer Society, multiple myeloma is a cancer formed by malignant plasma cells that develop in the bone marrow.

Plasma is a vital aspect of immunology. It's responsible for making the antibodies (immunoglobulin) that helps to protect a person against the infectious agents that enter the body.

Plasma cells are mainly found in the bone marrow. Out of control plasma cells evolve into the condition known as plasmacytoma. A solitary plasma cell tumor is called a plasmacytoma. The multiplication of plasmacytoma is referred to as multiple myeloma.

Mr. Jameison was suffering from great back pain because of this disease. I grew angry at the devil as I looked at Mr. Jameison lying in the bed. He had already suffered many physical ailments, but this was proving to be the worst. The doctor's diagnosis was that the condition was very aggressive and demanded immediate intervention. Upon hearing that, I said in my spirit, "I know a doctor who has the power to remove the aggression from any condition and render it ineffective."

The weapons of the devil will be formed, but they shall not prosper, says the Lord God of heaven. I rehearsed the Word of the Lord. When he says that no weapon formed against thee shall prosper, he means just that. Sickness will come, but it will not tarry forever. Every tongue pronouncing sickness upon the servants of the Most High God is already judged and is condemned. The blessings of the Lord are upon the righteous.

We shall overcome by the words of our testimony and by the blood of the Lamb. We are residing in a system that was set forth by the Word of God. Open your mouth and begin to decree and declare. Our tongue has been blessed with power. We are the oracles of God; therefore, we are authorized to speak as God would speak.

Multiple myeloma must die, by the power of Almighty God. I began to intercede for Mr. Jameison. Like Abraham, I called the things that were not as though they were. I believed God for remedying the situation. Satan and his angels were on the one side of Mr. Jameison pronouncing death as I stood in the gap, on his other side, proclaiming life. The battle raged for weeks while we awaited the doctor's plans.

Anyone intending to stand in the gap for somebody must be prepared spiritually, physically, and emotionally, because intercession can be physically demanding and draining. Deliverance might take longer than expected. God chose stem cell replacement therapy and chemotherapy to deliver him. The battle was long and exhausting, but the Lord prevailed. He delivered this man. Cancer left his body by the all-prevailing power of the only wise God of heaven.

If you never challenge God, you'll never experience his power. There is power in the name of Jesus to break every chain. God broke the chain of multiple myeloma and stopped the spread.

How can one seek and worship a dead god? Seek the God of heaven today and allow him to work a miracle in your situation. Cast your burdens upon him, because he is a burden-bearer.

The manifestations of God through signs, wonders, and miracles have attracted people in every generation. The Bible is like a mine. The deeper you dig into it, the more treasure you find.

And by the hands of the apostles were many signs and wonders wrought among the people; (and they were all with one accord in Solomon's porch. And of the rest durst no men join himself to them: but the people magnified them. And believers were the more added to the Lord, multitudes both of men and women.) Insomuch that they brought forth the sick into the streets, and laid them on beds and couches, that at the least the shadow of Peter passing by might overshadow some of them. There came also a multitude out of the cities round about unto Jerusalem, bringing sick folks, and them which were vexed with unclean spirits: and they were healed every one. (Acts 5:12–16)

When God restores, he does it to the utmost, as Job attested: "And the LORD turned the captivity of Job, when he prayed for his friends: also the LORD gave Job twice as much as he had before" (Job 42:10). God heals us according to his loving kindness and according to his tender mercies. Do not charge God foolishly if your healing or deliverance does not come instantaneously.

Mr. Jameison's victory over multiple myeloma did not come immediately. It took a few months, but it came and has remained to this day.

God is still God, whether we acknowledge him or not. All other gods must bow at the mention of the name of Jehovah. At the name of Jesus, demons must flee. At the name of Jesus, diseases and infirmities must run. Sickness and health cannot co-exist in the same body. One must die. Let sickness die, because our bodies are the temples of the Most High God.

Believe and pray this prayer with me.

Prayer

I curse with the curse of death the existence of those intimidating, tormenting sicknesses in my body. God provided my healing in the atonement of Jesus Christ. Sicknesses must go, in the name of Jesus.

I break and utterly destroy the generational curses of sickness. My DNA dictated that I will suffer from the same physical maladies that my ancestors suffered from. That is a lie from hell. I reverse that dictation; and, I decree that I will not be stricken with anything that is within or without my ancestral bloodline.

Let God arise, and let the lying enemies of my soul and health be scattered abroad. I return every lying order back to the sender. I command, in the name of Jesus, that every infirmity, known or unknown, in my body be rooted up and die in the blood of the Lamb. Sicknesses, be ye rooted up and disappear. Go! Leave behind neither branches, nor foliage, nor seeds, nor buds, nor blossoms. Be gone, all of you! In the name of Jesus, die and disappear.

The Lord says it; I believe it, and my body receives it. Amen.

You have prayed this prayer. Now arise, blessed one, and go to your heavenly Father. Give him praise, honour, and glory, for he has done great things. Arise in faith and receive from him today that which he promised in the atonement. God is not a man; therefore, he does not lie. Believe as I believe.

Before you called, he'd already answered.

Chapter 6
The Authority of the Name of Jesus

"And whatsoever ye shall ask in my name, that will I do, that the Father may be glorified in the Son. If ye shall ask any thing in my name, I will do it" (John 14:13–14).

To understand the importance of the name of Jesus in prayer, one must understand the biblical concept behind names. We also need to understand the importance of the name of God.

A name, especially in days of antiquity, was much more than a title or an identification badge used to distinguish one person from another. A person was so intimately associated with his name that to change it would be equivalent to annihilation. A name stood as a prophecy as to the destiny of the bearer.

Becoming acquainted with a name is like coming into contact with the person's personality, character, reputation, and power. So great is a name that God would swear by no other name than his own (Genesis 22:15–16; Hebrews 6:13). The name of the Lord is exalted in the earth (Psalm 8:1, 148:13).

A person's name is his possession. You have ownership of your name. When I call John, James will not answer; when I call Jennifer, Mary will not answer. Jesus owns his name because the Father gave it to him.

A name speaks of ownership and authority; therefore, when one uses the name of Jesus, he is really operating in the authority of the owner of the name. When you come in the name of Jesus, you come in the authority of Jesus.

David knew the importance and authority of a name. When he approached Goliath, he didn't say "I come in the name of Israel" or "I come in the name of King Saul of Israel." David faced Goliath in the name of the Lord, who will always defend his heritage (1 Samuel 17:45).

David faced his giant in the power and authority of the God of Israel, whom he served. He fought valiantly, because he understood that the giant that towered over his head was under God's feet. David faced Goliath with boldness, because he knew that the name of the Lord is a strong tower. The righteous runs into it and are safe (Proverbs 18:10).

The one who says, "In the name of Jesus" is acting upon the premise that Jesus will intervene, because he has given permission to use his name. Jesus' name is excellent in all the earth (Psalm 8:1; Proverbs 18:10; 22:1; Matthew 21:9). No one can access the Father or the throne of grace except through Christ Jesus (John 14:6). Jesus has given us permission to use his name; therefore, he will honour his word.

Our pious deeds have no power to open the entrance to the throne of mercy. Our righteousness is inadequate (Isaiah 59:1–2, 64:6). As the scripture says, sin has defiled us and separated us from God.

Who granted us the freedom to enter boldly into the presence of God? Jesus. When God sees the blood of Jesus sprinkled upon the mercy seat, when he reads the memo that his Son has given him on our behalf, he will hear and hearken to our cries. God remembered his covenant with Abraham, Isaac, and Jacob; therefore, in the process of time, he heard the cries of the children of Israel, and he performed his own promise (Exodus 2:23–25).

The Lord must honour his own word. His word shall not return unto him empty; it will accomplish that which pleases God (Isaiah 55:11). Tantrums and sacrifices do not move the hands of God. They do not impress him. God moves his hands and rescues us according to his tender mercies. Even though we approach the mercy seat in the name of Jesus, God still requires us to be obedient to his Word and his will. He will always accomplish what he set forth to do (1Samuel 15:22–23; Psalm 51:16–17; Isaiah 55:8–11; Hosea 6:6).

Because of Jesus and his atoning blood, we can come boldly to the throne of grace to obtain mercy and find grace to help in time of need (Hebrews 4:16).

Before the crucifixion, ordinary man could not approach God. To do so would mean death. God dwelt among man from behind the Cherubim situated on the mercy seat, first in the tabernacle of Moses in the wilderness, and then in the temple that Solomon built. The tabernacle in the wilderness and its furnishings were pregnant with Messianic imagery. Everything pointed to Jesus Christ. Entering the holy of holies was to enter the presence of God.

Before Christ, and under the Mosaic Law, God chose the high priest to stand as mediator between him and the children of Israel. Man could not disrespectfully scamper in and out of this most holy throne room. Man, being crimson-stained and filthy with sin, could not appease the wrath of God. If he entered the holy of holies uninvited, he would die. The veil separated the most holy God from sinful man. The high priest entered this compartment once a year on the prescribed Day of Atonement and offered atonement for the sins of man. Before he made his appearance, he would burn incense. The smoke would shield and protect him from having a direct view of God (Hebrews 9:1–11).

We have heard the story told many times that on the day that Jesus was crucified, the veil of the temple in Jerusalem was rent from top to bottom. It was a supernatural occurrence, because the veil was much too high and much too thick for man to have torn it from top to bottom. The temple was constructed using the same architectural design and blueprint as the tabernacle of Moses in the wilderness.

The average bystander had his first glimpse of the holy of holies on the day Jesus was crucified. The torn veil symbolizes his flesh that was broken for us at the cross. Jesus' utterance, "It is finished," announced the accomplishment of his redemption work. The sacrificial system was now fulfilled.

The sacrificial system served as our school master or tutor, pointing and guiding us to Christ. The story of Sarah and Hagar, and Isaac and

Ishmael, was an allegory. Ishmael had to go when Isaac came, because he was the child of the bondwoman who leadeth unto bondage. Isaac was the child of promise, the son of the free woman, who leadeth unto the grace of God and freedom through Christ. Isaac and Ishmael and Sarah and Hagar could not coexist together, hence the order: "Cast out the bondwoman and her son: for the son of the bondwoman shall not be heir with the son of the freewoman" (Galatians 4:30).

Jesus was the ultimate sacrifice. He entered the holy of holies after the crucifixion and presented his blood to the Father (Hebrews 9:24–28).

God authorizes us to come to him. Jesus bids all those who are weary and heavily laden to come. The angels in heaven have no legal right or authority to stop us from approaching the Father. The devil has no legal right or authority to stop us. Demons have no legal right or authority to stop us. God alone, for whatever reason, exercises the right to stop us or not hear us.

When we come to the Father as instructed by Jesus, "in his name," those words place a demand on the Father. God honors the word of his Son, because he was obedient even unto death on the cross. We, being adopted children, become heirs and joint heirs with Christ. The adopted children are entitled to the same rights, benefits, blessings, and privileges as the only begotten Son.

In the name of Jesus, we have victory over the enemy. Be aware that the blessings of answered prayer do not rest only upon the fact that we approach the mercy seat in the name of Jesus. We need to bear in mind that apart from Jesus, we have no rights or access. Approaching the mercy seat of God "in the name of Jesus" is not a magical formula. Many folks are under the impression that they can wave their magic wands, and God will act.

We cannot manipulate God into doing anything. If God could be manipulated like a puppet on a string, he wouldn't be God.

The Word of God clearly states that God will not hear us if there is iniquity in our hearts. You forfeit your privilege to use the name of Jesus in prayer or to chase devils if you have not kept yourself attached to the vine (John 15:5, 7).

Note that you can approach God on behalf of somebody else. Know also that even when we come to the Father in the name of Jesus, he might not answer our petition. Why? Prayer must parallel the will of God. Our will must coincide with the will of God. Even if you don't hear from God promptly, continue to trust him.

Jesus made a request in the Garden of Gethsemane that God denied. Jesus knew that God wouldn't answer him if the request was outside of his will. God will never give you more than you can tolerate. He places great value on the name of Jesus.

"Wherefore God also hath highly exalted him, and given him a name which is above every name: that at the name of Jesus every knee should bow, of things in heaven, and things in earth, and things under the earth; and every tongue should confess that Jesus Christ is Lord, to the glory of God the Father" (Philippians 2:9–11).

In Jesus' bodily absence, the believer has been given the power of attorney to act in his name. I have been granted permission by the king to use, with authority, his name. Every principality and power must crumble at the mention of the name of Jesus. No messenger of Satan can take up permanent residence in a place where God is glorified or where the name of Jesus is celebrated. There is power in the name of Jesus to pulverize every chain.

Pray with Me

At the name of Jesus, satanic fortresses must crumble. At the name of Jesus, the cycle of barrenness must be broken. At the name of Jesus, the spiritual darkness in your life must be dispersed, and the perpetual radiance must take up eminence.

In the name of Jesus, I break the cycle of penury from your life and lineage. In the name of Jesus, I come against the spirit of sabotage in your life. In the name of Jesus, the power of the underworld, the power of the prince of the air, the power of the prince of the seas, and the power of the prince of darkness is broken and destroyed.

Christ has redeemed you with his precious blood; therefore, the host of hell has no power over you.

I decree and I declare, in the name of Jesus, that your bondage(s) are broken and you are free. Whom the Son has set free, is free indeed.

In the name of Jesus, be thou delivered from thine infirmities. Amen.

Chapter 7
The Efficacy and Uniqueness of the Blood of Jesus:
Part A

"For the life of the flesh is in the blood: and I have given it to you upon the altar to make atonement for your souls: for it is the blood that maketh an atonement for the soul" (Leviticus 17:11).

"And they overcame him by the blood of the Lamb, and by the word of their testimony; and they loved not their lives unto the death" (Revelation 12:11).

Those of us who have read through the Bible will notice that it is a blooded book. The blood runs from Genesis to Revelation like a lifeline. Every living soul is aware of the efficacy of the blood.

An anemic person will not function as optimally as the person who has a healthy supply of blood flowing through his veins, because the life of the body is not the brain, the heart, or the lungs. It's the blood.

The blood gives life and power to our prayer, preaching, and teaching. Without the blood applied, our expositions have no life, our prayers have no life, and we have no life.

The writer of the book of Hebrews tells us that the Word of God is alive and powerful; it is sharper than any two-edged sword. It has piercing power; it has power to divide asunder the soul and spirit, and joints and marrow. The Word is so powerful and alive that it has eyes that discern the thoughts and intents of the heart (Hebrews 4:12).

What gives the Word life? The blood that runs through the arteries, veins, and capillaries of the Bible give the Word life. The spoken Word is alive and potent because it is mingled with blood. Jesus overcame Satan by the power of the Word.

In Genesis 4:9–10, Cain kills Abel. The breath leaves Abel's body, but his crimson blood, swallowed by the earth, tarries and cries out when the Father comes by. You cannot silence a good man. There is a tongue, a voice, a speech, and a language in every drop of blood. The life of the flesh is in the blood.

I'm taken back to the scene in Jerusalem on the day of crucifixion. With my spirit's ears, I listen to hear Jesus cry: "Guilty! Guilty! Guilty! You are all guilty! Death shall be your portion." Yes, they were all guilty and deserving of death, but the Father in heaven turned the intercom on so that the tender voice of Jesus could be heard over the brawling rebels. Jesus didn't ask the Father to destroy them; he asked him to forgive them.

Every time a sinner comes home to God, he must pass through the blood. The blood of Jesus continues to cry out for sinners. The blood of Abel cried out and exposed the sin of Cain, but the blood of Jesus cries out and covers the sin of man (1 John 1:9). As the scriptures says, the blood of Jesus speaks better things than that of Abel (Hebrews 12:24).

I stand on the Word of God, which says that the life of the flesh is in the blood. My prayer receives double power when I utter it according to the will of God, when I utter it in the name of Jesus, and when I apply the blood of Jesus to it.

Human DNA contains within it forty-six chromosomes, which are received from the mother and the father. Jesus' blood was devoid of any human male chromosome. This makes his blood more unique than the blood of mankind. The life of all human flesh is the blood. Human blood has the power to give life, but it has no power to save from sin.

The blood of Jesus Christ is doubly precious, because not only does it give life, but it gives a more abundant and eternal life.

Another important aspect of blood is that it's not stationary, but mobile. This tissue travels the entirety of the body, imparting nutrients and oxygen to every cell. At the same time, it collects waste matter and dumps it into the organs of excretion. If the blood is polluted, the body will expeditiously suffer systemic contamination. Any cell in the body that is deprived of blood will quickly infarct. It will die and then rot.

Spiritually speaking, the blood of Jesus traverses the circulatory system of every born again believer and the collective body of Christ. Any mortal man who is transfused with the blood that is not his "type" will react adversely, and sometimes tragically, to it. Biologists tell us people possessing blood type O negative are universal donors. There's no guarantee that a person receiving a transfusion of O negative blood won't react badly to something in the blood. The blood of a human universal donor will sustain life, but it will never have an effect upon the sin factor.

Christ is the only universal donor whose blood will transform both body and soul. The blood of Jesus counteracts sin and cleanses the soul. It gives life to those who are spiritually dead. It revives those who are dying. How can a brown cow eat green grass and produce white milk? It's a mystery, but God can dip a sin-blackened sinner in the crimson blood of Jesus Christ and causes him to come out as white as virgin snow.

Friends, our denominational names or hierarchical positions do not impress God. He isn't interested in our church polities, because some of our behaviours do not even give credence, honour, or respect to our own endorsements. We have been sitting in the seat of the hypocrites. We say one thing with our lips, but our actions defeat our own words.

What matters to God is that you are a believer who has been washed and made clean in the blood of the Lamb. A church building could be filled with the choicest proselytes of the earth, but unless this church is washed and purified in the blood of the Lamb, it's not God's church, and neither does she have life. The life is in the blood.

Adam's blood became polluted when he ate of the fruit of the tree of the knowledge of good and evil. Biologists agree that whatever man consumes enters his bloodstream, where it's distributed in a metabolized form to the body. Thousands of years have elapsed since the sin fruit entered man's blood in the Garden of Eden; however, the potency of the poisonous effluvia still circulates in the bloodline of the progeny of the first Adam. The stench of sin is everywhere. Man is spiritually dead, because the blood of Adam bears with it the sentence of death.

Man is alive spiritually because of the blood of Jesus, which bears with it the verdict of life. God introduced the sacrificial system in Old Testament because it would take blood to cleanse and atone for sin. God had to purchase man's deliverance with the blood of Jesus, because there was no human male involvement in his conception. A pregnant woman's circulation is separate from the baby's. There is no intermingling of blood and blood. Jesus did not inherit the tainted blood of Adam. Being born of a woman, he was sinless. He was the seed of the woman that the Father promised in Genesis 3:15.

While the world waited for the fullness of time to come, God used the sacrificial system and the shedding of blood to illustrate to humanity the concept that without the shedding of blood, there is no remission of sin. The sacrificial system was temporary, because God had in mind a new and better covenant. The sacrificial system was prototypical of Jesus' one-time sacrifice.

We've already examined Adam and Eve's choice of clothing. Their choice wasn't indicative of life, because no blood was shed; neither did it offer permanence, because fig leaves were highly perishable. God made Adam and Eve coats of skins. The blood of a substitute had to be shed to make those coats. Adam and Eve covered themselves with aprons of figs. An apron only covers part of the body. God made them coats of skins, which offered a fuller covering. This act of God was a shadow of better things to come.

The book of Ruth addresses the concept of kinsman redemption. It's a love story that serves as a prototype of Christ and his bride—the church. The Lord reminded me that the blood of bulls and goats wasn't sufficient for lasting atonement, because a kinsman redeemer had to qualify in several categories.

1. **A kinsman redeemer had to be a genetic or biologic relative.**

"And Naomi said unto her daughter in law, Blessed be he of the LORD, who hath not left off his kindness to the living and to the dead. And Naomi said unto her, The man is near of kin unto us, one of our next kinsmen" (Ruth 2:20).

As per Genesis 3:15, the redeemer who would crush the head of the serpent would be born of the seed of the woman. Jesus was a blood relative of man. He was conceived of the Holy Ghost and born of the Virgin Mary (Luke 1:26–38). The seed of the man played no role in the conception of Jesus Christ. This was a one-time occurrence in the history of humanity.

2. **A kinsman redeemer must be able to pay the full redemption price.**

"And Naomi had a kinsman of her husband's, a mighty man of wealth, of the family of Elimelech; and his name was Boaz. And Ruth the Moabitess said unto Naomi, Let me now go to the field, and glean ears of corn after him in whose sight I shall find grace. And she said unto her, Go, my daughter" (Ruth 2:1–2).

"When Jesus therefore had received the vinegar, he said, It is finished: and he bowed his head, and gave up the ghost" (John 19:30).

Like Boaz, Jesus Christ paid in full the price of redemption. The law dictated that no sin could be remitted without the shedding of blood. The laws governing purification varied, which is why Hebrews 9:22 states that almost all things are purged with blood, and that without shedding of blood is no remission of sin. Jesus Christ paid for sin with his blood. According to the law, some things were purified by fire and/

or water (Leviticus 16:26, 28; Numbers 31:23–24). Some things were also cleansed with the ashes of the red heifer (Numbers 19:2–10). The blood of Jesus appeased the wrath of God against sin. The blood of the victim, Jesus, was sufficient for the forgiveness of sin. Under the dispensation of the law as well as under the dispensation of grace, the blood was/is the purchase price for redemption from sin.

The blood of expiation was divinely arranged from the beginning. Revelation 13:8 teaches that the Lamb of God was slain from the foundation of the world. The Lamb to be slain was implied in Genesis 3:15; the shedding of blood was also evident when God made Adam and Eve coats of skins for a covering. Jesus paid it all.

3. **A kinsman redeemer had to be a willing participant.**

"And now, my daughter, fear not; I will do to thee all that thou requirest: for all the city of my people doth know that thou art a virtuous woman. And now it is true that I am thy near kinsman: howbeit there is a kinsman nearer than I. Tarry this night, and it shall be in the morning, that if he will perform unto thee the part of a kinsman, well; let him do the kinsman's part: but if he will not do the part of a kinsman to thee, then will I do the part of a kinsman to thee, as the LORD liveth: lie down until the morning" (Ruth 3:11–13).

Therefore doth my Father love me, because I lay down my life, that I might take it again. No man taketh it from me, but I lay it down of myself, I have power to lay it down, and I have power to take it again. This commandment have I received of my Father. (John 10:17–18)

Boaz willing played the part of a kinsman redeemer. Jesus was a willing kinsman.

4. **A kinsman redeemer should be free and not in bonds or a slave who needs redemption.**

"And she said, These six measures of barley gave he me; for he said to me, Go not empty unto thy mother in law. Then said she, Sit still, my daughter, until thou know how the matter will fall: for the man will not be in rest, until he have finished the thing this day" (Ruth 3:17–18).

"For he hath made him to be sin for us, who knew no sin; that we might be made the righteousness of God in him" (2 Corinthians 5:21).

No animal is a blood relative to man. Faithful believers in God denounce the theory of evolution. God uniquely fashioned and created man. Man did not evolve from apes. Man is God's masterpiece.

The blood of goats and bulls sufficed for a period; however, the animal never offered itself willingly. Many animals came to the slaughter, but not without a fight. No animal ever said to its master, "Here am I; I will go and die." An animal being prepared for the slaughter was singled out from the rest and kept in bonds.

Boaz was a free man. He foreshadowed Jesus, our kinsman redeemer, but he was not the king.

Jesus is the only one who qualified to be kinsman redeemer for fallen humanity. There is power in the blood of the risen Lamb. The blood of Jesus is still rich. Jesus Christ is the Lamb of God, which takes away the sins of the world. (John 1:29)

The blood of Jesus Christ prevails. It gives power to your prayer.

Chapter 8
The Efficacy and Uniqueness of the Blood of Jesus: Part B

Satan, the Blood of Jesus Is Against You

We know from Genesis 3:15 and onwards in the Old Testament that God had a salvific plan in mind. Throughout the Old Testament, God never ceased to present us with a picture of this redeemer, whether in type or in shadow. The prophet Isaiah gave one of the most vivid descriptions of the messiah. He also described the nature of his bishopric. He listed identifiable signs that would surround the conception and birth of the Redeemer (Isaiah 7:13–14, 9:2, 6–7, 53:4–5).

I have examined the findings of the rhetoricians of my time. They have come up with possible reasons why the blood clots. They can analyze and differentiate blood components. They can even manipulate the flow of blood through the system so that they can conduct a surgical operation. The blood of Jesus is powerful because of its makeup. Any normal blood composition bearing under or above forty-six chromosomes would be considered an aberration of nature. Jesus was 100 per cent man and 100 per cent God. He never inherited Adam's tainted blood. That's what made his blood so powerful.

Mary was the catalyst God used in his plan of salvation (Isaiah 7:14; Matthew 1:18–25).

The Son had the rich, red, righteous, untainted blood of the Father flowing through his veins. The child that was born carried within him the Son that was given. The child could be seen with the naked eye, but the Son had to be discerned.

He saith unto them, But whom say ye that I am? And Simon Peter answered and said, Thou art the Christ, the Son of the living God. And Jesus answered and said unto him, Blessed art thou, Simon Barjona: for flesh and blood hath not revealed it unto thee, but my Father which is in heaven. (Matthew 16:15–17, emphasis added)

Jesus Christ, the sinless man, was the visible manifestation of the living God. At the age of twelve, he astounded the learned men in the temple at Jerusalem. They marvelled at his knowledge about God. He was about his Father's business. "And she shall bring forth a son, and thou shalt call his name JESUS: for he shall save his people from their sins" (Matthew 1:21).

Even after this revelation, man didn't comprehend that the child born was the Son given. Jesus Christ was the anointed Son of God who came on a rescue mission to save his people from their sins. This is why his interrogators had to ask him if he was the King of the Jews (Matthew 27:11).

At the crucifixion, one cried out saying, "Truly this was the Son of God" (Matthew 27:54b).

They were too late. Peter caught the vision prior and had made that annunciation.

The world might not understand all there is to be understood about God, but I know that the world and the devil understand blood. The devil tried on the days of temptation to talk Jesus out of going to the cross. He was concerned about his head, and he was also aware of the fact that once the royal blood of Jesus Christ was shed, salvation's plan would be accomplished (Matthew 4:5–6).

When a person prays, "Satan, the blood of Jesus is against you," he's not repeating a religious incantation; he's saying, "I come against you, Satan, with the power that is in the shed blood of Jesus." To the ordinary ear this sounds like just another prayer, but in the ears of the enemy, it sounds like a powerful battering ram directed towards bringing down his ramparts.

The powerful blood of Jesus already flows through the veins of the redeemed. The power of the blood energizes your prayer made in the name of Jesus. The Holy Spirit seals you, and no devil can break this seal. You are forever sealed, if you continue to do the will of God and abide in him.

The devil fears the child of God because of the hedge of blood God has placed around him. Remember that before the devil could venture near Job, he had to go to God first (Job 1, 2). Satan can only touch you when God permits him to for a purpose. When the devil looks at you, he sees the blood of your commander.

No healthcare institution will allow novices to infuse blood into a patient unless they are trained people of experience who know to monitor for a reaction. That healthcare giver must know what to do in the event of an emergency. Likewise, not just anybody can walk around pleading the blood. It doesn't work that way. Satan cannot cast out Satan. A person using the name of Jesus in prayer, or proclaiming that there is power in the blood of Jesus, must be born again, saved, and sanctified. He must be given authority to use the name of Jesus and the blood. The blood has the power to destroy sin and liberate man: "For this purpose the Son of God was manifested, that he might destroy the works of the devil" (1 John 3:8b). At the same time, being under the blood of Jesus doesn't exempt you from the attacks of the wicked one: "Yea, and all that will live Godly in Christ Jesus shall suffer persecution" (2 Timothy 3:12). The devil and his emissaries will come after you to try and torment you to death. They will try to shoot you down before you shoot them down.

The devil will release strange creatures from the abyss to frighten you if he thinks that you're a threat to what he considers his territory. I had three encounters that I will never forget. Had I not been covered under the blood of Jesus, my family and I would have been long dead. Jesus delivered us with his strong and mighty hands. I know what prayer can do. I take no credit for what he has done.

Encounter with a Half Man/Half Horse

Some years ago, I sat with family members watching the Olympic games. My ailing mother was having a nap in bed. Suddenly, I saw a very awful thing. A man was coming down the street garbed in a full suit of purest white. His shoes were white, and the felt hat upon his head was white. His hair was snow-white, and he was handsome. He seemed to be of mulatto descent. This was a very horrible sight, because from his head to the waist, he resembled a man, but from the waist down, he was like a horse. I began to pray and call upon the Lord.

For a moment, I lost sight of him; but, then he surfaced again and was now standing outside the side window across from my mother's bed. He lifted his hands, which looked like forefeet, and placed them on the window ledge. He intended to enter my mother's room.

I leapt from my seat and cried aloud, "Satan, the blood of Jesus is against you." We dashed to the bedroom, surrounded Mama, and prayed. We asked the Father to cover us and to cover the property within and without with the blood of the Lamb. At the mention of the blood of Jesus, that half man/half horse disappeared and was never seen or sensed again.

I described the encounter to a friend, who told me that in Greek mythology, this half man/half horse creature was called a centaur. Personally, I don't indulge in myths and such things, but this creature troubled my spirit. I know that this was a demonic force. As a child of God, I chose to believe that this creature, whatever it was called, was a satanic monster released by the devil to torment and terrorize my mama's home. Why it manifested as a half man/half horse remains a mystery. All I know is that the Lord visited us that evening and expelled the enemy. I know what prayer and the blood of Jesus can do.

Although strange, this was not a figment of my imagination; it was a real encounter. I didn't read it in a book of mythology. This happened, not in a dream, but in my waking hours while I was watching the Olympic games.

Battle with a Persistent Lizard

Two weeks before my mother passed, I beheld a small lizard crawling up the verandah rails. It was on its way into the house. I didn't think much of it at the first, because lizards are common in the West Indies. Every now and then they crawl into your house, especially if there are trees close by and if the weather is hot. Some poly lizards and croaking lizards might even take up residence under the eaves of the buildings. Well, there were no trees near the house.

I was sweeping the floor, so I raised the broomstick high and landed a blow to the lizard. It rolled over onto its back and appeared dead. As I walked away, the Holy Spirit spoke: "Do not turn your back on that lizard; it is not dead." I turned around and saw the lizard crawling back towards the steps attempting to re-enter the verandah. It stopped at the bottom of the stairs and looked up at me. I stood on the top stairs and looked down at it. I had the broom in my hand. Speaking to the lizard, I said, "If you are sent here, come to me."

That lizard crawled to about twelve inches from me. I lifted the broomstick high and flattened the lizard with another blow. It turned over onto its back and appeared dead again. Seconds later, that lizard shook itself back to life and stared at me again from the bottom of the steps. I felt like a raging bull in the spirit. The live-in helper looked on. The devil was persistent, but I was even more persistent. I was in a battle with a messenger of Satan. Since we couldn't co-exist together, one had to go—and it was not me. I was paying the bills, and no devil was going to chase me from my own home.

Once again, I spoke to the lizard, "If you are sent here, come to me." The lizard came as it did the other times. Again, I whacked it with the broom. "Satan, the blood of Jesus is against you." The same thing happened. It rolled over on its back as if dead. Then it shook itself back to life and stood at the bottom of the stairs and looked up at me. The yellow eyes were now red.

This happened some four times. The fifth time, I spoke to the lizard saying, "Enough is enough. Satan, the blood of Jesus is against you. Go back from whence you came, in the name of Jesus. In the name of Jesus, I reverse this order, and I return you to the sender. I send you back to hell, in the name of Jesus."

I lifted the broom high and came down on that lizard with strong blows, while asking the Lord for coverage. I beat that lizard until it lay on the concrete like minced meat. I dealt with it so militantly that even the broomstick broke into pieces. It was fatally wounded.

Looking at the lizard, I said, "If you are sent here, come to me." It didn't budge. It was as dead as a door nail. The remains stayed on the ground until the rain came down at 2:00 p.m. and washed it away. Strangely, the chickens in the yard passed without touching it. The flies and the ants passed it by without touching it. That was not normal.

This occurred. It wasn't taken from fairy tale books or from the Strange but True encyclopedia. The spirits of torment and torture are let loose today to scare you to death. You need to be covered under the blood of Jesus.

I overcame the wiles of the forces of darkness by the power of the blood and by praying in the name of Jesus. The devil came, embodied in a tiny lizard, but Jesus detected and exposed him. It's a good thing to trust and believe in God. God delivered me and my mother's house, again, that morning. The Lord already told me that I was going to encounter demons. For this reason, I was fearless. The Lord promised to protect me from all evil, and he kept his promise.

The blood of Jesus prevailed another time. God protected and delivered me from the noisome pestilence and from the destructive force that should have struck me dead at noon. No weapon formed against the children of God shall prosper.

Visit from a Strange Iguana

It was 2:00 p.m. on a Friday. I was getting ready to go to the grocery store to buy bread. A voice spoke to me saying, "Behold, the iguana comes. Go out to meet it." I said to the housekeeper, "The iguana is come; I am going out to meet it." Together we hurried to the verandah. Seated on the rails was a young iguana. I knew it was young, because it was light green rather than dark green. It was about ten inches long from snout to tail, and it had yellow eyes.

I asked the housekeeper to get the broom. She brought it, and I lifted it high. In the name of Jesus, I came down on it hard. It flew into the air and disappeared without a trace. We prayed and asked God to deliver us, again. The tempest that was raging against my mother and the rest of the family must cease. The blood of Jesus will never lose its power to deliver.

The Holy Spirit had told me two weeks earlier that God was about to change my mother's address. He was going to take my mother home to glory, so I kept a keen watch on her daily. I prayed and asked the Lord to take my mother home in the daytime and not in the night. I didn't want to wake up in the morning to find her cold, blue all over, and dead. I wanted to see her when she left. "Lord, let me see my mama when she leaves." I asked the Father not to let it rain either.

God granted my request. Two weeks later, on Monday, October 7 at 10:00 a.m., the Lord called my mother home. She passed from this life while I was doing her morning care. I attempted CPR, but the Lord said to let her go, so I did. As she drew her last breath, I spoke to her. "Goodbye, Mama. You've been a good mother. You've worked hard and done well. The Lord awaits you. Go and rest in peace. Goodbye, Mama."

On Wednesday, October 9 at 11:00 a.m., my sister arrived from Florida. She stood beside the stove making tea. I went in after her and beheld a great iguana perched on the wall, high above the stove. I knew it was a grandfather iguana, because the colour was a very dark green. It was two times the size of the younger one of two weeks back. My sister didn't see this creature. I said to her, "Don't move! The iguana comes again." She looked up and backed away from the stove.

We began to pray and call upon the name of Jesus. "Satan, the blood of Jesus is against you," we decreed and declared. It disappeared at the mention of the blood of Jesus, but apparently it didn't leave. About fifteen minutes later, I saw it under the eaves outside the living room window.

Two of my brothers joined me and my sister. One of them grabbed a can of strong insect spray and began to spray the iguana as it began to crawl away. At each blast of the spray it stopped, shook itself, and then looked at us with yellow eyes, as if to say, "Catch me if you can."

"Stop spraying," I said to my brother. "This one doesn't call for spray. It calls for the blood of Jesus." We called upon the name of Jesus.

At the name of Jesus and at the mention of the blood, this iguana disappeared without a trace. I know that this was no ordinary iguana. It was a messenger from hell, in disguise. We called upon the name of the Lord, and he protected us. God delivered us one more time.

The Lord could have stopped the half man/half horse creature, he could have stopped the persistent lizard, and he could have intercepted and stopped the grandfather iguana and its son. God did not. God allowed them to appear before me. He gave me a personal demonstration of his mighty power. I believe that God is who he says he is. He is the Great I Am, and I believe in his power to save and to deliver. Satan, the blood of Jesus is against you.

Jesus Christ has a name that is above all names. At the name of Jesus, every man-made kingdom must crumble. He is the mighty God—the God we serve. I know what prayer can do. I know that there is wonder-working power in the blood of the Lamb. I know that there is power in the name of the Lord. The name of the Lord is a strong tower into which the righteous can run and be safe. The Lord God of heaven and earth is still able. He is more than able to keep safe that which I have entrusted unto him. I know Christ defeated the devil at Calvary.

When the believer says, "Satan, the blood of Jesus is against you," he declares that he is not standing on his own, but in the power of the spirit and the blood of Jesus. The devil already knows that the only power that he has is what he has been allowed by God.

Christians do not have to "plead" the blood of Jesus. The Merriam-Webster Dictionary defines the word "plead" as asking for something in a serious and emotional way; to try to prove a case in a court of law; or to say in court that you are either guilty or not guilty. The Free Dictionary describes "pleading" as: an earnest appeal; to beg or to make an emotional appeal. In view of the meanings of the word "plead," we can draw the conclusion that we do not have to plead the blood of Jesus.

No child of God needs to beg or emotionally appeal to God for the blood of Jesus. His blood has already been shed, and it's still the only agent presiding in the work of salvation in the world. The blood of Jesus still does its work in the business of healing. Words are powerful. I believe that all we need to do is remind the devil that the blood of Jesus Christ is still against him, and that he is already defeated. Satan, the blood of Jesus is against you.

The revelator assures us that the saints will overcome the serpent by the word of their testimony and by the blood of the Lamb. (Revelation 12:11) There is still power in the blood of the Lamb.

The Lord rebuke you, Satan, and the blood of Jesus is against you. No demonic forces can take up residence in an atmosphere that is saturated in the blood of Jesus.

Satan, the blood of Jesus was against you when it was shed at Calvary, and it is still against you today.

Chapter 9
Agonizing in Gethsemane

On the night Jesus was betrayed, he went into the Garden of Gethsemane and prayed until he experienced the condition called hematidrosis, a rare clinical phenomenon which occurs when the tiny capillaries near the surface of the skin break and spill blood into the sweat.

Matthew reports that Jesus took with him Peter, James, and John to the Garden of Gethsemane. He began to be sorrowful and very heavy. He said unto them, "My soul is exceeding sorrowful, even unto death: tarry ye here, and watch with me" (Matthew 26:37–38; see also Mark 14:33–34). Luke, the physician, tells us, "And being in an agony he prayed more earnestly: and his sweat was as it were great drops of blood falling down to the ground" (Luke 22:44). The writer of the book of Hebrews stated:

Who in the days of his flesh, when he had offered up prayers and supplications with strong crying and tears unto him that was able to save him from death, and was heard in that he feared; Though he were a Son, yet learned he obedience by the things which he suffered; And being made perfect, he became the author of eternal salvation unto all them that obey him; Called of God an high priest after the order of Melchisedec. (Hebrews 5:7–10)

We understand from these verses that the prayer Jesus prayed in Gethsemane was no ordinary prayer, but a prayer that was indicative of intense emotional pain and anguish. This prayer was painfully sorrowful. Agony is derived from a Greek word that means "contest." This denotes severe pain and the struggle which an athlete undergoes. Agony denotes the kind of force that is applied in a chariot race.

Jesus demonstrated that purposeful praying takes a toll on the physical and emotional aspect of a person's being. He didn't hide the fact that he was painfully oppressed. I don't know what troubled his spirit the most, but I know, from his own admission, that he suffered the kind of emotional distress that an athlete, a charioteer, or a wrestler would feel prior to and during a contest. That prayer took such a toll on Jesus' physical being that God had to dispatch an angel from heaven to strengthen him (Luke 22:43).

Jesus Christ, the anointed Saviour, took on the sins of the world. The great anointing upon his life didn't alleviate the great mental pain he felt. The anointing gave him strength for the journey, but it didn't shield him from the anguish. He cried unto his Father and asked him to allow the cup to pass from him. Not even the selected three who went with him could understand what Jesus went through. They felt a little of what he was feeling. We are told that they fell asleep because of the sorrow (Luke 22:45).

"If thou be willing, remove this cup from me: nevertheless not my will, but thine, be done" (Luke 22:42). What cup was Jesus speaking about? It was the wrath of God upon humanity because of sin. Sin separated man from God, as symbolized by the veil of the tabernacle in the wilderness (Jeremiah 25:15–18; Revelation 14:9–10).

I don't think Jesus agonized over his impending suffering and death, because he knew that his mission to earth was for that purpose. His destiny was not vague or indiscernible. He even made mention of his destiny in a conversation with Zebedee's sons and their mother (Matthew 20:20–23). Jesus came of his own free will to be the kinsman redeemer to purchase man's salvation. Because he took upon himself our sins, he was subjected to the contents of that cup—the cup of God's wrath (Psalm 75:8; John 18:10–11). Jesus came to do the will of the Father (Psalm 40:7–8; 2 Corinthians 5:21).

The cup presented to Jesus Christ was filled with the wrath of God against sin, the effect of sin, and the payment required to appease it. The sin of man was imputed into Jesus' account. For a moment, Jesus felt alienated from God. His final words on the cross said it all (John 19:30). Those words were the annunciation of victory. What he came for was accomplished. He bowed his head and gave up the ghost.

Suffering isn't the worst thing that could ever happen to a person. The worst thing that could ever happen is feeling forsaken by God and his Son when you are experiencing trouble and tribulation. The Lord quenched the flames of God's righteous indignation when he drank of the cup. Today, we can come to the throne of grace and drink freely of the cup of his blessing. As far as the price of salvation is concerned, the cup is empty.

Conium maculatum, more commonly known as poison hemlock, is native to certain regions of Europe, West Asia, and North Africa. It is highly poisonous. In ancient Grecian dynamics, the poisonous substance extracted from this plant was forced upon prisoners who were condemned to die. Etymologic findings reveal that the poison affects the nerves and muscles of the respiratory system. The victim would die shortly after ingestion. It's rumoured that the great philosopher, Socrates, died when he was infused with hemlock poison.

If the stories of the witnesses and scribes of ancient history are precise, we can safely assume that those who drank of the cup of poison hemlock did not do so willingly. Jesus, when served the bitter cup, drank it willfully (Isaiah 53:6–10). Jesus drank all of it. Thank God! Jesus took the cup and drank the entirety of its contents. Over two thousand years ago, he died for our trespasses, but he arose again from the grave (Romans 4:23–25; 1 Peter 2:21–25).

Jesus made prayer a part of his ministry. His last prayer in Gethsemane was not without blood. His sweat came forth as drops of blood. He who prays must have an unmovable faith in God. Miracles happen in an atmosphere of prayer and faith (Hebrews 11:6). Earlier I wrote about the importance of a watchman for the watchman. Yes, he who is engaged in warfare prayer can expect to agonize like Jesus; therefore, he needs back-up. God sent an angel to strengthen Jesus, and God will strengthen you as you engage in those times of "virtue draining" prayer.

Chapter 10
Not by Might, nor by Power, but by the Spirit of the Lord of Host

The Holy Spirit

"Then he answered and spake unto me saying, This is the word of the LORD unto Zerubbabel, saying, Not by might, nor by power, but by my spirit, saith the LORD of hosts" (Zechariah 4:6b).

I've heard many people refer to the Holy Spirit as an "it." Let it be established that the Holy Spirit is not an "it." The Holy Spirit (also called the Holy Ghost) is the third person of the Godhead. God the Father, God the Son, and God the Holy Spirit are three distinct persons, yet one God (1 John 5:6–8).

The Holy Spirit existed with God before the foundation of the world. He was present when the world was created. The earth was without form and empty, and darkness was upon the face of the deep. Then the Spirit of God moved upon the face of the waters (Genesis 1:2). Some translations say that the Holy Spirit flutters, or hovers, like a dove upon the face of the waters.

The Holy Spirit quickened that which was empty, barren, and dead, awakening it so that it could produce as the voice of God commanded (Job 26:13; John 6:63).

From the book of Genesis, we learn that the Holy Ghost is a live, active, and powerful person. Anyone he touches cannot remain cold, dead, barren, or dry. He must arise and in the power of the Spirit take charge and produce as God orders. Most people identify with the manifestation of the Holy Spirit on the Day of Pentecost, because they don't realize that he was operating here long before that.

Not only was the Holy Spirit an equal co-partner with God in the creation of the material world, but he was an active participant in the making of man. Bible scholars understand that when God said, "Let us make man in our image, after our likeness," he was speaking to both the Son and the Holy Spirit.

Like the Father and the Son, the Holy Spirit is aware of every aspect of man's being and can discern man's thoughts. The Holy Spirit can see deep within the hidden recesses of my mind, so he is able to trouble my conscience when I do that which is unacceptable to God. The Father, the Son, and the Holy Spirit are one. The Spirit says what the Father and the Son say. The one does not act contrary to the other. They are in total agreement with each other. Their words and actions are congruous.

The Manifestation of the Holy Spirit in the Old Testament

The Holy Spirit has always had a profound effect upon mankind. God never left man destitute. He knew that it was not good for the man to be alone, so he provided for him a helpmeet who was compatible to him mentally, physically, emotionally, and spiritually. God made Eve for Adam. Also, the triune God made himself available to man. God presented himself in the Garden of Eden in "the cool of the day." When

Adam and Eve sinned, they hid themselves from God at the time they knew he would visit them.

How deceptive is the wicked one to beguile man into thinking that God is limited by distance, time, or place! God is omnipresent, omnipotent, and omniscient. You cannot see God, but you know that he is here (Psalm 139:7–12). The Holy Spirit was present when the devil tempted Eve.

I present for consideration Genesis 3:1–10.

After Adam and Eve partook of the tree of the knowledge of good and evil, their eyes were opened and they came to the harsh reality that they were naked. Conscious of their error, they realized that they were in jeopardy of the fierce judgement of God.

One of the offices of the Holy Spirit is to convict man and make him conscious of his trespasses against God. In the biblical narrative, we see a woman caught in the act of adultery. Her accusers were careful to remind Jesus that the Law of Moses demanded that she should die, but Jesus gave them a word: "If you've never trespassed against God, then you cast the first stone at her." Convicted by their own conscience, the accusers left the scene without casting a stone at the woman (John 8:1–11). If they had no conscience, or if the Holy Spirit wasn't present, they wouldn't have been convicted (John 16:7–11; Romans 9:1).

God gave Adam and Eve the moral faculty of conscience. When we step out of alignment with the Word of God, conscience kicks in to bring us back into alignment. One of the tragedies of the fall is that man gained knowledge of what is right and wrong—he gained wisdom. Alas! In the process, he lost the power to control and subdue his own wanton mind; therefore, he continually gets himself into deep quagmires. Without the blood of Jesus, man would be forever lost.

In his zeal to capitalize on wisdom and knowledge, man forgot to get understanding: "Wisdom is the principal thing; therefore, get wisdom: and with all thy getting get understanding" (Proverbs 4:7). Having wisdom and knowledge without understanding is a tragedy. One could have all the degrees in the world, or be more intellectually endowed than the wisest man, but nobody benefits from his genius if he has no understanding. Without understanding, we can't properly process or utilize the wisdom and knowledge acquired: "Be ye not as the horse, or as the mule, which have no understanding: whose mouth must be held in with bit and bridle, lest they come near unto thee" (Psalm 32:9).

The Ethiopian eunuch gained much wisdom and knowledge from reading Isaiah 53:7–10, but he had no understanding of what he was reading (Acts 8:26–33). "The righteousness of thy testimonies is everlasting: give me understanding, and I shall live" (Psalm 119:144).

When the conscience is cauterized because of sin, the person loses sensitivity to sin. The desensitized person can no longer feel the pricks of guilt piercing his heart or stabbing at his brain. The rancher on a cattle farm brands his cattle with a hot iron. Those persons whom Satan has branded will apostatize and follow false prophets, heresies, seducing spirits, and doctrines of devils. They will speak lies in hypocrisy, forbid to marry, and command to abstain from meats that God has created to be received with thanksgiving by those who know the truth (1 Timothy 4:1–4).

The Holy Spirit Moved Samson

After the episode in the Garden of Eden, the Holy Spirit continued to operate in the lives of humans, but he did not infill them.

For example, the Spirit of God moved (came alongside and nudged him into action) Samson in the camp of Dan. Samson felt the move of the Spirit of God upon him and went after the Philistines, and destroyed them (Judges 13:25, 14:6, 19, 15:14, 16:1–31).

In Judges 16, Samson loses the seven locks of his head. Samson tried to shake himself into action, as at other times, because he didn't realize that God had departed from him. The Philistines overpowered him, gouged his eyes, and brought him in captivity to the house of their god, Dagon. The seven locks of Samson's head served as a symbol of his identity. Long hair was unique to a Nazarite, who was a person who voluntarily decided to be set apart, or consecrated, for service to God.

Numbers 6:1–21 lays out the vow of the Nazarite with the following requisites:

- The position is voluntary.

- The person can be man or woman.

- The person must follow specific instructions and restrictions.

- The person must serve for a specific period.

- If the person defiles himself during the period of consecration, he must shave his head, and the priest must offer up a sin offering and burnt offering unto God for him. He could not redeem or transfer the former days that he was consecrated. They are lost. The priest alone could render him fit to operate in the office of a Nazarite again.

- At the end of the period, the person must offer a sacrifice unto God.

Samson (Judges 13:1–7), Samuel (1 Samuel 2:8–28), and John the Baptist (Luke 1:13–17) were chosen from before birth to be Nazarites. A Nazarite was to refrain from drinking vinegar, wine, or any fermented drink. He was to abstain from eating fresh grapes or dried grapes, nor could he drink any liquor of grapes. He should eat nothing made of the vine tree, the kernels, or the husk. The Nazarite should not cut his hair for the period of his vow. He was not to defile himself with a dead body, even if it was a family member, because this would render him ceremonially unclean.

At the end of the Nazirite's term, the hair would be shaved at the door of the congregation and burned in the fire under the peace offering sacrifice. The priest would place a certain portion of the offering upon the hand of the Nazirite after his hair was shaven. This would be for a wave offering before the Lord. After this, the Nazirite could drink wine. The Nazirite must fulfill his vow according to the law of his separation.

Samson's hair symbolized not only his strength, but his identity. Every Nazirite had long hair, but not every one of them had the strength of Samson. God endued Samson with special power. To cut the hair of his head was equivalent to backsliding and abandoning the faith (Judges 16:17, 20–22). Samson toyed with his sanctity and lost that which identified him as a separated vessel unto God the Father.

Although the Lord removed himself from Samson for a season, his eyes were constantly upon him. There was never a place Samson ventured where God didn't see him. The eyes of the Lord were upon Samson even when the Philistines were making a public ridicule of him.

Shaving the seven locks of his head was symbolic of the ministry or the mission that was not perfected. He was cut off prematurely before his term was concluded. It amazes me that Samson never called unto the Lord throughout Judges 13–14, even though he was walking contrary to his calling. Samson prevailed against the Philistines simply because God promised to deliver his people, and he used Samson as a conduit in the process. Samson did call unto God to restore his strength when he found himself in prison amongst the enemies.

Notice that Samson didn't have to ask for his hair to grow again; it automatically began to grow. Why? Once a person restores his broken relationship with God, God will receive him again and make him new.

Samson messed with his consecration. In the New Testament era, we are called upon to keep our bodies in a state of separateness from the sinful things of the world (Romans 12:1–2).

The Attributes of the Holy Ghost

✣ The Holy Spirit is a person with characteristics such as feelings and emotions; therefore, it is possible to grieve him (Ephesians 4:30).

✣ He is intelligent, knowledgeable, and intellectually endowed. He is an infallible, authentic expert; therefore, he can and has taught us all things (John 14:26).

✣ The Holy Spirit has been here from the beginning. He makes wise, intentional decisions. In the Old Testament, he moved upon whom he would. In the New Testament, he infills and then bestows the gifts of the Spirit upon believers. He is active in the setting forth of the saints for kingdom work and building. He equips and empowers believers for service (Acts 13:2, 4; 1 Corinthians 12:11).

✣ The Holy Spirit is a teacher. He teaches us all things and brings all things to our remembrance; therefore, we can spiritually discern things and compare spiritual things with spiritual (John 14: 26; 1Corinthians 2:13–14).

✣ As an intercessor, he intercedes for us with groanings that cannot be uttered (Romans 8:26).

✣ The Holy Spirit reproves the world of sin, of righteousness, and of judgement (John 16:8).

✣ The Holy Spirit loves the soul of man in the same way that the Father and the Son do; he bears witness of the Father and the Son (John 15:26, 16:13–14; 1 John 5:6).

- The Holy Spirit bears witness that we are the children of God, the Father (Romans 8:16).

- He is a discerner; therefore, he reveals the deep things of the Spirit. He declares that which is about to come to pass. He searches the hearts and knows the mind of the spirit, because he makes intercession (Luke 2:26; Acts 5:1–11; Romans 8:27; 1 Corinthians 2:10–11; 1Timothy 4:1).

- The Holy Spirit is powerful and authoritative. He commands, and the believers execute the imperatives. The believer also has delegated power and authority. Authority means that one has been given the right to do something. Power is indicative of the ability to accomplish the mission (Acts 8:29).

- The Holy Spirit assists us in crucifying the flesh and mortifying the deeds of the body (Romans 8:13).

- Like the Father and the Son, the Holy Spirit was here from the beginning (Genesis 1:2; Job 26:13, 33:4; Psalm 104:30).

- The Holy Spirit is our comforter. He is the promise of the Father (John 14:18; Acts 1:4).

The Manifestation of the Holy Spirit in the New Testament

The Holy Spirit manifested his presence and is very much apparent in the New Testament era.

The Holy Spirit came upon the Virgin Mary and impregnated her with the Lord Jesus Christ (Matthew 1:18–20; Luke 1:35). Elisabeth was filled with the Holy Ghost when she heard Mary's announcement (Matthew 3:11, 16). Zacharias was also filled with the Holy Ghost and prophesied (Luke 1:67).

The ministry of Jesus Christ was not without power. When Jesus was baptized, the Holy Spirit descended upon him in a bodily shape like a dove (Matthew 3:11, 6; Luke 3:21–22). Jesus, full of the Holy Ghost, returned from his baptism and was led of the Spirit into the wilderness (Luke 4:1). After his wilderness experience, he returned to Galilee in the power of the Spirit, and his fame spread through all the regions round about (Luke 4:14).

Every born again believer is indwelled by the Holy Spirit. From the moment of conversion, your body becomes a residence of the Holy Spirit (John 14:16–17, 26, 15:26, 16:7–11).

A Rescue Mission to Earth

For what purpose did Jesus come to earth?

- ✣ Jesus came to seek and to save those who are lost (Luke 19:10; 1Timothy 1:15).

- ✣ Jesus came to call sinners to repentance (Mark 2:17; Luke 5:32).

- ✣ Jesus came to lay his life down as a ransom for many (Matthew 20:28).

- ✣ Jesus came to bear witness to the truth (John 18:37).

- Jesus came to fulfill the will of His Father (John 6:38).

- Jesus came because he is the Light of the world (John 12:46).

- Jesus came that men might enjoy a more abundant life (John 10:10).

- Jesus came to establish the good news, or the gospel (Mark 1:38).

- Jesus came in order that the law might be fulfilled (Matthew 5:17).

- Jesus came to be a propitiation for our sins (1 John 2:2, 4:10).

- Jesus came because, like the Father, he had compassion for Adam's fallen race (John 3:16–18).

- Jesus came to bless mankind and to turn him from his iniquities (Acts 3:26).

- Jesus came to redeem mankind from the curse of the law (Galatians 4:4–5).

- Jesus came so that the righteousness of the law might be fulfilled in us who do not walk after the flesh but after the Spirit (Romans 8:3–4).

Mission Accomplished

Why did Jesus have to go? Jesus' tenure on earth would soon be finished. As we learned before, He came on a rescue mission to redeem man, who was eternally separated from God. This would be accomplished at his crucifixion on the cross of Calvary.

Jesus was the visible manifestation of the invisible God. Once His mission was accomplished, there was no need for Him to remain on earth. He had to return to his Father, but He would not leave his people comfortless. He sent them the Holy Ghost.

The ambassador of God needs the ministry of the Holy Spirit. The Holy Spirit brooded over the elements, and at the command of God, everything came into existence. The word "moved" is derived from the Hebrew word "rachaph." It means to brood, as a hen broods over her chicks. Our heavenly Father did wonders through the power of the Holy Spirit. The unity between the Father, the Son, and the Holy Ghost is the greatest demonstration of team spirit. Jesus told the disciples:

Verily, verily, I say unto you, He that believeth on me, the works that I do shall he do also; and greater works than these shall he do; because I go unto my father. (John 14:12)

The greater works Jesus speaks of aren't greater in power or magnitude. Jesus' ministry on Earth didn't take him to the far reaches of the world; however, he gave the apostles the Great Commission. He further told them that when the Holy Ghost was come upon them, they would be his witnesses in Jerusalem, Judea, Samaria, and unto the uttermost part of the earth (Acts 1:8). The apostles would venture into areas that Jesus never did.

Jesus also had said that signs would follow the believers. On the day of Pentecost, the Holy Spirit descended upon those tarrying in Jerusalem. They were endued with power for service. Under the influence of the Holy Spirit, the disciples performed miracles. Signs followed them, as the Lord said in Mark 16:15–18.

Immediately following the baptism of the Holy Ghost and fire, Peter boldly stood and ministered to the listeners. At least three thousand people were saved in that crusade. The Lord added to the church daily (Acts 2:14–47).

In Acts 3, God wrought a miracle in the life of the lame man at the gate of the temple called Beautiful. This man was crippled from birth, and he was now over forty years old (Acts 3:2, 4:22). This tells me that God isn't limited by time frame; he can reverse orders, even the orders that were decreed before birth.

Under the power of the Holy Ghost, the believers prayed. After they prayed, the place where they were assembled together shook. All were filled with the Holy Ghost, and they spoke the Word of God with boldness (Acts 4:13–31). In Acts 5, the Lord dealt with Ananias and Sapphira because of their sinful deeds. In this instance, their crime was discerned through the power of the Spirit.

Miracles continue throughout the book of Acts. The church was advanced, as Jesus decreed. Revival broke out everywhere the apostles were driven. The Holy Spirit never left them. He continued to baptize believers and equip them for kingdom duties. Not only did the Holy Spirit baptize believers, but He also imparted gifts to them. From the book of Romans throughout Revelation, the Holy Spirit continued to demonstrate His mighty power.

The Holy Spirit Seals Us and Is Our Earnest

"Now he which stablisheth us with you in Christ, and hath anointed us is God; Who hath sealed us, and given the earnest of the Spirit in our hearts" (2 Corinthians 1:21–22).

The English word "earnest" is derived from the Greek "arrabon," meaning, "a part payment in advance for security; a large part of the payment, given in advance as a security deposit that the whole will be paid later; an installment; a down payment which guarantees the balance or the full purchase price" (Strong's Concordance).

The Lord promised in John 14:1–3 that he would come again to snatch his bride away. He assured us that he would not leave us without hope; therefore, we are given the gift of the Holy Spirit. The Holy Spirit seals us. Nobody places a deposit on something that isn't valuable or important.

With this understanding, we know that the Ekklesia (the church) is highly important to God. She is the expected bride of his Son, Jesus Christ. The Holy Spirit is given to the church as a guarantee or down payment. This is ample proof that God will not forsake us, but will finish the work he started within us (Ephesians 1:13–14).

This is not the end of all things, because at the end of this life we will be with the Father, the Son, the Holy Spirit, and the heavenly host in heaven. What we experience here is only a foretaste of what is to come. The promise did not stop at the apostles or the first century saints. The Holy Spirit has also been given to us (Acts 2:38, 5:32; Romans 5:5, 8:9, 8:11; 1 Corinthians 6:19). He is faithful who promised.

Baptized with the Holy Ghost and Fire

"And, behold, I send the promise of my Father upon you: but tarry ye in the city of Jerusalem, until ye be endued with power from on high" (Luke 24:49); "And they were all filled with the Holy Ghost, and began to speak with other tongues, as the Spirit gave them utterance" (Acts 2:4).

Imagine being in that facility on the day of Pentecost. Imagine the aura—that visible emanation of powerful energy coming down upon those brethren. What the believers saw and experienced was distinct and tangible. I can feel a surge of power passing through my fingers as I pen these lines. This was no hocus pocus. It was the fulfillment of the prophecy of the prophet Joel (Joel 2:28–32; Acts 2:16–21).

According to scriptures, the first Adam was made a living soul, but the last Adam was made a quickening spirit (1 Corinthians 15:45). As we lift our hearts and voices in prayers unto God, the Holy Ghost helps our infirmities by making intercessions for us with groaning which cannot be uttered. Why? We do not know what to pray for as we ought (Romans 8:26).

The rule of thumb is this: those who live by the Spirit and walk by the Spirit will not fulfill the lust of the flesh (Romans 8:5–17). With the Holy Spirit in full operation in our lives, we will manifest the fruit of the Spirit (Galatians 5:16–25).

Processed in the Furnace of Affliction

My greatest desire, after conversion, was to experience what the believers experienced on the day of Pentecost. I yearned to be baptized with the Holy Ghost and with fire. I stood in the intercessory prayer line several times, but nothing happened.

One Sunday afternoon while I was standing in the prayer line, a mother said something that made me angry. She said, "You want the Holy Ghost? Do your homework!" This offended me, because I thought she was saying that something was wrong with my walk with God. When I got home that afternoon, I picked up the telephone in readiness to dial her and give her a piece of my seething temper. But as I touched the dial, the voice of the Lord thundered in my ears: "Do not touch that dial. Mother told you to do your homework; put down the telephone, and do your homework." Frightfully, I backed away from the telephone.

It was scary. I realized that what Mother meant was that I should continue to reach out to God, not only when I was in the sanctuary, but when I was without. I repented and began to do my homework, as ordered.

In a spiritual encounter one Sunday morning, I fought a great battle with the forces of darkness. I was speaking in the English language, but the forces still came at me. Suddenly, the Lord placed another language in my mouth, and I began to speak in an unknown tongue. Immediately, the darkness dispersed. I wasn't in the church, but at home in my bed. I continued to speak as the Holy Spirit gave utterance.

I began to leap and shout for joy. I was baptized with the Holy Ghost and with fire. The feeling inside was beautiful. I felt as light as a feather. Breakfast had no taste that morning. A stream was bubbling within me. I went to church, but didn't voice my experience.

During that week, the devil crushed my spirit. I was at a bible study session. It ended with a sacred song and then prayer. I closed my eyes, as I sang, and was suddenly taken to another place, a resplendent place. I heard voices singing, but they weren't the voices of the saints. The voices belonged to angels. I heard musical instruments playing, and a wind enveloped me. It caressed my cheeks and then brushed my lips. I felt warm all over my body. It was happening again.

I began to speak in another language. A sister interrupted me, shouting, "You are filled with the Holy Ghost. You are filled! You are filled!" She was ecstatic.

I opened my eyes. A great dazzling light filled the place. I felt as if I was suspended in the air, but what happened next brought me back to earth. Somebody shouted angrily, "Filled! Filled … what? You need to be ministered to!" I felt crushed and embarrassed. I couldn't hold back the tears, which meandered down my cheeks like a rivulet.

By the time I reached my abode, I felt like a lifeless rag doll. I felt as if I'd gone to the butcher's shop, because my spirit was slaughtered. I slumped in the sofa and wept bitterly. That experience really floored me.

I received a knockout punch. I entered the spiritual doldrums and didn't want to speak in tongues ever again.

I recalled the excitement and rejoicing when a brother received the baptism with the Holy Ghost and fire. There was singing, shouting, and dancing. There was the giving of thanks unto God. Everybody rejoiced and prayed with the brother, but I was immediately chopped down when I was endued with power from on high. Why, Lord?

Nobody but God knew the pangs I suffered. Every time I felt the Spirit of God moving upon me, I did something to quench Him. Every time I did that, I suffered more. I was young in the Lord and had yet to learn how to rise above persecution and use it as a launching pad to bring me to the next dimension of the Spirit. The war was on. This was when I learned that prayer should be a priority in the life of the believer. I learned to call upon the name of the Lord in a deeper way.

Misery Likes Company

It happened on a Sunday morning. The Lord showed me a vision that was imminent. He said that during the preaching of the message (whether in the morning or evening I knew not), a young woman would interrupt the service and begin to speak in tongues. Three people would try, without avail, to calm her. The Lord said that he'd prepared a song to be infused into the stormy atmosphere to restore order and still the tempest.

I began to pray, because I'd never had anything like this happened to me before. I was so timid, because I was new in the Spirit. The vision manifested exactly as the Lord had said. Ten minutes into the evening message, a young woman began to speak, nonstop, in tongues. Everybody whom the Lord showed me was there doing exactly what the Lord had said—trying to take control, to no avail.

Being young in the Spirit, I didn't quite understand how to carry out the imperatives of God, so I consulted with those having authority and waited until I was given deployment to sing. As soon as I uttered the first line of the song, there came a shift in the atmosphere. The young woman calmed down and took her seat. The speaker attested that God had given her the same vision. God is not a dream ... he's a reality, but God does give dreams and visions. He said that he would pour out his Spirit in the last days—that is now. Sons and daughters would prophesy. The young men would see visions, and the old men would dream dreams.

I believe that everybody, whether you're a new convert or not, should have a spiritual mentor or teacher. A mentor or teacher has the capacity to guide us so that we'll not stumble, even with the gifts that God has blessed us with. Joseph had a revelation from God, but he didn't know how to execute it. He needed a mentor, a spiritual mother or father, to guide him and teach him how to use the gift of God effectively. Embarrassment can kill, especially if the person is a babe and suckling in the Lord. A mature Christian needs to remember where he or she is coming from. We do not want to kill anyone; rather, we want to bring them up in the nurture and fear of the Lord.

A series of events followed that left me in misery and mental confusion, but it would not be edifying to list them individually. After the fact, I didn't want to sing anymore or pray in public anymore. I didn't want to testify. Every time I opened my mouth to say something, I heard a voice saying, "Shut up, you are ignorant." I knew it was the voice of the enemy.

I was confused and nervous. I was also hysterical, because I was receiving revelations and didn't know whether they were from the Lord or from the devil. Being endued with the gifts of the Spirit should be a wonderful experience, but my experience left me embarrassed and afraid.

I was caught between a rock and a hard place. My mind was messed up, and I felt that I had nobody to talk to. I cried and prayed. I cried and prayed again. Why did I not feel better?

I barricaded myself in my own private mental prison. Negative thoughts began to infiltrate my mind and left me trapped in a state of psychological trance. I felt as if I was anesthetized. I was bound and kept under maximum security—in my own mind. I didn't know what to do with the anointing God had placed on my life. The devil said to run and hide and not let anybody in. He convinced me that I'd be chopped down again, so I became a victim and hid within myself. I felt stupid and insignificant. I was emotionally wrecked.

I was physically still in God's army, but my mind was in the wake of a riot. Coming into the presence of the Lord should be a joyful experience, but I felt no joy. The thoughts of worthlessness mocked and silenced me each time I tried to say something in the presence of the Lord. There had to be a way out, so I prayed and I prayed again, but I was still bound.

I thought that the best way out was to stay away from the house of the Lord, but I soon realized that sitting at home wouldn't be wise, because the devil would always find employment for idle hands and minds. I continued going to the house of God. Folks thought that I was "quiet." They didn't realize that I was silently suffering. I felt disconnected, not from God, but from the assemblage. I never had a spiritual mentor; therefore, I became a mental recluse and bore my woes alone—until. As I wrestled with the dragon that wanted to bankrupt me spiritually, I heard the voice of the Lord saying: "Will you be freed from that mental shackle? I am come to break you free. I am your God. Walk with me."

Newborn babies need the nourishment of the unadulterated Word of God. They need tender loving care and nurturing. I needed to learn to nurture and encourage myself. And so, I did. I arose from the state of stagnancy and bitterness and spoke with all I needed to speak with. It was painful, but I did it. Before I could be used mightily of God, I had to confront the first monster—self and self-pity. I confronted all other monsters after the first one was dead. I could blame everybody and remained sedentary, but the anointing on my life was too great and would not be stifled. The more I pulled into myself, the more God reached in and pulled me out. One evangelist told me that I had an end-time ministry. I had to get out of the rut.

Three months had elapsed after the last incident. One Friday afternoon, I was encouraging a friend. She had a people problem and was asking God to fix them. I poured out words of consolation from the Bible into her and repeated what the Lord told me to tell her: "Do not ask me to fix them, but rather ask me to fix you so that you can cope, because you cannot run from yourself. Everywhere you go, you are going to meet some of them.

The Lord then said to me, "Stop asking me to fix them. Ask me to fix you so that you can cope, because everywhere you go, you will find some of them." Oops! The Lord told me that I needed to be fixed. Yes! I needed to be fixed, because as an ambassador for God, I'll be faced with persecution. My faith will be tested. I must pass through the refiner's fire. God has a way of fixing everyone according to his agenda and timing. This word is for all of us who are followers of Christ and doers of the Word of God (Romans 8:36–39). We are all targeted. In the name of Jesus, be fixed so that you can cope.

I am my worst enemy, because I allowed persecution to shut me down. Growing pains are common to all who come to Christ. All of us must be processed in the furnace of affliction. We must endure and overcome fiery trials (1 Peter 4:12–19).

I wanted the palace, but not the pit, the prison, and the wilderness. I wanted the mountaintop experience, but not the experience of the desert and the valley. I was one of those people who wanted to be a golden Christian without passage through the refiner's fire.

Dear readers, it doesn't matter how we get there, as long as we get there—even on broken pieces of the ship. I braced myself and like a baby learning to walk, I stood. The Lord gave me this prophetic word: "Stand upon your watch! The devil is afraid of your prophetic destiny and that is why he is trying to kill you. Take unto you Psalm 45 and meditate upon it."

I shook myself free of the dust and broke loose from the mental chains that held my mind captive. It was a struggle, but God sent me revival fire and soaked me with the Holy Ghost. He picked me up from the rut and set me upon my feet so that I could stand again. Like the man at gate of the temple called Beautiful, I began to walk, and then I leapt and praised God. Satan, you lost again. I'm not there yet, but I'm going on towards total perfection.

I'm pressing on, because I want to see Jesus (Philippians 3:10–14). God granted me the power to pray. It's dangerous to live without the anointing of the Holy Ghost. (Psalm 40:1–3, 51:11–13, 85:6). Every child of God will have his own Jordan to cross, but the God of heaven will make a way. He made a way through the Red Sea when all looked bleak before and behind. I know what prayer can do. It is a necessary and important weapon.

God doesn't want us to just cross over—he wants us to possess and take authority. When the children of Israel left Egypt, they were harnessed (Exodus 13:18). Harness in Hebrew nomenclature refers to a suit of defensive armour, or armed men fitted together. A person coming from a setback is dangerous. When God brings you out of the doldrums, you are harnessed. You are armoured to fight and very dangerous. You're fitted together, or harnessed, with the Holy Ghost. His power is your power.

I say unto all who read this book: do not leave empty. Keep holding on to the horn of the altar and cry out unto God. The Holy Spirit waits to usher your petition to the throne room of heaven. I speak to you from my heart. Had it not been for the God of heaven who answers prayer, I would be long dead, but God, who is plenteous in mercy, looked down from heaven and answered my prayers. Hold on a while longer; God is about to show up and change your situation.

When God was about to emancipate the children of Israel out of Egypt, he told them to eat the Passover meal and dress themselves in travel clothes (Exodus 12:11). God is telling us today to dress ourselves for the occasion, as he is about to take us places.

God is about to pass through your situations with the blood of the Lamb and turn them around for good. This is the time of your turnaround. This is the beginning of your new beginning. Your latter shall be greater than your former. I learned to pray. I learned to trust the God of heaven and wait upon him. God has renewed me many times when, like the eagle, I molted.

I must confess that every now and then, I find myself in moping valley. My spiritual eyes and talons become calcified with the cares and pressures of life. Every now and then, I find myself naked and vulnerable, because my feathers are shed. Every now and then, the strength to soar, to rise and eat is absent, but I looked towards the holy hill of Zion and fastened my feet upon the Rock. Like the Shunamite woman, I cried, "It is well! It is well! It is well!"

Every now and then, I feel like Elijah under my juniper tree, complaining unto God about what he already knows. But blessed be the name of the Lord. I found strength; therefore, I arise and eat the spiritual food God has provided for all those who are weak and famished.

My sisters and my brothers, arise and eat, because the journey is not finished yet. There are still a few more miles to cover. The Lord is about to pass your way with a strong and great wind. He will break in pieces the mountains standing before you. He will shake the foundations of hell with a holy earthquake. He will send holy fire. Every golden Christian is processed in the furnace of affliction. Stand firm and do not lose ground. You are an overcomer.

Chapter 11
Praying in the Spirit

Let us first establish the fact that being spirited is quite different from being spiritual. Likewise, praying in the spirit is different from spirited praying. A person praying in the spirit doesn't seek a "wow" from the audience. His thoughts are focused on the Lord; therefore, he prays as unto God. As he prays, he listens for the direction of the Holy Spirit. God uses the spiritual person as an oracle.

A spirited person is a lively person. When he prays, he exudes such exuberance that others might think, Wow! This is it! But is that what praying in the spirit denotes? Bear in mind that Satan has placed counterfeit messengers all over the world. Some people who are expressive and fluent in prayer can, at the same time, be as far away from God as the east is from the west.

Simon the sorcerer won over the audience in Samaria by means of satanic power. He exalted himself as some great one. Anointed with the Holy Ghost and fire, the apostles stormed the city, and people were converted to Christianity. The sorcerer also professed to be converted and followed the ministry of Philip, but in the process of time, he sought to purchase the power of the Holy Ghost with money. In religious terms, this is called "the sin, or act, of simony." The Lord used Peter to rebuke him sternly (Acts 8:9–25).

Some people have the gift of verbosity and can articulate words, but their prayers are nothing but "stock" prayers prayed out of the abundance of their vocabulary. Did the Pharisee not pray out of the stock of his storehouse? (Luke 18:10–14) When a prayer is fuelled by the Holy Spirit, it always touches the audience. No matter what the magnitude, soft or thunderous, it will trigger a response from the listeners. God will be glorified, and breakthroughs will come.

What Is Meant by "Praying in the Spirit?"

Praying in the Spirit is recorded about three times in scripture (1 Corinthians 14:14–17; Ephesians 6:18; Jude 1:20). There is a marked difference between praying with/in my spirit and praying in the Spirit.

Praying in the Spirit/praying in the heart

Often, we use heart/mind/spirit interchangeably to express silent speech. A thought conceived in my heart, a thought conceived in my mind, or a thought conceived in my spirit are the same. We conceive things in our hearts even before we voice them. It's out of the abundant storehouses of our hearts that we speak.

I have prayed in my spirit many times. Nobody hears or sees me praying, but God, who knows the thoughts of my heart, knows that I am praying. The devil acts according to what he hears. He cannot read what's in your heart; however, when you pray aloud, he hears and can marshal his emissaries to bombard you. The "spirit" as used in John 11:33 and Ephesians 4:23 refers to man's inner core. When I pray with my inner core, nobody besides myself is edified, because nobody hears. I am the only person who benefits from that prayer.

"Now Hannah, she spake in her heart; only her lips moved, but her voice was not heard: therefore, Eli thought she had been drunken" (1 Samuel 1:13). Eli wrongly accused Hannah because she was praying in her heart, or in her spirit. Her lips moved, but no audible words came forth. She was misunderstood. To Eli, she was high on wine, because it was a time of feasting. Hannah, in fact, was praying from a sorrowful heart unto Jehovah.

Praying in the Spirit can refer to praying in the heart with no audible words coming forth. Ultimately, it's divine communication between your spirit and the Spirit of God. No third party is necessarily involved.

"The Spirit itself beareth witness with our spirit, that we are the children of God" (Romans 8:16).

As children of the Most High, we sometimes feel the need to speak to him in our hearts rather than with our voices. We know that whether we speak aloud or whether we speak in our hearts, God hears us. The children of God are privileged to speak with him in the spirit.

I once visited somebody whom medical experts had declared brain dead. He had zero brain or bodily function for three days and would only be on life support until family could come and visit him. His vital statistics were at rock bottom. He was as frigid as an icebox. We sang and prayed, and I stretched over him like the prophet Elijah did with the Zarephath woman's dead son. I spoke the words "come forth" unto him. Those words beckoned to his spirit.

When deep called unto deep, the brain dead responded by moving his entire body in the bed. He kept on moving at subsequent intervals as we continued singing and praying in that intensive care ward. His vital signs increased. He was not unconscious, but brain dead; however, God stirred him and he heard and responded with a sign—the moving about of his entire body in the bed.

Praying in the Spirit is synonymous with praying with the intervention of the Holy Spirit

"For if I pray in an unknown tongue, my spirit prayeth, but my understanding is unfruitful" (1 Corinthians 14:14). When a person prays in tongues, he or she is under the influence of the Holy Spirit, because one cannot truthfully speak in tongues unless the Holy Spirit gives the utterance to speak. The person speaking in tongues is in a divine dialogue with God. Unless there is an interpreter, the Bible says that the understanding is unfruitful.

Consider the following passages:

"Praying always with all prayer and supplication in the Spirit, and watching thereunto with all perseverance and supplication for all saints" (Ephesians 6:18).

"But ye, beloved, building up yourselves on your most holy faith, praying in the Holy Ghost" (Jude 1:20).

Praying in the Spirit in the context of these two scriptures refers to a prayer that is uttered according to the leading of the Spirit. It means to pray about the things the Holy Spirit leads us to pray for. In Ephesians 6:18, Paul instructs believers to pray in the Spirit always. Praying in the Spirit should be done under the authoritative unction of the Spirit of God:

Likewise the Spirit also helpeth our infirmities: for we know not what we should pray for as we ought: but the Spirit itself maketh intercession for us with groaning which cannot be uttered. And he that searcheth the hearts knoweth what is in the mind of the Spirit, because he maketh intercession for the saints according to the will of God. (Romans 8:26–27)

"And I will pour upon the house of David, and upon the inhabitants of Jerusalem, the spirit of grace and of supplications" (Zechariah 12:10a).

The Holy Spirit, who is acquainted with man's infirmities, steps in and gives a helping hand so that our prayers make sense to those who are listening. He also ensures that our prayers will ascend to the throne room of God as sweet smelling savours. They will not be offensive to God or man.

Praying always with all prayer and supplication in the Spirit, and watching with all perseverance and supplication for all saints, does not mean that we should pray in tongues, because not everybody has the gift of tongues. Some people speak in tongues occasionally, but they don't have the gift of tongues to speak always (1 Corinthians 14:2–5).

Praying always with all prayer and supplication in the Spirit, and watching with all perseverance and supplication for all saints, means that our prayers and supplication should be directed and guided by the Holy Spirit. Man should not cease from praying for all saints. The Spirit-led prayer ministers to the soul of man in the same manner as the preaching of the gospel of Jesus Christ. When one prays in the Spirit, he prays according to the prompting of the Holy Spirit.

It wasn't the preaching of a message that prompted me to turn my heart over to the Lord, but a scary vision and a sacred song entitled, "I'll be satisfied." Like that song, a prayer prayed with the Spirit's intervention can turn backsliders back to God and convict sinners so that they run to Calvary. The Holy Spirit indwells the believer and knows what he needs to pray for and how he should pray; therefore, when we bow before God, the Holy Spirit steps in. He is our Paraclete. He gives us a hand, because we don't know what to pray for.

A person praying in the Spirit prays from the depth of his being. He's not just a spirited person gifted with loquacity. He is led of the Holy Ghost, and his prayer stirs and edifies the souls of the listeners. Many of Jesus' public prayers were very short and he used simple words, but they always accomplished what they set forth to do. Jesus prayed in the Spirit always.

Often, I find myself praying towards things that had never crossed my conscious mind. I had no prior knowledge of the content of the prayer. All I know is that I felt a quickening in my spirit, and out of my mouth came things that surprised me. Countless times after prayer somebody tells me that they were blessed by my prayer, because it spoke to their needs. I had nothing to do with anything. I'm just an instrument in the hands of the Master Potter. I'm a recipient of the grace of God, and the object of his beneficence. I tapped into the promise that God promised the house of David—the spirit of grace and supplications. I give God all the glory.

The Holy Spirit is always sensitive to the needs of God's people. He has the affinity to bring the right words in due season. He helps us to pray in season and out of season (into the future). The Holy Spirit is intensely involved in the prayer life of the saints and the church, because spiritual growth progresses in an atmosphere of prayer, fasting, and the Word of God. Remove prayer, and everything in Christendom will come to a dead halt.

Paul, a Great Icon of Prayer and Faith

To the church in Rome, Paul gave this assurance:

"First, I thank my God through Jesus Christ for you all, that your faith is spoken of throughout the whole world. For God is my witness, whom I serve with my spirit in the gospel of his Son, that without ceasing I make mention of you always in my prayers" (Romans 1:8–9).

To the church in Corinth, Paul uttered these words: "I will pray with the spirit, and I will pray with the understanding also…" (1 Corinthians 14:15).

To the brethren at Galatia, he said: "My little children, of whom I travail in birth again until Christ be formed in you" (Galatians 4:19).

Paul's injunction to the church at Ephesus, and subsequently to us, was/is: "Praying always with all prayer and supplication in the Spirit, and watching thereunto with all perseverance and supplication for all saints" (Ephesians 6:18).

The apostle had this prayer for the church at Philippi: "I thank my God upon every remembrance of you, Always in every prayer of mine for you all making request with joy" (Philippians 1:3–4).

Paul had this word of encouragement for the Colossians brethren: "We give thanks to God and the Father of our Lord Jesus Christ, praying always for you …" (Colossians 1:3).

Unto the church at Thessalonica, he said, "Pray without ceasing" (1 Thessalonians 5:17).

Unto Timothy, Paul spoke: "I exhort therefore, that, first of all, supplications, prayers, intercessions, and giving of thanks, be made for all men; For kings, and for all that are in authority; that we may lead a quiet and peaceable life in all godliness and honesty. For this is good and acceptable in the sight of God our Saviour" (1Timothy 2:1–3).

"I thank God, whom I serve from my forefathers with pure conscience, that without ceasing I have remembrance of thee in my prayers night and day" (2 Timothy 1:3).

Unto Philemon, Paul said: "I thank God, making mention of thee always in my prayers" (Philemon 1:4).

Paul, the great icon of prayer, never ceased to pray and give thanks unto God for the brethren and the people with whom he came into contact. He endorsed what Jesus said: "…men ought always to pray and not to faint" (Luke 18:1).

Let us join together in the Spirit, and with the Spirit pray for men everywhere, as the Lord commanded.

Eulogy

In my studies of the blessings of God, I found something interesting. The Greek word rendered blessing is the same word for the English word "eulogy." According to Dictionary.com, "eulogy" denotes a speech or writing praising somebody highly who has just died. To bless somebody is to bestow upon them good things and to speak well of them.

If a eulogy is a blessing or an oration speaking good things about a person, it shouldn't be read after the person dies, but while the person is living. We need to follow the Lord's example and give blessings to others while they are alive. If you mean to bless me, do it while I'm alive.

"Blessed be the God and Father of our Lord Jesus Christ, who hath blessed us with all spiritual blessings in heavenly places in Christ" (Ephesians 1:3). The living God blesses us out of his never-ending economy. Bless somebody today. Do not wait until after death.

Prayer

I personally pray that the God of heaven and earth will pour upon you his manifold blessings. I pray that the Father will open unto you new and effectual doors.

I pray, in the name of Jesus Christ, our soon coming king, that he will drive out the adversaries from before you.

I pray in the name of our Lord Jesus Christ that you will not just overcome and cross over from your adverse circumstances, but that you will claim your inheritance and occupy every territory God has given you.

I pray, in the name of Jesus, that this year God will restore unto you all that which the enemy has devoured.

I pray in the name of Jesus that you will enjoy good health. You will increase in strength and wealth.

I pray that you and your loved ones will be blessed. You are the highly favoured of God. Before you were born, God knew you. You are a person of destiny.

Be blessed with all spiritual blessings in heavenly places in Christ Jesus. Amen.

Chapter 12
Praying in Tongues and Interpretation

"For if I pray in an unknown tongue, my spirit prayeth, but my understanding is unfruitful" (1 Corinthians 14:14). The Holy Spirit gives the believer utterance to speak in tongues. A multi-linguist can speak fluently in a diversity of languages acquired through studies and exposure; however, God through the Holy Spirit imparts the gift of unknown tongues to the believer.

With this gift also comes the gift of interpretation. The Holy Spirit places the language in the mouths of the speakers, and the speakers deliver in audible tones. This kind of speech isn't stored in the memory banks of the speakers; therefore, one cannot retrieve unknown tongues at will. It comes by the will of the Father in heaven.

The prayer prayed in the spirit has a divine objective. It should always be for the glory of God. Every now and then, the Holy Spirit will impress upon our spirit to pray special prayers for individuals, cities, nations, or conditions. When one prays in an unknown tongue, interpretation should follow, according to Paul. If there is no interpreter, nobody benefits. Paul made it clear that if his spirit prays but he doesn't understand what he just said, his understanding remains unfruitful. He is no wiser, because he doesn't comprehend what has been said. Likewise, those who are listening are not enlightened, and everything remains a mystery. Nobody can receive or agree with something that is not illumed.

Interpretation sheds a light on the prayer that is prayed in tongues. This is one of the gifts the Holy Spirit imparts unto the believers. A child of God, under the anointing of the Holy Spirit, can translate a foreign tongue into a language that will be understood by the listeners. The interpreter has no prior affiliation with the language being interpreted (Acts 2:4–12). This is the distinguishable difference between that which is spiritual and that which is temporal. The tongues spoken of in Acts 4 were foreign to the believers, but clear to the masses. God authenticated that the tongues were of the Holy Ghost, because every nation identified his own language.

Decades ago, I was in a youth service where a young man was summoned to pray the opening prayer during a time of devotion. For the first couple of minutes, he prayed in the English language, but every word for the next fifteen minutes was spoken in an unknown tongue. While he prayed in English, everybody agreed with him; but from the time he went off in tongues, there was total silence.

There could have been a word in that prayer for somebody, but nobody was edified, because nobody understood what was being said. There was no interpreter. He could have been giving thanks unto God, or sending forth a word for somebody seated in the audience (1 Corinthians 14:19–23).

I remember a time when I telephoned a sister. She answered the call. She probably was having an intimate moment with her Father at the time, because all I could hear on the other end of the line was a babble of tongues. It was confusing. I wondered why she'd answer the telephone if she was that high on the Holy Ghost. A person so deeply saturated with the Spirit wouldn't stop to answer the telephone. I hung up. I was not being edified by her tongues.

I understand that every now and then God will change our language for a purpose, but as Paul contended, nobody can say amen if he cannot identify with what has been said. To the unlearned it seems like nothing. They will think that we have all gone insane.

If your spiritual language is between you and your Father, then keep it between the two of you. If the language carries with it a message for the audience, then there has to be an interpreter.

Advocates in Prayer

Before you begin to pray, remember that you're not alone. If you abide in the Word and the Word in you, your ability to pray effectively will be profoundly governed by the abiding and perfecting presence of these two:

1. Jesus, the first advocate in prayer

According to Dictionary.com, an advocate is someone who speaks or writes in support or defense of a person or a cause; a person who pleads for or in the behalf of another; or an intercessor. Jesus plays a substantial part of the prayer life of the saints, because he is the mediator between man and God. Without Christ, we have no access to the throne of grace. Christ's mediatorial work enables us to approach the blood-stained mercy seat in holy of holies, where we can speak to the Father personally.

Jesus is our advocate. He sits at the right hand of majesty and speaks to God on our behalf (1 John 2:1–2). Jesus enlightened the apostles concerning the Comforter, whom he also termed, "The promise of the Father." Before the annunciation of the advent of the Holy Spirit, Jesus informed the disciples that if he did not leave, the Holy Spirit would not come.

The bishopric of the Holy Ghost is distinct from that of the Lord. The Lord saves us, heals us, and anoints us with the Holy Ghost and with fire. I reiterate the fact that in days of antiquity, the Holy Spirit didn't indwell man; instead, he moved upon them whenever God commanded. But now he indwells us. The Lord continues the work of the kingdom in us through the Holy Spirit who lives in our hearts.

Because of Jesus, we have been infiltrated with the spirit of power, love, and a sound mind. (2 Timothy 1:7) Believers can valiantly conquer the adversaries, because they don't walk alone. They walk under the banner of the blood of Jesus. Those who dwell under the secret place of the Most High shall abide in the shadow of the Almighty.

God has commended his love towards you; therefore, when you battle with the enemy or with the cares of life, you do not have to fear. You enter with soberness of mind and with confidence (see Ephesians 2:13–15, 18-22, 6:10–12; Proverbs 18:10; Hebrews 4:14–16). I have been in the ministry of prayer for many years and have discovered that prayer is labourious work, but God did not intend for you to labour alone. God has given us Jesus to lighten the load.

2. The Holy Spirit, the second advocate in prayer

The Holy Spirit endeavours to work in the believer always. The Holy Spirit cannot be separated from the Word of God, because the Word is God, and the Word is with God. The Holy Ghost issues from God, and the Holy Ghost must perform the will of the Father who sent him into the world.

The Holy Spirit teaches us and brings things to our remembrance so that we remain aligned with the Word of God. He revives and refreshes us when our spiritual and physical energy are depleted. The Holy Spirit sustains us and gives us the unction for service. He exposes the orders that the enemy has sanctioned against us. He also demolishes the gallows and the booby traps that the devil has erected to ensnare our necks and our feet. The Holy Spirit brings illumination to the Word of God so that we will be enlightened.

Because of the work of the Holy Spirit, the person who prays gains audience with God. God has delegated unto us his dynamite power. One cannot pray a prevailing prayer except he is charged with the Holy Spirit and led of the Holy Spirit. Every child of God has at least one gift. Those gifts differ, according to the inspired Word of God (1 Corinthians 12:4–12). Every gift of God is given for his glory.

God Stopped Children from Running Away

Once I was led of the Holy Spirit to pray for a college associate's marriage. It was 7:00 a.m. on a Sunday when I called her and expressed my concern about her marriage. I travailed with her in prayer and interceded for her two young sons. I told her that she needed to have a talk with them, because they were planning to run away from home. The trigger was the breakdown of the marital relationship between her and her spouse.

At 3:00 p.m. she called me back to inform me that while I was speaking with her that morning, her older son was in his room writing her a letter. The problems in her marriage had taken such a toll on the children that they were planning on running away the next day after school. They were going to leave the letter in the mailbox. She had a talk with them and was spared the agony of learning that her children had run away from home. The Holy Spirit stepped in right on time and stopped a potential tragedy.

God Stopped the Foreclosure

One morning while I was praying, the Holy Spirit prompted me to pray for a couple who had run into financial difficulties. Their home was about to go into foreclosure. I spoke with the wife after I prayed, and she told me that the situation looked bleak. We prayed again and asked God to intervene. We asked God turned back the contrary wind that was coming up against them. I said to her, "God will not allow you and your children to sleep under the trees. God is alive; you will not lose your home."

The odds were against them, but heaven granted them favour. They paid the mortgage before the deadline by the grace of God. Today they are the happy owners of an even bigger property. The Holy Spirit saw ahead and made provision to fix that which was imminent. God is concerned about every aspect of our being. God is alive and kicking. We give him all the praise, the honour, and the glory.

Three-Month Shut Down of Electrical Metre

I was caring for my ailing mother when the bank book went empty. What would I do, how would I pay my bills with no money? The next bill was expected to arrive in three months. Every day I stretched my hands towards that meter box and prayed. "Lord, I have no money to pay the bills; but you are Jehovah Jireh. You are my provider." Your words say, "Whosoever believeth on you shall not be ashamed" (Romans 10:11). Your words say, "...they that seek the LORD shall not want any good thing" (Psalm 34:10). I left all things in the hands of the Lord. One day the agent from Light and Power came to check my metre. I was very concerned and nervous because the man kept asking me to plug and unplug my electrical equipments. He kept asking me to switch things on and off. I asked, "What seems to be the problem?" He replied, "For the past three months your metre shut down and recorded only $9.99." He added, "You do not have to pay the $9.99. I will just reset your metre."

When he was gone, I jumped for joy and gave God the glory. God has the power to fix electrical metre. God is infinitely powerful. God can effectuate that which his infinite wisdom prompts him to do. God sent the Holy Ghost to shut down the metre because he knew I had no money to pay the bill.

Chapter 13
Praying According to His Will, His Plans, and His Purpose

The religionists, occultists, voodooists, witchcraft workers, sorcerers, necromancers, soothsayers, zodiac readers, astrologers, palm readers, diviners, crystal ball readers, and black magic workers all claim to have power.

As Paul attested, seducers creep into houses and lead away into captivity idle women who refuse to watch and be sober (1Timothy 4:1; 2 Timothy 3:5–7).

Paul preached boldly in the Jewish synagogue at Ephesus for three months. When he finished, he separated the believers from the hardhearted who had not received the truth. He moved to a schoolroom and there ministered for some two years (Acts 19:8–9). Paul knew the will of God, his plans, and his purpose, so he spared no effort to separate himself from those who hardened their hearts against biblical precepts and doctrine. God says that the believers should have no fellowship with the counterfeit.

Jesus found himself amongst beasts, but he prevailed. He lives and has the keys of death and hell. Time invested in prayer and supplication to God is never time wasted. The devil gets another death stroke when saints everywhere begins to honour God and offer prayers unto him. How can one pray according to God's will, plan, and purpose? As I traverse the pages of the Bible, I'm cognizant of the fact that the whole duty of man is to fear God and keep his commandments (Ecclesiastes 12:13). I'm also aware that man's highest incentive should be to bring glory to the name of God (1 Corinthians 10:31). We bring glory to the name of the Lord when we know his will, do his will, and pray according to his will and purpose.

The only way to know the will, plan, and purpose of God is to ask him (Mark 11:24; James 1:5–6). The person who desires to know what God has in his mind must ask God in faith. If one lacks wisdom, he should seek God, who blesses us liberally.

When Hannah was pressed by her adversary, Peninnah, she went into intercessory prayer before God. Hannah desired children; but she was not getting pregnant. Children are important in every generation, and the greatest desire of a woman after she marries is to bear children. Society and her own innate tendencies pushed her to have children, especially sons. Hannah knew that children are the heritage of God; therefore, she prayed according to the will of God, and God opened her womb and gave her a son (1 Samuel 1:9–28).

God delivered Daniel from the mouth of the lions. Daniel's prayer life didn't begin in the den of lions. It began before he was cast into the den. I am certain that he continued in prayer while he was with the lions. Circumstances did not drive him to pray. He prayed ahead for the circumstances that he and the children of Judah and Jerusalem would encounter (Daniel 6:1–28).

Praying according to God's will, plan, and purpose demands that we search the scriptures (John 5:39). God bids us to pray for our enemies; pray that the Lord of the harvest will send forth labourers into the harvest; pray that we might escape temptation; pray for those who are labouring in ministry; pray for governments and those who have the rule over us; pray for those who are oppressed with maladies and infirmities; pray for the salvation of the people; pray for mercy and forgiveness; and pray for boldness to minister (Psalm 51:1–2; Matthew 5:44, 26:41; Luke 10:2; Acts 4:29; Colossians 4:2; 2 Thessalonians 3:1; 1 Timothy 2:1–3; James 5:13, 16).

Praying according to the will, plans, and purposes of God cannot be overemphasized. The scriptures are filled with references. God teaches that if we walk in the Spirit, we will not fulfill the lust of the flesh (Galatians 5:16–26).

God gives gifts even to those who have not asked him or deserve it. God blessed Samson's mother with a little son who would begin the work of deliverance at a time when the Philistines were oppressing the children of Israel. Forty probationary years, and God was ready to send deliverance. Samson's behaviour wasn't always congruous with his consecration, but God did not strike him. God used him as an instrument in the ministry of deliverance.

Many so-called prophets are under the false notion that they can twist God's hands into delivering. We have yet to learn that if God works miracles by our hands, he alone gets the glory. When the supernatural occurs, it's not because of our "prophetic" prayers and utterances. It's because of God's mercy. It's offensive to God to hear prayers that command him to act. Therefore, we need the guidance of the Holy Spirit when we pray, because we do not know how to pray as we ought to

We can make prophetic decrees and declarations until the cows come, but nothing will happen. It will happen when God says it will happen. It will happen when we submit ourselves to God's fashioning hands. It will happen when we decrease and when our lives are lost in his. It will happen when our will aligns with God's will. God will do it when we begin to walk in obedience to his words and leading.

There are those who believe they are the practitioners of the prophetic, and that the supernatural only happens when they pray or perform. If God wishes to put a prophetic word and a prayer in the mouth of a donkey, he can. God used the whale, the worm, and the gourd to teach Jonah valued lessons. A donkey spoke to Balaam. God spoke a word through the donkey, but he never made the donkey a prophet.

Peter was headed for demise when the cock crew. The cry of the rooster jolted Peter back to reality, and he realized his own weaknesses and vulnerability. If it weren't for the mercy of God, we'd all be consumed. All the glory belongs to God.

The spirits of witchcraft, manipulation, and control are prevalent in the world and have infiltrated the house of God today. If we aren't careful, we might be led into captivity by these seducing spirits.

A Healing Service Ritual

Some years ago, on a Friday night, a sister invited me to what she called a "healing service" at a local church. I was annoyed in my spirit from the time I set foot inside the door. Service began, and immediately the pastor began speaking in tongues. He commanded the people to begin speaking in tongues. About 95 per cent of the people obliged. Then he directed them to begin prophesying to each other, which they obediently did.

He alternated between speaking in English and speaking in other tongues. The people followed in hot pursuit. It sounded as if they were quarrelling as each person tried to outdo the other. He turned the service over to his wife, and she did the same thing. She spoke in tongues and prophesied; then she prompted the people to do the same.

When she got tired, she turned the service into the hands of another person, who continued with the same ritual. It was appalling. They behaved as if the Holy Spirit was a tap one could turn on and off at will. The control the leaders had over the audience was amazing.

The speaker spoke from Acts 3:1–11. At the end of his short message, they brought forth white sheets. People took turns going to the altar to be prayed for. The speaker wouldn't move to the next person until the present one fell to the floor. As soon as the person fell, they covered her with a sheet. Within a minute, the person who had just fallen to the floor removed the sheet and return to her seat. The next person came and the same thing occurred. This continued for the rest of the service.

I rebuked my friend sternly and refused to visit that place with her again. She eventually stopped going when they refused to pray for her. "Get out of the prayer line with your cancer and disease," they told her. She ran and never went back.

God the Father, God the Son, and God the Holy Spirit are not robots. They're not mechanical gadgets that you turn on and off at will. The Holy Spirit gives utterance to speak.

And this is the confidence that we have in him, that, if we ask any thing according to his will, he heareth us; and if we know that he hear us, whatsoever we ask, we know that we have the petitions that we desired of him. (1 John 5:14–15)

We don't have to manipulate the situation. God is not a robot. The scripture says that if we ask any thing according to his will, he hears us.

The Spirits of the Prophets Are Subject to the Prophets

The children of God need to become acquainted with the Word of God, because there are many end-time counterfeits on the prowl. They come to seek and to destroy and to make the Word of God of none effect. Counterfeits bring confusion, and they have shipwrecked the faith of many in the body of Christ. The healing service ritual above was totally confusing.

The Bible says that the spirits of the prophets are subject to the prophets (1 Corinthians 14: 29–32). God explicitly refers to the "spirits of the prophets," not the "Spirit of God." Prophets can make a conscious choice (the lead of his spirit) to speak or not to speak, but they can't initiate a true prophetic utterance. Neither can they command others to prophesy to anyone. One can speak into the lives of others, and one can quote prophetic verses of the scriptures to others, but when it comes to prophesying, that's the work of the Holy Spirit.

The Holy Spirit is not a mascot or a religious mantra. He is the Spirit of the living God—the third person of the Trinity. He comes and goes of his own free will … not when we chant.

Unknown tongues are divine utterances given through the Holy Spirit as a sign to the unbeliever.

Prophesies are divine inspiration from God to the believers. They are initiated by the wonderful working of the Holy Ghost. One does not stand in the congregation and flippantly speak in tongues or frivolously prophesy and then ask others to become involved. It is the spirits of sorcery and manipulation that do this.

The apostle Paul encourages believers to follow after charity and desire spiritual gifts, that they may prophesy (1 Corinthians 14:1). The gift of prophecy or prophesying and the gift of the prophet are two distinct entities. Some people function dually in the gifts of prophet and that of prophecy. Jeremiah sought God for his people. It took ten days before God sent them words. The prophet had to wait upon God before he could utter a word to the people (Jeremiah 42:1–22).

"For the prophecy came not in old time by the will of man: but holy men of God spake as they were moved by the Holy Ghost" (2 Peter 1:21). Prophets are placed in position by divine selection. One does not arbitrarily choose to become a prophet. The gift of prophesying or prophecy is given by the Holy Spirit. Through the working of the Holy Spirit, a person operating in the prophetic anointing will bring forth an inspired utterance from God to the people. Through prophecy and prophesying, the Holy Spirit reveals the heart of God in an audible voice. The people hear and are edified, exhorted, and comforted (1 Corinthians 14:3–4).

It is a lie from hell that causes one to believe that he or she can orchestrate, activate, or manipulate the move of the Holy Spirit. He comes of his own free will when believers humble themselves, gather in unity, and pray towards the will, plan, and purpose of God. God issued this indictment against the false prophets:

> The prophets prophesy lies in my name: I sent them not, neither have I commanded them, neither spake unto them: they prophesy unto you a false vision and divination, and a thing of nought, and the deceit of their heart. (Jeremiah 14:14)

One of the ascension gifts Jesus gave to the believers was the gift of the prophet. He gave some apostles, some prophets, some evangelists, some pastors, and some teachers (Ephesians 4:7–16). These gifts have specialized functions. They are equipping ministry gifts. People should be divinely appointed to give leadership in these areas.

There's a vast difference between being led of the Holy Spirit and being driven by a seducing spirit.

God uses believers as catalysts to minister deliverance to the spiritually bound. Do not become so fascinated with the gifts that you forget the reasons for the gifts. The gifts are for the perfecting of the saints, for the work of the ministry, and for the edifying of the body of Christ (Ephesians 4:12).

Indeed, we can pray over folks and over situations. We can ask God for his intervention. Yes, we can speak a word into the atmosphere and see satanic interferences and activities aborted (Isaiah 46:11b). God has given us the authority and power to shut down the works of the devil.

Joshua commanded the sun to stand still upon Gibeon, and moon to stand still upon Ajalon (Joshua 10:12–13).

Elijah prayed until fire came down from heaven on Mount Carmel (1 Kings 18:38).

Elisha poured salt into the contaminated water at Jericho, and it was healed (2 Kings 2:19–21).

When in Melita, a venomous snake bit Paul. He shook the venomous reptile into the fire and watched it die (Acts 28:1–7).

God can involve us in his miraculous manifestations. At the end of the day, God gets the glory. Many people try to control others because of their giftedness. There is not a word that God has placed in my mouth to deliver to his people that he has not placed in the mouths of the former prophets. Search the scriptures and have a talk with Isaiah, Jeremiah, Ezekiel, and Daniel. God has done it before, and he will do it again. I am careful in my testimonies of the goodness of God to ascribe all the glory unto him. When Satan tried to exalt himself above God, God kicked him out of heaven. His fall was quick. He came down like a bolt of lightning.

If the result of prayer depended upon the person praying, there would be no room left for God to be manifested. If healing was up to the physician, no physician would die from debilitating diseases. He would heal himself. But physicians die, because they are not God.

You'd be surprised to know that many folks who pray or intercede for you are themselves in bondage. Many folks can pray you happy, but then go home miserable and unfulfilled. They need deliverance. While they pray you out of your rut, they return to their places bound and unhappy. Folks pray over your marriage while theirs are falling apart. Some people are praying your prodigals back to Calvary while theirs are rebellious and still at large.

When we pray according to God's will, plans, and purpose, we leave the door open for him to enter and perform wonders. If we continue to knock and wait upon God, he will open unto us his good treasures. He is our Father. A woman might abandon the child she gave birth to, but God says he will not forget us. God says that he has graven us upon the palms of his hands; therefore, we are always before him (Isaiah 49:16). This means that every time God opens his hands, he sees us. Wait upon God and exercise faith while waiting.

A person with the gift of the prophetic will avert confusion by keeping silent and forebear to speak until the Holy Spirit gives him the go-ahead.

Anyone speaking as an oracle of God will do so in a decent and orderly manner.

Chapter 14
Coupling Fasting with Prayer: Part A

What is fasting? Like prayer, fasting is a neglected spiritual discipline. By fasting, the candidate makes a conscious decision to abstain from all foods and drinks, or to exclude certain foods and drinks from the diet for a period of time.

An absolute fast is normally defined as abstinence from all foods and liquids for a defined period, usually a single day (twenty-four hours) or several days. Other fasts may be only partially restrictive, limiting particular foods or substances. The fast may also be intermittent in nature. Fasting practices may preclude sexual intercourse and other activities as well as food.

A person might also be ordered to fast totally or to refrain from certain foods and drinks for a certain period of time for medical reasons. Fasting requires that the person bring his mind under strict spiritual discipline and control.

Biblical Fast

A biblical fast is the willing abstinence from food or drinks for the purpose of soul cleansing or other spiritual reasons. No matter what the reasons are, fasting will be beneficial to both soul and body.

Biblical fasting is not an optional discipline for the believer, but a mandatory requirement, especially for those seeking a more intimate relationship with God, empowerment, and breakthrough. In a biblical fast, the pursuant focuses on God.

Jesus introduced himself in scripture as the bridegroom. After his death, his disciples would suffer many things; therefore, consistent and intense fasting would be required (Matthew 9:14–17). Under the old covenant, the people fasted according to the precepts of the Law, but once the bridegroom paid the price of redemption on the cross, the new covenant was ushered in.

Jesus Christ was the fulfillment of the Law; therefore, the people of God did not have to be ritualistic in fasting while he tarried with them. After his ascension, the body of Christ would need to fast in order to continue to experience the deep things of God. The visible manifestation of the living God was wrapped up in Christ Jesus. He was also called Emmanuel—God with us. When he made his exit from the world, there was left an aching longing to be close to him. This was filled when the Comforter came.

The wonderful thing about Christ's absence is that his beloved, the church, doesn't have to mourn for him, because she has access to the throne of grace. She also has the indwelling presence of the Holy Spirit to comfort her. The church doesn't have to sit around and bemoan her lover, because he's not dead. Her bridegroom is alive and has made himself accessible to her by means of the gifts of prayer, fasting, and the Word. All we need to do is call him up. The royal spiritual telephone line is always open, because God is expecting our call. The more our souls thirst after him, the more he fills us (Matthew 5:6).

The Condition of the Vessel Matters

There should always be a purpose for fasting. One of the reasons I fast is to get my vessel ready to receive enablement for the next dimension in the Spirit. Any person who is releasing virtue and pouring out needs to be poured into and be replenished. The minister is in constant need of refreshing. It's dangerous to give out of your reserve; therefore, it's imperative for the minister to be ministered to.

When the woman with the issue of blood touched the hem of Christ's garment, healing power went from his body. The woman tapped into the power source of Jesus and immediately was delivered from that which had plagued her for twelve years. She drew healing from the healing reservoir of Jesus Christ (Luke 8:45–46). This was a strategic and timely move. It is written in the Torah or the Pentateuch that the children of Israel should make fringes/tassels/tzitzit on the borders of their garments. This carried with it great spiritual significance for the children of Israel (Numbers 15:37–41; Deuteronomy 22:12). Each time the Israelites looked at the fringes, they would remember the commandments of God and that there is only one true God. This woman must have heard of or read the prophecy of Malachi 4:2. She knew exactly what she was doing when she touched the hem of Christ's garment.

It was prophesied that the messiah would be a healer and a bondage breaker (Isaiah 53:5; 60:1–3). Jesus did not give out of his reserve. He had a constant flow of the anointing, because he fasted and prayed regularly; he kept his vessel pure.

The Lord doesn't pour his anointing into dirty vessels or broken cisterns that cannot accommodate it (Jeremiah 2:13). God mends brokenness and cleans vessels before he pours in the new wine. The condition of the wineskin matters; therefore, when I fast, I pray and ask God to cleanse my vessel so that I will be ready for what he must impart into my spirit. As the scripture says, new wine must be poured into new wineskin. No scripture is new except to those who have never heard it. There can never be a downpour without an outpouring.

The other day I stood by my window during a hail and thunderstorm. The slanted drops of rain descended heavily. As they hit the ground, they formed little puddles. Those puddles extended outwards and joined other puddles. As puddle met puddle, they formed a little rivulet and meandered down the side of the street. Rivulets joined with other rivulets until the entire road was under water. The water spurted into the air as the vehicles dashed by. It was wonderful to look at. The water ran towards the manhole and disappeared down the drain. Most amazingly, when the rain stopped, the road, the trees, the lawn, and the cars in the parking lot were splendidly clean.

I feel exceptionally clean after I've gone through a season of prayer and fasting. Each time I couple fasting with prayer, I experience something new. I feel a new surge of electricity permeating my body. For days after, I have no appetite for food. All I want is more of God and the Holy Spirit. God cleanses me so that he can fortify me with new visions, new dreams, and new and effective way of preaching and doing his work.

Who Should Fast

All the people of God should fast. Nobody should restrict himself from this wonderful, soul-satisfying, and cleansing experience. If one has a prevailing medical condition that prohibits an absolute fast, then he can do a partial fast for a shorter period. Use wise judgment and fast only as you are able to. Fast as the Lord directs.

Fasting involves mind, body, soul, and spirit. Fasting disciplines the flesh and brings it into subjection so that God can become the principal person in our lives. Many people have made their bellies their gods, and they cannot give up food for a season. When a believer fast, he gains mastery over his flesh. Looking back into the Garden of Eden, we see that the devil used food to entice Eve. Adam followed in hot pursuit (Genesis 3:1–7).

In the Old Testament, God instructed his children to fast and pray (Leviticus 16:31, 23:32). On the Day of Atonement, the children of Israel fasted before Jehovah. This practice became known as "the day of fasting" (Leviticus 16:29–31; Jeremiah 36:5–7). Other people in Old Testament subjected themselves to fasting and prayer for personal reasons, for their brethren, and for the nation (2 Samuel 1:11-12; 2 Chronicles 20:1-4; Nehemiah 1:1-4).

The New Testament worshippers also fasted and prayed, Jesus being the chief example. Those holy men and women realized that prayer was of the utmost importance in their lives, but fasting cleanses the entire man so that when we pray, we will be able to focus on God. Fasting helps to silence the flesh so that the spirit can be rejuvenated. In fasting, the flesh is abased and disciplined in such a way that God and the Holy Spirit can take full control (see Matthew 4:1–11).

When you fast, your body hankers for that to which it's accustomed. Food is made for the body, and the body for food. The devil will try to use hunger as a weapon against you; therefore, gird up the loins of your mind so that the craving for food will not defeat you (Luke 2:36–37; Acts 13:2–3, 14:23).

While fasting, the born again believer empties his mind and thoughts of the things of the world so that the things of God can come alive. The flesh and the spirit are diametrically opposed to each other. Fasting helps us keep our minds open so that the Holy Spirit of God can impart into our spirit the nuggets that are required to maintain our consecration.

Some people have no trouble praying, but fasting is one spiritual discipline that compels us to deny the lusts of the flesh. Fasting affects us holistically. One can pray for hours without the prayer having a physical impact, but during a fast, the physical, emotional, and spiritual man will feel the effects sooner or later. Once again, it is imperative that we enter this season soberly and wisely.

When the groom is gone, the children of the bridal chamber will fast and pray. Jesus has now been gone for over two thousand years. As the years go by, I see a great need to fast and pray. Perilous times are here. The children of God need to buckle their seat belts tightly around their waists. Gird your heavenly armour on—we are in for a bumpy ride. Fast and pray for the abiding presence of the anointing.

We need to fast and pray and call upon the Lord to revive us again. One of the mistakes we make is to fast only when we are in a battle. We need to fast before the battles of life begin. As children of God, we will be engaged in warfare. Daniel prayed before the battle, during the battle, and after the battle.

Fasting prepares you for what you'll have to face during the tests of life. If you discipline yourself to fast now, the flesh will not fail you when you encounter the beasts in the wilderness of trials (Luke 4:1–15). The devil began challenging Jesus when he knew Jesus was hungry. Why? The devil knew that after such a fast, the flesh needed food. He tempted Jesus to turn the stones into bread. Jesus would not be defeated, because he had disciplined his flesh before the trial. His flesh was subdued, and the devil lost the battle (Luke 4:3–4).

Satan looks for our vulnerability and works on it. If we discipline our bodies before our fiery trials, we'll be able to win when we are tested. Fasting prepares you for your tests in life.

Chapter 15
Coupling Fasting with Prayer: Part B

The Fast That God Has Chosen

When you fast, there are principles to follow (Isaiah 58:4-9). First, we need to remember that we don't fast so that man can see us and hear us; we fast because it's required and necessary. We shouldn't fast because we want man to applaud us for our piety; we should fast so that we'll be able to fulfill the will of God, according to his words.

Second, God is holy, and his people must be holy. Without holiness, nobody shall see God. When we fast and pray, we should remember that we are coming before the holy God. According to Isaiah 58:6–7, the type of fast that God has chosen is the one that loosens the bands of wickedness, undo the heavy burdens, sets the oppressed free, breaks every yoke, deals bread to the hungry, returns the outcast to their homes, and clothes the naked.

Our fasting must not be done in an atmosphere of strife and contention (Isaiah 58:4). God is not the author of confusion (1 Corinthians 14:33). We don't come to tell God how wicked our brother or the world is and that he should smite them; we come with an attitude of repentance, because we know that none of us are righteous (Isaiah 64:6). Our demeanour should be one of humility, because we know that we aren't worthy of God's mercies. We must prostrate ourselves before God and confess our sins and ask him for forgiveness so that we can win our unsaved brothers and sisters for God's kingdom.

God is not oblivious to the fact that the world is in gross darkness and spiritual slumber. The world waits with eager anticipation and zeal for the persons who are sold out to God to point them to the way of salvation. We are in the age of grace, not the age of condemnation.

Judgement belongs to our God.

One of our duties is to bring man to the awareness that the sinner who has not repented of his sin will be judged and condemned when he stands before the judgement seat of God. Our duty is to invite the backslidden and the unregenerate to the reality of the cross. Like the apostles of old, we need to preach Jesus Christ and that he was crucified. We need to tell mankind that the only way to heaven is through Jesus Christ. All other ways are the broad ways, or detours, that lead to hell.

In this age of grace, we have been empowered and authorized by the Great Commission to go and teach all nations, baptizing them in the name of the Father, and of the Son, and of the Holy Ghost, and teaching them to observe all the commands of the Lord. The Lord promised that he will be with us always, even to the end of the world.

A desperately thirsty deer will hasten to the source of water. He runs to the brook. He has no time or desire to attend to every little thing that demands his attention. He must find the water source. Therefore, anyone lacking wisdom should seek God. The Lord knows best. When a Christian is fasting, he has no time to trouble his soul with striving or petty quarrels. His spiritual ears must be sensitive; and his eyes must be kept keen so that he doesn't miss his target. How often have we missed our season because we were deafened and blinded by the things that have little or no value to our souls? Don't miss your season.

God honours the fast geared towards bringing the lusts of the flesh under subjection to the Holy Spirit. Jesus had to bring the flesh under subjection to the rule of the Holy Spirit when he was in the wilderness of temptation. Jesus had a dirt body like the first Adam. The extraordinary thing about Jesus was that he had total control over his flesh. The lust of the eyes and the flesh had no power over him. All power has been given unto him both in heaven and in earth.

Why Do We Fast?

1. We fast because Jesus endorsed it.

Jesus led by example (Matthew 4:2). Our first duty is to obey God and his instructions. Any instruction that God gives us will be for our benefit. God's leading is always right.

2. We fast when we need to have a closer relationship with God and for victory over the oppressors.

Intimacy with God brings us into position for breakthroughs. When the enemies surrounded King Jehoshaphat, he engaged himself and the people in a season of fasting and prayer (2 Chronicles 20:1–13). Relationship matters. Lovers cannot conceive unless they become intimate. Nobody can be intimate when they are far apart. Intimacy demands that we get up close and personal.

3. We fast when we need strength to overcome the wiles of the wicked one.

Adam and Eve lost spiritual strength. They became weak and vulnerable to the devil because of association. They crumbled under temptation. They gave up power. Whatever or whoever you surrender power to becomes your master, and you his servant (John 8:34).

If we spread our beds in hell, God can see us there. If we take the wings of the morning and fly away into yonder wilderness, God can find us there. Using the law of double reference, God passed a verdict on both man and the devil (Genesis 3:14–24). Man had to find his way back to God on God's terms.

Jesus, the second Adam, washes our crimson stains. We tap into his power when we fast and pray (Isaiah 65:24). God has a way of giving us things we didn't even ask him for, because he knows what we have need of. Abraham also has this testimony.

4. We fast because fasting helps to break generational curses and bondages.

Rachel found herself in dire need of deliverance. She had an innate desire for children. Every couple who came into marital relationship in that era was pressed to procreate. The woman would be blamed if she wasn't able to produce children. Some men would take a second wife if their first was barren.

There is absolutely no curse the enemy can hurl at you that God cannot destroy with his mighty power (Genesis 25:21). Sarah was barren, but God opened her womb and Isaac was born. Rebekah was barren. Isaac could have married another wife and procured children by her, but he did not. He interceded on behalf of Rebekah, and she conceived and gave birth to twins. Years later, we see God open the womb of barren Rachel. These are clear indications that God has power over generational curses and bondages.

Bondage of Barrenness Broken

Joanna and her husband, Joseph, had been trying to have children for years. They were at the point of frustration. During a time of prayer and fasting, Joanna requested special prayer concerning employment issues and a business venture. The Holy Spirit whispered to me saying, "She is yearning to conceive, but it's not happening because she is suffering from the condition called endometriosis. Pray over her womb." She hadn't told me her story prior to this.

I laid my right hand over her womb and prayed, in the name of Jesus, for babies to come forth. She fell to the floor and screamed as a woman in travail. She related her medical diagnosis later. Within nine months, she pushed forth multiple births. God is faithful concerning his promises. Joanna triumphed over the bondage of barrenness and the curse of endometriosis. God broke the cycle and set her free.

Give God the Glory; It Is a Girl

The telephone rang. "Hello!"

This is Carmelina. I desperately need you to come to my house and pray. I cannot sleep in my bedroom. I had to set up my bed downstairs. There's an overwhelming heat throughout the house, and it's killing me. Strangely, my husband and my two girls aren't feeling this great heat, only I am. It's driving me crazy.

"What seems to be the problem?" I questioned.

"I have no idea," she continued. "I went to the doctor a month ago, and he said I was pregnant. I went back for another examination, and he said I'm not pregnant. It was a false alarm. He suggested dilatation and curettage. It's booked for the middle of next month. I'm very concerned about this, because I really feel pregnant. I know my body. I know how

I felt when I was pregnant with the other two girls. Something's wrong, and the doctor's missing it. Will you come and pray for me? Please?"

"I'll fast for you," I said, "and then on Saturday, I'll bring a few intercessors to your house and pray."

While I fasted and prayed, the Holy Spirit spoke to me. saying: "She is pregnant, but the doctor cannot detect the baby because a demon is obscuring the child. No matter how many tests the doctor performs, the baby will not be detected. The enemy is trying to kill her, and the plan is exsanguination. The dilatation and curettage is a carefully orchestrated setup from hell to cause her to bleed to death. Everywhere she goes, the demon stalks her."

Saturday came. I sought the Lord and went alone to Carmelina's house because, for various reasons, the other intercessors couldn't come. I stepped into the house and was hit in the face by extreme heat. I felt as if I was in an inferno turned up high. The extreme heat was caused by a demonic presence. The young woman was flushed and feverish. She was sweating profusely. Except for underpants and bra, she wore no clothing. She was alone at home.

Looking at her, I remembered Jesus' encounter in the country of the Gadarenes. I began to sweat also because of the heat wave, and I was wearing heavy clothing. I started prayer meeting. I gave orders to open every window and door in the house, even the garage doors. The supernatural was about to take place. God was about to purify the house and deliver Carmelina and her unborn baby.

We called upon the name of the Lord. We travailed until I felt as if I was giving birth. Yes, I was. I was giving birth to her deliverance through the power of God the Father, God the Son, and God the Holy Spirit. The Holy Spirit stood at the mouth of my spiritual birthing canal. I felt something move from within me. I didn't see it, because it was in the spiritual realm, but I knew I had pushed out something. The stronghold that was erected against this young woman began to crumble. The spiritual Philistine garrison began to go down, until something in the spirit realm crashed. It was over by the power of God.

There came a shift in the atmosphere. The extreme heat went out through the opened windows and doors. When it was all over, God air conditioned the house. She, her house, and her unborn baby were set free by the power of Almighty God. The demonic interference was gone for good. It was now cool, and the temperature was bearable. We shut every window and door that we'd opened and gave God thanks for the victory.

I told her about the revelation from God. She had a friend who worked in the lab; therefore, she knew how to analyze urine. I told her to bring a urine sample and have it tested for pregnancy. The test result came back positive. She also tested her urine at home. She was greatly pregnant. She brought the results to her doctor the next Monday morning. The doctor did his own examination and tests. What do you know? To his utter consternation, a healthy, developing baby girl showed up.

Months later, Carmelina gave birth to a bouncing baby girl. Today this baby has blossomed into a beautiful, healthy, brilliant girl. The baby that was not is a girl. Give God the glory. God extended mercy and stopped the death of mother and baby when we prayed. The devil would have massacred this darling girl had God not stepped in. Do not destroy that baby. This might be your only child. Have a little talk with Jesus.

God is a mighty God. We can reach him through Jesus and the Holy Spirit. We can access him through prayer and fasting. God can see what the doctors cannot see. Before you do anything, seek Jesus. See if God will not provide an alternative. God is mighty to save the living, the maturing, and the unborn. God answered by fire when Elijah called (1 Kings 18:37–39).

I bow before the living God who answers by fire and by water (Judges 6:36–40). God specializes in the things that seem impossible. Your seemingly impossible situation can be an opportunity for God—if you believe.

Difficult situations are no respecter of persons. You might have to stand in the gap or stand in proxy for somebody else. The next story was quoted before but not in its entirety. In Mark 9:14–29, a man brought his son who was stricken with a dumb and deaf spirit to Jesus. The man explained that whenever the spirit came upon his son, he foamed and grinded his teeth. He explained that the disciples were unable to deliver the lad. Right there in the presence of Jesus, the spirit overcame the boy. He fell to the ground, wallowed, and foamed at the mouth.

First, Jesus dealt with the man. He would have to exercise faith for his son's deliverance, because the son was not mentally able to believe for himself. He couldn't hear or speak. Daddy had to speak and believe for him. The father cried to Jesus and asked him to deliver him from unbelief. Jesus rebuked the foul spirit and drove it out of the boy.

When the disciples asked why they were unable to cast out the spirit, Jesus told them that if they wanted to be successful in the realm of the supernatural, they would have to fast and pray. If we fast, we will see more manifestations of the supernatural. We'll see more people healed of diseases and set free from demonic oppression. God promised that his power would be manifested not only in the lives of first century believers, but in all who will allow him to work through them (Joel 2:28–32). The God of Peter and Paul is the same God of today. He has not lost his power, neither can he be limited by time or distance. He is omnipresent. Our God reigns, and he is here. Hallelujah.

5. We fast and pray for salvation of the lost, spiritual growth, and revival of the nations.

Daniel fasted and prayed for the captives of the Southern Kingdom of Judah (Daniel 10:2–3). Revival will happen when those who know the worth of fasting and prayer begin to genuinely get on their faces in sackcloth and ashes, weep before God, and repent. Daniel was that conduit who stood in the gap for God's people (see also Numbers 16:44–47; 2 Chronicles 7:12–14).

When we fast and pray, the hopeless will receive hope, the discouraged will be encouraged, and the one who has lost the will to live will be revived. For thirty-nine years, the children of Israel wandered in the wilderness. In the fortieth year, they were ready to go over and take possession. God didn't leave them there to die. The next generation was ready. When they had no way, God showed them the way.

We can't overemphasize God's faithfulness to his promises. God doesn't desire the death of a sinner, but that the sinner should repent and turn to him. You are the catalyst that God wants to use to revolutionize the world and bring about local and national revival.

6. We fast for physical, emotional, and psychological healing (2 Kings 20:1–7; 3 John 1:2).

Because of the increase in technology and scientific discoveries, people today are inundated with more knowledge than ever before. But even with the increase of knowledge, man is still dying from debilitating diseases such as cancer, diabetes, cardiovascular diseases, and many more. We are terrorized by epidemics, pandemics, and other plagues.

Jesus had a healing ministry. Everywhere he went, the people thronged him because he healed their diseases. Every stripe he received at the crucifixion was for our healing. Jesus was conceived by the power of the Holy Ghost. He was born with power. He was baptized with the Holy Ghost. He preached and taught with authoritative power. He came back from the grave with resurrection power.

Jesus gave his servants the power and authority needed to accomplish their assignment (Mark 16:17–18). If you should survey a given church audience, you'll find that over half of the people are suffering from one malady or the other. They are under the care and supervision of various doctors: the neurologist, the ophthalmologist, the audiologist, the odontist, the ENT specialist, the cardiologist, the respirologist, the hepatologist, the hematologist, the oncologist, the nephrologist, the osteologist, the orthopediologist, the immunologist, and all the other ologists that you can think of ... but they aren't being healed. Even the little children are under the care of the pediatrician.

I believe it's time for somebody to initiate an upper room convocation and place these medical conditions on the altar of God. We need to shut down the supper room more often and summon both young and old to join hands and hearts together in the upper room and see if God will not cause these plagues to disappear. This is "cry out" hour. Cry out to God to stop the plagues. Our healing has been paid for by the atoning blood of the Lamb. We can see the power of God manifested in physical, emotional, and psychological healing.

Many people have been called into places of ministry, but they're kept down by some menacing diseases. They cannot maximize their potential because of infirmities. You can rise above it in the name of Jesus (Matthew 8:13–17). The entire eighth chapter of Matthew deals with healing and deliverance.

Even the storm and tempest obeyed Jesus' command. Exercise faith in God. King David cried out unto God when he was distressed. King Hezekiah cried out to God when he learned that his condition was terminal. Elijah cried unto God when the Zarephath woman's son died. Elisha cried unto God when the Shunamite woman's son died. Both Mary and Martha cried unto the Lord when Lazarus became sick and died. When Naaman acted on the Word of God and dipped seven times in the Jordan River, he was healed of the leprosy that was destroying him (2 Kings 5:1–14).

It's time for Canada, the United States of America, and the world to cry unto the Lord God, our Maker. God is not only a giver of life, but a sustainer of life also. God is veracious. He says what he means, and he does what he says he will do (Isaiah 40:28–31).

Tap into the power of God. Stay plugged into the source and see what God will do. God is still our refuge and strength. He is still a present help in trouble. Be still and know that God is God. He is exalted in all the earth.

The purpose of a fast is not limited to these six points. There are many other reasons why one might call a fast. Whatever your reasons, do it as unto the Lord. Whatever you do in secret, God promises to reward it openly. Fasting and prayer can bring deliverance. As Jesus promised, miracles will happen when we fast and pray.

Chapter 16
Coupling Fasting with Prayer: Part C

Types of Fasts

Fasting is a means by which we bring ourselves into submissiveness to the will and purposes of God. In fasting, you seek to gain mastery over food and the flesh, or self-will ... not the other way around.

The Bible provides several examples of people who involved themselves in periods of fasting. I don't believe that there is a model, per se, set out for fasting. You choose to fast, or you're commissioned by God to fast. When you voluntarily fast, you set the type, the duration, and the boundaries. Having said this, many people, including myself, agree that fasts can be categorized as follows.

Regular

In a regular fast, the person(s) lays aside all food types. Some people might choose to drink water only during this time. The apostle Paul,

Ezra, and Moses engaged in this type of fast (Deuteronomy 9:9–10; Ezra 8:23, 10:6–17; Acts 9:1–9).

Partial Fast

In this type of fast, the participant excludes only certain foods and drinks from the diet (Daniel 1:12, 10:2–3). Daniel fasted partially and prayed when he needed to understand the vision (10:1–3). He consumed roughage (vegetables, lentils, beans, nuts) and water. There was no allowance of meats, pastries, pleasant bread, fried foods, or wine. Many Christians today engage in the Daniel fast quite frequently.

Full Fast/Absolute

A full fast is one in which no food or drink is allowed for the duration of the fast. Ezra engaged in a full fast for the exiles from Babylon. The Bible doesn't specify the length of the fast, but we know that he consumed nothing during that time (Ezra 10:6).

Esther found it necessary to fast, because the enemy of God was planning to annihilate the exiles of Judah. Haman was behind this plot of genocide. Mordecai related this to Esther, but it wasn't lawful for even the queen to appear before the king except by invitation. That person could be executed (Esther 4:11). Esther and Mordecai entered a season of fasting. God heard and delivered the Jews.

Paul voluntarily fasted after his encounter with the living God. He was on his way to Damascus to detain the Christians when he had a life-changing experience. The Lord met him by the way, and he was converted. Fasting and prayer strengthened his relationship with God (Acts 9:9).

The record shows that the teachers and prophets at the church at Antioch fasted and prayed until they had a revelation from the Lord (Acts 13:1–3). They fasted and prayed until they had a word from God. After the revelation, it appears they continued fasting and praying before releasing Paul and Barnabas into ministry.

Before You Begin Fasting

1. Establish your objective

As you establish your objective, you need to think about your reasons for fasting. Is it for a renewal of your spirit and walk with God? Is it for guidance and protection? Is it for healing of mind, soul, body, and spirit? Is it for God's special grace to handle a trying situation, or for the resolution of a menacing problem? Is it to seek the face of God in order to know his will?

Once you've identified your objective for the fast, you'll be able to pray in a more specific and strategic manner. A person with no directive in fasting will find himself going around in circles. Work out a plan and follow the plan.

2. Discipline your thought processes and your mind

The mind is the greatest battlefield. There are internal battles and external battles. You cannot fast effectively if you have many things weighting down your minds (Judges 7:3–4; 2 Timothy 2:4; Hebrews 12:1–2). God told Gideon not to bring any soldier who was fearful into the battle. Of the thirty-two thousand soldiers, twenty-two were fearful. Gideon went from thirty-two thousand to three hundred. How effective would that army be if God had not stepped in?

Paul tells Timothy that any soldier going to do battle cannot become encumbered with the cares of life. A person waging war against the enemy needs to be able to concentrate on what he's doing. He does not want to be shot down.

A person entering a time of fasting and prayer needs to enter it with a clear mind so that he can focus his attention on the Lord. He needs to keep his mind clear of anything that will cause him to be defeated. He needs to be sober and vigilant. Prepare your mind, because fasting will take a toll on the body as well as the mind. Plan the type of fast you are about to undertake.

God expects us to behave intelligently and use wisdom in all that we do. You are aware of the condition of your body; therefore, plan wisely. Allow the Holy Spirit to guide you. The Lord is acquainted with who you are and knows how much your body can handle.

3. Get rid of the Martha syndrome

It's helpful if your fast can be done during the times when your life isn't too busy and encumbered with many things. It's harder to concentrate on the things you should when you're busy. Get rid of the Martha syndrome. Keep out of the fast lanes, if you can.

Many people are fasting, yet they get themselves caught up in a flurry of things, such as shopping sprees, watching the television, surfing the Internet, talking on the telephone and texting, or listening to the radio. All these things should be done in moderation, if there is really a need.

You need to position yourself so that you can hear from God. Martha busied herself with many things, but Mary chose the better part. She stayed at the feet of the Master so that she could learn from him. During your fast, you need to divorce yourself from anything that will hinder the effectiveness of what you're trying to accomplish.

It's wise to stay physically active, because your brain functions better when it receives a constant flow of oxygenated blood. The brain will become lethargic and fall sleep if it lacks proper blood flow.

4. Wean your body slowly from regular diet before you begin a prolonged fast

Your body is a unique machine. It will crave that which it is used to. Consider the physical implications of an extended fast and proceed with care. There are certain foods you do not want to deprive your body of suddenly. If you do, your body will scream at you.

Prepare your body by beginning to eat smaller meals about a week prior to the fast. In this way, you won't place a sudden, drastic demand on it. Plan a dietary regimen well. Wean yourself from treats and snacks gradually before you begin fasting. If you break away from your favourite foods slowly, you'll be less likely to crave them in the thick of your fast. Many people cheat on their fast because they give up certain foods too rapidly.

5. Plan to finish strong

Demands on the mind and body can cause one to quit fasting. As stated before, fasting takes a toll on the body eventually, but if you rely on the Lord to help you, you'll be able to stay the course and finish at the time planned.

Fasting is a discipline, and the tempter is always present to entice you with what you love and desire. This is the tactic he used in the Garden of Eden. He enticed Eve, and she began to lust after that which was forbidden. Eve became curious and ate of the tree of the knowledge of good and evil. Curiosity killed the cat, as the saying goes.

Stay the course. Every day you fast bring you one day closer to the finish. Keep in mind the objective of your fast, and plan to finish strong.

Chapter 17
Coupling Fasting with Prayer: Part D

During Your Fast

1. Place liberal, scrumptious servings of the Word on your daily menu.

Select and choose specific verses from the Bible to memorize and meditate upon. You overcome the enemy with the power of the Word of God. The Word of God is the food of champions. Jesus overcame the devil with the power of the Word.

Scripture says that the Word of God is active and alive. It has the capacity to cut through and dissect. The Word of God is also a discerner. It is like a mirror. Anyone who stands before the mirror of the Word of God will always see a true reflection of himself.

The Library of Congress in Washington, D.C. is the world's largest library. It's the repository of millions of volumes of books and other printed publications and manuscripts. I'm certain that the books found there are very interesting; however, no book in the world can equate itself with the Bible. No written word has been described as alive and at the same time powerful. No other volume claims to have the capacity of a two-edged sword, which can pierce and divide asunder the soul, spirit, joints, and marrow. No book in the world boasts its capacity to discern the thoughts and intent of the heart.

The Word of God is God. God is alive and well; therefore, his Word is alive and well also. The Word of God has been rejected by many, but even this has not diminished its relevance in the world. The Word of God has the power to motivate, invigorate, transpire, and inspire. The Word of God informs, transforms, and reforms. It has a word for every situation. The Word of God is still a viable document.

If you're in need of comfort, go to the Word of God. If your need is healing, go to the Word of God. When your soul is famished and you feel the need for restoration and invigoration, go to the Word of God. As you fast, meditate upon the Word of God. It is a lamp and a light. It will help you overcome temptations. It will shine forth its light into the dark places of life and expose that which should not be there—it has discerning potential.

2. Pray and confess your sins and the sins of others.

One of the greatest enemies of our fasting and prayers are sins that have not been confessed and repented of (Psalm 66:18–20). There is true confession and there is diplomatic confession.

A genuine confession acknowledges the sins committed. A person who considers himself guilty of a crime will show some sorrow and remorse. This should lead to repentance: I am guilty. I am sorry for my sins.

A diplomatic confession is one in which the person does not acknowledge his sins directly. He makes use of the word "if." If I am guilty, I repent. One is either guilty or not guilty. You know whether you're guilty or not guilty. The only person who knows you better than you know you is God. Examine yourself and make restitution accordingly.

David admitted that he sinned; this admittance led to genuine confession and repentance (Psalm 51:3–4). As you fast, be wary of the fact that we might even sin and not know that we have sinned; therefore, it's imperative that we ask God to forgive us of sins of which we are unaware. Accept the forgiveness God has granted you and forgive yourself.

Commit yourself as planned. God can keep that which you have entrusted unto him against the time of testing. Golden Christians are produced in the refiner's furnace. God will not allow you to be burned, but he will be in the furnace with you to regulate the thermostat.

3. Worship the Lord in the beauty of holiness.

The one who expects to receive from the hand of God will not wait until he has received before giving thanks. As he begins to pray, he praises, worships, and gives thanks unto God.

The person who is fasting realizes that God inhabits the praises of his people. He also knows that prayer will usher him into the presence of the divine. He knows that prayer demolishes strongholds and clears the way of any demonic interference that is sent to block prayer in the spiritual realm. Prayer, praise, and worship bring you into the realms of the spirit, where spiritual oppositions cannot venture to oppose and bombard your mind (Galatians 5:16–17).

God is a spirit, and all those who worship him must do so in spirit and truth. The Holy Spirit will guide you in all truth. He will empower you and elevate you higher and far above your enemies. Every time you enter a season of fasting and prayer, expect that the enemy will send his juggernauts to try and devour that which you have sacrificed. The intent is to render your sacrifice ineffective. You must learn how to drive them away (Genesis 15:7–11).

I admire Abram's tenacity towards the sacrifice he laid before Jehovah. No scavengers came when there was no sacrifice, but as soon as Abram laid down his sacrifice, the fowls came down to capitalize on it. Abram drove them away. Good thing he was watching his sacrifice keenly. Good thing he wasn't afraid of those scavengers! The greatest battle you fight usually comes just before you receive your breakthrough, so while the battle is raging, you'll have to pull out the weapons that you've kept sharpened and ready and wield them.

Prayer, praise, and worship are powerful weapons that can enhance your fast and usher you into the presence of divine providence. Just think of Paul and Silas in the Philippians jail. The angels in heaven worship God around the clock. They sing the song, "Holy, holy, holy is the LORD of hosts: the whole earth is full of his glory" (Isaiah 6:3).

When Isaiah caught the vision, he wrote that the posts of the door moved at the voice of him that cried, and the house was filled with smoke. A prayer from the heart, genuine praise, and worship will enter the throne room of God and move heaven (Revelation 15:3–5). God is worthy of our worship from the rising of the sun unto the going down the same. God is to be praised always.

4. Wait patiently on the Lord.

We live in a microwave, push button era. Everybody wants everything fast and easy. Everybody seems to be in a hurry. There are many alternatives to choose from. The problem with alternatives is that they might not be the right thing for you. A person who has confidence and trust in God will wait patiently for him (Psalm 27:14; Isaiah 40:31).

As Christians, we don't walk around in fear as those who have no hope. We walk with our heads held high, because we know that he is faithful. God is not unfaithful concerning his promises; his words are yeah and nay. He will deliver that which he has promised. Those who wait for him must do so in the spirit of trust and confidence.

There is a time for everything, and God is never a minute too early or a minute too late. He is always right on time. The prophet Jeremiah emphasizes the blessedness of waiting on the Lord. In his lamentation over the children of God, he expresses his innermost feelings towards the God who never fails. Like David, he boasts about the goodness of Jehovah. God is a God of provision. God never disappoints those who seek him and wait patiently for him. Having experienced the goodness of God, he exhorts us to place our hope in God and wait quietly for his salvation. He waited patiently for God.

Those who are in a hurry to get there need to listen to the voice of experience. It's been discovered that a person usually gives better care to the things he waited patiently for. Man has the tendency to abuse and mishandle the things that come too easy. Over the ages, many men and women have acted apart from God's advice because they grew impatient and could no longer wait upon Him. They become discontented, because things weren't happening as fast as they thought they would.

David found himself in the cave of Adullam with four hundred men who were distressed, in debt, and discontented with life (1 Samuel 22:1–2). Everything looked grim, but David trusted God. God sent a word by the prophet Gad to tell David that it was time to evacuate the place in which he had taken refuge. Cave life was over. The days of confinement were over. "Judah" means praise. The prophet brought a word from the Lord to tell his son to get out of the cave and go to the place of praise and worship. Praise is comely. Worship God.

You've been too long in the cave of despair. It's time to start praising the Lord. Give him praise and glory. You have fasted and you have prayed. Now praise your way out of the rut. Be like the eagle. Don't allow the storm to pull you under; allow it to lift you higher. Do not die in the storm; rather, ride out the storm.

Wait upon God and watch as he uses that which should have killed you as a stepping stone to lift you up. Wait on the Lord. God and the blessed Holy Spirit will instruct and guide us. If you never tapped into the power of God, you'll never experience its strength. Thank God for your trials.

God promised Abram that he was going to bless him and make him a great nation and make his name great (Genesis 12:1–3). As Abram waited for the promise of God, the spirit of impatience showed up. In the heat of impatience, he brought forth an Ishmael by Hagar, the Egyptian handmaiden. Ishmael offered only temporary relief in the life of this man of God, because he was not the child of promise; therefore, when the appointed time came, Ishmael and Hagar had to go (Galatians 4:22–24, 28–31).

The eternal will of God was to bring forth Isaac, who was a prototype of Christ Jesus. Ishmael was born because of the will of the flesh; nevertheless, God did not slay Ishmael, but spared him for a purpose. Ishmael falls into the category of God's permissive will. He was not a part of God's original plan, but because of the mercies of God, he became a part of God's permissive plan. God permitted the lad to live for a purpose. The same cannot be said for the first son David had by Bathsheba. God forgave David, but he took the child (2 Samuel 12:1–31).

Many of us have brought things into our lives because we were impatient. Wait upon the Lord and be of good courage, and he will strengthen our hearts. Again, I say, wait!

We learned earlier about the children of Israel and their wilderness wandering. They would not make their entry into the Promised Land at the time of God's appointment, because they'd insisted on sending spies into the land. As a result, they spent forty years wandering in the wilderness. God had promised to give the children of Israel the Promised Land for an inheritance. You will get what is coming to you if you wait on the Lord. Move when God says move.

God can answer our petition with a yes, no, or wait. If God has promised, he will deliver.

Don't push the hold button when God says act. Don't push the mute button when God bids you speak. Don't place a period in your life where God meant for a comma. Act upon what God bids you to act upon.

God rewards those who patiently wait for him. Don't get frustrated and abort the vision or the mission. Like the prophet Habakkuk, write it down so that you don't lose sight of it. Wait for it. Delay does not mean denial.

5. Shout now and begin to give thanks.

"O Give thanks unto the LORD; for he is good: because his mercy endureth forever" (Psalm 118:1).

We need to learn to give God thanks for the things he has done, the things he is doing, and the things he is about to do. Even if you don't receive what you ask God for, you should still give him thanks.

We should thank God for all his marvellous acts in our lives. King David was a man of praise and worship. Interestingly, David didn't begin to praise and acknowledge God after he became king ... he began while he was yet a shepherd boy. When he became king, he didn't cease worshipping God because of his inflated ego—he worshipped God even more. He brought the children of God to a place of worship. He was grateful to God for everything, and blessed and praised the name of the Lord always. When he looked at his body and saw the excellent work that God, the Master Potter, had wrought, he gave God praise and glory. I don't know about anybody else, he said, but I'll bless God's holy name always. His praise will continually be in my mouth. (See Psalm 34:1; 51:5, 139:14–16)

It's paradoxical, but the same body that's conceived in sin and shaped in iniquity is also fearfully and wonderfully made. Sin and iniquity mar and spoil, but God, the Master Builder, knows how to shape us and remake us so that we will become the vessel of his likeness.

Thank the Lord for the fact that you're a designer's original. You are uniquely you, and there is nobody else quite like you—not even your identical twin. You are one of a kind.

I bought two exceptionally beautiful dresses for separate weddings. They were very expensive dresses, and I was told that there was no other dress of that calibre in the store. That boutique purchased all their garments from a special manufacturer outside of the country. Those dresses were natty and designed with sartorial elegance.

The first was a two-piece dress. The jacket was accentuated with pearls and sequins. A designer's two-piece appliqué kept the front of the jacket together. I attended one wedding and stood afar off and looked around. Behold! Somebody else was in what seemed like the same two-piece dress as mine. I immediately felt sad, because I thought my dress was the only of its kind and would be distinct from every other dress at that wedding.

I stayed as far away from the other woman as much as I possibly could. All evening long, those who passed by admired and complimented my beautiful dress. The other person probably received similar sentiments. Apart from the bride and the wedding party, I thought I would be the belle. Oops! There was no such luck.

When I did get close to her, near the end of the reception, I realized that although the garments looked alike, they were very different. Who duplicated who? I knew not. I made myself miserable for nothing. The material, the appliqué, were all different.

I went to the second wedding and saw a woman in a dress that looked like mine. The colour and the design were the same as mine (purple and lilac), and the styling was the same; however, when I checked it closely, I noticed that the fabric was as coarse as calico, and the designers were different. It was a two-piece dress. My under-piece was made of lilac Dacron, and the overcoat was made from chiffon with mauve and lilac patterns. They looked alike from afar, but they were far from similar. They were duplicates. Who duplicated who? I knew not.

Every now and then we settle for second best or duplicates when God has originals and much more in store for us. I was not the diva that I thought I would be at those weddings. My dresses were duplicated … or could it be that mine were the duplicates?

You are the handiwork of God's creative genius. He fashions you with his own hands. Man was flawless when he was created. When God came to the crescendo of his creative narrative, he commended himself for his great work by declaring that it was very good. It is good to give God thanks, because there is no other designer who could have shaped our body parts in such definite proportions as he did. You are not a duplicate of me or a carbon copy. You are uniquely you—God's original masterpiece.

We are bound to give God thanks not because we expect him to give us something, but because of what he has already given us. God has been good to us. We thank God for his faithfulness. When our souls need restoration, he leads us beside still waters and causes us to lie down in green pastures. He anoints our heads with oil so that we will not become infested with the parasites of sin.

Give God thanks for the gospel of Jesus Christ, because it is the power of God unto salvation (Romans 1:16). Some envision the gospel as only doom and gloom, but it's the opposite. The gospel of Jesus Christ points out sin, death, and hell; but, it also offers salvation, a hope of heaven, and eternal life for those who will receive it. We thank the Father for his compassion in that while we were still lost in our trespasses and sin, Christ died for us (Romans 5:8).

Praising God and giving him thanks is a personal choice that one must make (Psalm 69:30–31, 103:1–5; 2 Corinthians 9:15; Philippians 4:4–7). Shout now, because you have already won the victory.

Other things to do or not to do during your fast

As stated earlier, fasting, especially extended fasting, can take a toll on the physical man. It is therefore imperative that you rest appropriately and not over-exert yourself. Do not become lazy, but at the same time ensure that activities and rest are balanced. You want to maintain equilibrium in your system.

1. Get enough sleep and rest so that you don't feel fatigued during the day.

2. Don't discontinue prescription drugs without the advice of your physician.

3. Choose the kind of legumes, grains, fruits, and vegetables you need in your diet.

4. Water is preferred over pops. Avoid chewing gums.

5. Avoid foods that are high in fats and complex sugar.

Don't limit yourself to these five points. There are other things that you might think of to do or not to do. Do as you see fit or as instructed by the Holy Spirit.

Fasting and the Married Couple

"Let the husband render unto the wife due benevolence: and likewise also the wife unto the husband. The wife hath not power of her own body, but the husband: and likewise also the husband hath not power of his own body, but the wife. Defraud ye not one the other, except it be with consent for a time, that ye may give yourselves to fasting and prayer; and come together again, that Satan tempt you not for your incontinency" (1 Corinthians 7:3–5).

Apart from food and drink, people entering in a time of fasting for whatever reason will also restrict themselves from other activities. The married couple has a big decision to make concerning their sexual activities during times of fasting.

According to scripture, the married couple's bodies belong to each other. The Bible advises that a couple should not deprive each other of sexual intimacy except by mutual consent. If they need to engage themselves in prayer and fasting, they should talk it over together. If they do restrain themselves from the pleasure of sex, it shouldn't be for extended periods of time, because temptation has a way of knocking on the door of the mind when the body is deprived of what is customary.

To avoid infidelity, the married couple should come together again after the fast.

God doesn't embrace abstinence for the married couple. Don't assume that your partner will expect a lack of intimacy because you're on a fast. You might be surprised to find out that what you and your spouse expect differs. Talk it over with each other so that there is no misunderstanding or conflict. Too often I hear married people describe sex as "a dirty business." The excuse for refraining from the act during fasting and prayer is: "I want to feel clean."

If I understand the Bible correctly, God foreordained sexual relationship between a husband and his wife (Genesis 1:27–28, 2:24, 4:1–2, 5:4).

Adam and Eve were both naked when they were created. They didn't know that they were naked, so they weren't ashamed. But when sin entered, they discovered their nakedness and were so ashamed that they covered up and hid from God. Nakedness was never meant to be a shameful condition.

Sexual intercourse was never meant to be a dirty business. Sin, infidelity, and the laxity of man's morals have caused the act to be visualized, by some, as nasty. What God ordained is never a dirty business. God will judge fornicators and adulterers, but he holds the marriage he ordained between one man and one woman in high esteem and honour (Hebrews 13:4). God encourages the married couple to pay each other due benevolence—that is, sexual fulfillment. The married couple belongs to each other. Copulation is a decision that must be established between the man and his wife during periods of prayer and fasting.

For medical reasons, a couple might not be able to enjoy each other sexually. You and/or your physician will decide how to approach this matter. Pray that God will deliver you or your partner from the restrictive conditions that prevent you from enjoying each other.

God designed sex to be enjoyed within the confines of marriage; therefore, it is against the will of God for the married couple to use prayer and fasting as a means of avoiding sexual relations with each other. One should never use the Word of God or the ministry to defraud each other of the pleasure of sex. Be sensitive to the needs of each other. Love, understanding, affection, caring, sharing, and empathy go a long way.

Until marriage, the single person is called to celibacy. He or she must maintain chaste living. Married couples, when you come to the great congregation in a time of fasting and prayer, be mindful of the way in which you display your affection towards each other. Remember that there are single people around. Some have not yet conquered and subdued the hormones that are racing through their system. Be sensitive to their stages of growth and development. Some behaviour belongs within the confines of your bedrooms. Do not behave inappropriately with your spouse before them. We are children of the Kingdom of God, so let's not place a stumbling block in the way of each other. Remember that you weren't born married. You passed the way of singleness before.

Chapter 18
Coupling Fasting with Prayer: Part E

Breaking Fast

You thought you couldn't do it, but you did it. The following suggestions concerning the breaking of a fast are presented from personal experiences. These suggestions might not be suitable for everyone in the same manner. You began your fasting using wisdom, and now you are going to break it using wisdom also.

Now that the last day of fasting has been completed, you are about to reintroduce your normal diet to your body. Breaking a fast is as important as beginning one. Important precautions need to be taken. When you begin to eat again, don't start with a big "all you can eat buffet." Reintroduce foods gradually.

Remember that your body breaks down during a fast; you have lost some weight, and physical energy might or might not be depleted. You haven't consumed a lot of calories; therefore, to compensate for the loss, your body converts the protein stored within your skeletal muscles into fuel for energy so that you don't collapse.

One of the worst things you can do to your digestive system and your body after a prolonged fast is reintroduce solids with a bang. The foods that you eat when breaking your fast should not place a great demand upon your system. You don't want to exhaust your energy supply; you want to rebuild it. The foods you eat when breaking fast should be ones that are easily digested and distributed, in a timely manner, throughout the body.

Hydration

I try to rehydrate my system without overloading it. I find that natural fruit juices and fruits are easily digested, because they have a high-water content. I break my fast with fruit juices and fruits such as melon or pears. I stay away from citrus fruits because of the acid contents, which might bring about gastric irritation. My stomach is sensitive.

I don't drink tap water; I drink filtered or purified water to rehydrate my body quickly. I am a water person. Decaffeinated tea and chicken or beef broth are very helpful in rehydration. Watch the sodium contents, because wherever salt goes, water follows. You don't want to deal with edema, which is a medical condition in which excess fluids collect in the cavities, or interstitial spaces and tissues of the body, causing swelling.

Reintroducing normal diet

When I've fasted for seven days or more, I give myself an allowance of at least four to five days before I reintroduce heavier foods into my diet. My system has been adjusting to the present diet. I don't want to confuse my body.

Coming out of a fast of one to five days, I allow myself at least two to three days before reintroducing heavier foods. Everybody is different.

Some people might need more time to reintroduce heavier foods; others might need less time. I wouldn't recommend a hasty reintroduction of heavy foods. Any abrupt reintroduction of heavy foods might lead to one complication or another, as mentioned earlier.

I discovered that a heavy, complex diet places the kind of demand on the digestive system that can lead to complications such as gastro-abdominal cramping and discomfort, flatulence (gassiness), eructation (belching), borborygmus (a rumbling or gurgling noise caused by the movement of fluid or gas in the intestines), diarrhea, constipation, or bloating. I can personally attest to a few of these. I learned my lessons from experience.

Resist the urge to include junk foods and processed foods in your diet. They are high in salt, complex sugars, carbohydrates, saturated and hydrogenated trans fats and oils, and other chemicals that might irritate the digestive tract. Break your digestive system in gently.

Many people are turning to organic foods instead of the regular counterpart, because organic foods are supposed to be free of pesticides and other harmful chemicals. They are also naturally higher in antioxidants. This is a matter of choice, because organic products come with higher price tags. Those on a limited budget might not be able to afford organic foods. Some people use swish chard, kale, iceberg lettuce, and cucumbers to restore the body's energy level.

The solids I consume when breaking a fast are always very small, light, and soft. Keep close observation on your stomach's behaviour. During the season of fasting, your body underwent some detoxification. You have also lost weight, as stated before. It might be a good idea to try and maintain your new weight. Always keep in mind your medical condition. The foods that you can use when breaking your fast are not limited to the choices I have supplied. Use good judgement and speak to your Father in heaven.

Chapter 19
With Jesus in the School of Prayer

Part A: Praying Intelligently

Earlier I introduced the constituents of prayer. Now I'll share the benefits of praying intelligently, or the dangers of praying unintelligently.

Jesus was praying in a certain place. When he was finished, one of his disciples said unto him, "Lord, teach us to pray, as John also taught his disciples" (Luke 11:1).

The disciples had been walking with Jesus for a good while. They must have heard him praying before, because such was his regular practice.

Looking at Matthew's narrative, I'm led to believe that this request might have been precipitated by the contents of Jesus' teaching on the mount (Matthew 6:5–8).

Jesus gave an outline of the way that the hypocrites pray. They took pleasure in praying in the open places, because their desire was to be seen and heard of men. Having heard this, the disciples discovered that they needed to make an unselfish move to the next level of prayer. Therefore, they requested to be taught to pray as John had taught his disciples.

Notice that this disciple didn't ask Jesus to teach them how to pray. Every intellectual would like to think that he or she knows how to pray. The request of the disciples spoke to this. We don't need to learn how to pray … or do we?

As we analyze the format of the Lord's Prayer, we'll notice that Jesus took the liberty of teaching them how to pray properly, and not as the heathens and the hypocrites pray. It's an embarrassing shame to hear the tone that some prayers assume. There are prayers that are suitable for the closet.

It's imperative to learn not just to pray, but how to pray, so that we don't place a stumbling block in the paths of the innocent. I'm aware that prayer is a personal conversation between you and the Father, but if you're praying in public, your prayer is no longer between you and the Father, because there's an audience listening. We are praying unto God, who is intelligent and wise. We don't have to sport a doctor's degree or a bachelor's degree to speak to the Lord, but we do need to pray wisely and intelligently.

In the eyes of God, we are nothing but specks of dust. Looking down from an airplane, one is brought face to face with this reality: man is nothing but dust. From certain elevations, man is not even visible. Had it not been for the blood, we would have been as nothing in the sight of God. If anyone would boast about anything, let it be about the divine exchange that Jesus made when he went to the cross on Golgotha's hill. It was considered a curse to be hanged on a cross, but look at what God did—he took the shame that I might be able to lift my head and my eyes up in the presence of the accuser of the brethren (Galatians 6:14–15).

When Jesus declared, "tetelestai," a Greek word meaning, "It is finished," he meant that the work of redemption was completed. Like sheep we went astray, but we are no longer bound by the letter of the law. The grace of God still stands in bas relief for those who will receive it. Modernists, do not allow the enemy to bewitch you into thinking more highly of yourself than you should. Do not become vain. Remember, "Pride goes before a fall."

Paul had enough in his background to boast about. He could have flaunted his apostolic prowess, his rhetoric power and fluency of speech, and the fact that God had given him the gifts of prophecy, tongues, and revelations. He could have bragged about his acumen in business, or his planting and organization of churches. Paul was a high-pedigree Hebrew, educated in the law of the Torah. He was brought up under the tutelage of the renowned Gamaliel. Standing next to Paul, some of us intellectuals would fade into nothingness.

Paul looked in the mirror and saw a wretched man who had to battle daily with the flesh. He was a persecutor, an oppressor of them that believed in Christ, but he obtained undeserved mercy from God. He wanted to do good, but evil always presented itself. He didn't want to be an intellectual fool having all the accolades in the world; he wanted Jesus. Paul chose to boast about the transforming power of the blood of Jesus Christ and the vicarious work of the cross. Man's ego would fade into nothingness if he saw himself as he really should. Be like the apostle Paul and seek to know Jesus and the marvellous work that he did to purchase our salvation.

Jesus is excellent in all the earth. He is majestic. He is glorious, and he is honourable. Jesus maintained grace and composure during his trial and crucifixion.

Pilate washed his hands, because he found Jesus faultless (Matthew 27:24).

The seemingly remorseful betrayer, Judas, confessed that he was a sinner, but Jesus was guiltless (Matthew 27:3–5).

As Jesus gave up the ghost, the centurion gave witness that Jesus was the Son of God (Mark 15:39)

When you pray, remember that God already knows that you are coming (Isaiah 65:24).

When you pray, don't be as the unlearned and hypocritical, but pray so that your prayer will be palatable unto God and unto the hearers. Do not be braggadocios, or arrogant, in your prayers. We need to knock those chips off our shoulders, because God already knows all things.

Part B: The Danger of an Offensive Prayer

Not only should we not be boastful or lift ourselves in pride when we pray, but we must ensure that our prayers target the right object.

Many years ago, I officiated at a prayer conference. One of the prayers I heard almost blew my mind. It was embarrassing. One person was asked to pray over a certain subject matter. That person walked about, moving his hands frantically as if chopping down something. Then came these tumultuous words: "Lord, kill them! Lord, move them!" I chose to believe that the prayer was geared towards the devil and his minions and not towards any person in the audience; however, to the listening ears, it was harsh, irritating, and offensive. Everybody became hushed as the person thundered. A few left the room.

Many were offended and commented on the questionnaire that this person might have good intentions, but was desperately in need of training. There were times when Jesus went off by himself to pray. Jesus told the disciples, "I have yet many things to say unto you, but ye cannot bear them now" (John 16:12). Some folks aren't ready to hear some things; they cannot handle them. Be wise and intelligent when you pray. Even a prayer geared against the devil must be prayed wisely and intelligently. We cannot allow our disgust to take precedence over the Holy Spirit's work and action. There is an appropriate forum for everything. God is not the author of confusion.

God has given us wisdom, because he doesn't want us to place a stumbling block in the way of others, especially those who are not yet saved or matured in the Spirit. A prayer can be strong and powerful, but not offensive.

A wise chef tastes as he cooks so that he'll detect what is not palatable before it's served. If the meal lacks flavour to the server, it will also lack flavour to the consumers. Folks will vomit that which is unpleasant. Don't feed others what you would never eat. Serve that which the Holy Spirit places on the menu. He is sensitive to the present needs and situations. God is wise and has imparted unto us his wisdom. Let us use wisdom to the glory and honour of God, and not become an offense or a stumbling block to others or to the ministry (Romans 14:16; 2 Corinthians 6:3–10).

God requires us to correct each other in the spirit of meekness. We also need to avoid offending others. If we offend them, we might just lose the opportunity to win them to Christ. It's impossible to stop people from being offended, but if anyone would be offended, let it be for the truth of God rather than a bad attitude.

Your ministry is as good as dead once people lose interest, confidence, trust, and respect for you as a minister (Proverbs 18:19).

God has distributed gifts to individuals as it pleases him. We use our gifts for the advancement of the Kingdom of God. Failure in any area affects all within the body.

Prayer is a ministry that should not be neglected or undermined in our daily ministrations. Those who are gifted to expedite this ministry in public must seek the Lord. We are not orphans. God has sent us the Holy Ghost to help us when we're stuck and don't know what else to say. Let the Holy Spirit speak to you and through you. We are not our own; we belong to Jesus.

I don't mean to insult anybody's intelligence. We have not yet attained. We are still in a world where sin abounds; nevertheless, God knows that even the most intelligent people need help every now and then because they're human, and humans are often infirmed and ignorant in their ministrations. Also, the deceiver has a subtle way of coming upon us, like a flood, to trip us when we need to behave soberly.

The Holy Spirit anticipates those times when we're about to go the wrong way and helps our infirmities. The key to being effective in the things that we say and do is listening keenly and attentive to what the Holy Ghost is saying and where he is leading. The Holy Ghost subdues the flesh so that it doesn't get in the way of what the Lord wants to do. He forewarns us so that we don't overstep our boundaries (Romans 8:26).

Somebody is always listening; therefore, we need to know how to pray. Both Jesus and the Holy Spirit intercede with groaning. The Holy

Spirit is never at a loss for words. He has a word or a groan for everything. The person who prays can respond accordingly as moved by the Spirit of God.

There is a vast difference between an aggressive, militant prayer prayed against the wiles of the devil and an offensive prayer spat out because of the workings of inner personal conflicts and emotions. Some prayers must be prayed in the spirit or in the closet. The Father who hears in secret will reward you accordingly.

Jonah had a judgmental attitude towards the inhabitants of Nineveh. He wanted God to destroy them (Jonah 3, 4). He forgot that the same merciful God who delivered him from death didn't desire the death of the sinner, but that the sinner would turn to him. God had to use the worm and gourd metaphor to correct his error.

God didn't answer Jonah's prayer in the manner that he wished, but God is plenteous in mercy. Jonah cried, "O LORD, take, I beseech thee, my life from me; for it is better for me to die than to live!" (Jonah 4:3). The disturbing undertone of Jonah's prayer rings like a bell in my spirit's ears. I'm inclined to believe that Jonah wanted the entire city wiped out.

The disciples needed to be taught to pray, because prayer is the hub around which everything would turn in Christendom. The prayer-saturated church will not die; it will remain alive, powerful, and strong so that it can evangelize effectively. Prayer will keep the bloodhounds and the predators at bay. The enemy comes to kill, steal, and carry away captives. Prayer and the discernment of the Holy Spirit will expose the whereabouts of the wicked one and chase him away so that he does not devour the nestlings.

Chapter 20
Dissecting the Lord's Prayer: Part A

Looking at the Lord's Prayer, we can readily see that there is a divine order to this prayer. The Lord's Prayer is comprised of several components. It consists of elements that are vertical, meaning that they are directed towards God and speak of his love for us, his exaltedness, his glory, and his majesty. Other segments speak of the horizontal relationships we share with those around us. We extend forgiveness and mercy to those who have offended us in the same manner that God has forgiven us.

God already knows what we have need of; therefore, the major focus of our prayers shouldn't be on what we can receive from him, but on giving him the worship that is due him. Prayers should be filled with gratitude and thanksgiving. God is our Father, and by his own words, he is under obligation to supply the needs of his children (1Timothy 5:8).

The greatest commandment is to love God with our entire being. Second to this is the commandment to love our neighbour as we love ourselves (Exodus 20:2–7; Deuteronomy 6:4–5; Mark 12:29–31).

God must be addressed first in our prayers. He should take priority in our lives. While adoring God, who we cannot see except in the spirit, we must give thought to those we can see. All who love the Lord will set time aside to get intimate with him. The more intimate we become with

God, the more spiritually prolific we will be. There is a vast difference between acquaintanceship and relationship.

For a relationship to grow, it must be nurtured and watered. God does not want to be casually acquainted with us; he wants lasting relationship with us.

Our Father, which art in heaven

Jesus is highly intellectual, and he knows theology. He knows that the world has a pantheon of gods and beings that they call father. Jesus ensured that his disciples understood the importance of identifying whom they called father.

A person who begins prayer with "father" is not necessarily addressing the God of heaven, so Jesus directed the disciples, and subsequently us, to give adoration to the Father who resides in heaven, but also has dominion and power in the earth. Identifying his place of residence is important. We pray not to the gods made with hands, or the gods of this world (which are not gods, as stated by the prophet), but to the only true, the only wise, the only living, the only omnipotent, omniscience, omnipresent God of heaven.

When we enter prayer, we should expect that there might be other gods present; therefore, it's imperative that we identify which one we want to direct our prayers to. Every god wants to be acknowledged, praised, and worshipped. The devil or his agents are present at every church service and prayer meeting, because Satan wants to be adored and glorified. The devil and his agents seek magnification (Job 1:6–7, 2:1; Revelation 12:7–13).

The passages of scripture in Job and Revelation referred to above attest to the fact that the devil is a very busy spirit. He presented himself before God so that he could accuse the brethren.

He came to earth with vengeance on his mind. He has no power to take revenge on God; therefore, he wages war against the subjects of God—the saints. He accused Job before God of being a user. He dared to mess with the authenticity of Job's love and worship of God (Job 1:8–12).

God had the power to bind Satan and chase him out, but he didn't. God listened to him as he spilled his guts. We need to be able to discern what's in the mind and gut of the devil so that we can direct our prayers strategically. Don't waste precious shots. Aim for the head of the matter and open fire expecting to hit and not to miss. Be not afraid. God is with you. (Psalm 23:4, 34:7, 91:1). The LORD is omnipresent; he is encamped around us on every side. He protects and defends his children with militaristic power. No devil can come into combat with us without first meeting a battalion of God's military force.

The Lord surrounded his people in the Old Testament. In the New Testament era, we are still surrounded by the Lord. Not only this, but the Bible says that our lives are hidden with Christ in God (Colossians 3:3). This tells me that we have comprehensive coverage. The all-encompassing Jesus covers us on every side.

This doesn't mean that Satan won't try to attack us, because he will. He doesn't want to admit defeat. The devil will always try to bring us into bondage. He will dive into the sea and try to fish up our past. But know this: whom the Son has freed, is free indeed (John 8:36).

You need to pray that God will confuse the demons so that they miss your address. The devil went too far at the Tower of Babel; therefore, God confused them so that none could understand the other. God saw Satan and exposed him. "Where have you been, Satan?" God asked. Satan replied that he'd been going to and from, and up and down, in the world. We know that Satan is never up to any good.

When we come to pray, we must let the devil know that he is not the centre of attraction.

Sometimes when we pray, we need to keep the devil's name out of the prayer and just adore God. When it's time to expose the devil, expose him. When it's time to adore and bless the name of God, do so. There is a time to blast the devil. God already knows that he's in our midst. God saw him coming. Your focus must be on God. He keeps his words to his people.

God is the person of distinction when we come to worship services. The Christian is monotheistic and serves the only true and living God. Everyone must speak to God individually. God inhabits your praise.

If he is your Father, give him the praise and the glory. "Our Father, which art in heaven" indicates personal acknowledgement. God is my Father; therefore, I will serve him and call upon him in the morning; I will call upon him in the noontide; I will call him up in the evening; and I will call him in the midnight hours. If he is your Father, then give him honour.

Let Us Exalt His Name Together

Father in heaven, I praise, worship, and adore you. You are my everlasting portion. You are my provider and my protector. You are my high tower and my escape from the snares of the fowler and from the noisome pestilence. You are water when I am thirsty, and a rock when I need a place to anchor. You are the wings stretched out when I need shelter from the storm.

The enemy would daily swallow me up: for they are many that fight against me, O thou Most High. But if ever I am afraid, I will trust thee. I will not fear what man can do unto me. When I cry unto thee, O God, every enemy must turn back, because they know that God is for me. I praise you, Lord, and I praise your Word. I praise thee, Father, because thy vows are upon me until I die. You have delivered my soul from death. Will you not deliver my feet from falling, that I may walk before thee in the light of the living? (Psalm 56:1–13, paraphrased).

I praise you, Lord, because you have seen the wickedness of the wicked and have put their deeds to naught. I worship and adore you, Father, for I have seen your mighty power. You try the hearts and reins, and you establish the just for your righteous name's sake. Yes, Lord, the enemy conceived mischief and brought forth falsehood. He has made a pit, digged it, and is fallen into the ditch he made. His mischief shall return upon his own head, and his violent dealing shall come down upon his own pate. But thou, Lord, have prevailed; therefore, I will praise you because you are righteous. I will sing praises unto you Lord, most High (Psalm 7:9-17, paraphrased).

Lord, I praise, worship, and adore you, because when I think of who I am, I realize that I would be nothing if you hadn't made me a somebody. If you, Lord, should mark iniquities as you could mark them, who would be able to stand? But there is forgiveness with thee. My soul waits for you, Lord, more than they that wait for the morning (Psalm 130:3-6).

I give you praise because you are the God of heaven before whom I stand. You have never let me down. Sometimes I cannot feel you, but I know that you're always right where I left you.

Amen.

Chapter 21
Dissecting the Lord's Prayer: Part B

Hallowed be thy name

The word "hallowed" comes from the Greek word "hagiazo" and the Hebrew "quodesh," meaning "to make holy, consecrated, sanctified, distinct, to dedicate, or separated." God created man in his image and his likeness. Man sinned and marred his image; however, God is separate from sin and cannot sin (Exodus 15:11; 1 Samuel 2:2; Isaiah 6:2–3; Revelation 4:8, 15:4).

Everything about God speaks of his moral perfection. Everything about his essential nature is good. God is Almighty. We should not dishonour his name or use it profanely. We should be careful to reverence his name always. He who dishonours the name of God will be held guilty (Exodus 20:7).

I have seen under the sun that people of eminence are honoured.

One dare not approach the Queen of England on a first name basis. We address her thus: Her Majesty, the Queen of England, or Queen Elizabeth. We address princes as Your Royal Highness. We address the prime minister of a democracy as Mr. Prime Minister. When we come before His Majesty, we approach him as one who is honourable and deserving of the honour of his people—Our Father.

The name of the Lord is not a swear word, but a strong tower. The righteous takes refuge in the name of the Lord. Man must honour the sacred name of the Lord. David reverenced God (Psalm 50:1–2), and the disciples reverenced the Lord (Luke 24:19). It was a violation to dishonour the king in ancient times. The perpetrator would be seen as challenging the king to a fight, so they would be dealt with as an enemy.

To speak of God irreverently is considered contempt. Why deal treacherously with God when he has not dealt treacherously with us? We cannot enter the arena of conflict with God and win. We profane the name of the LORD when we profess to know him yet fail to live according to his statutes (Titus 1:16). "If I am God, says he, where is my honour?" (Malachi 1:6, paraphrased).

The Christian is under divine obligation to defend the name of the Father. Why? Covenant partners have the weapons belt of each other; therefore, they must defend each other.

The righteous are in a blood covenant relationship with the Father, through Jesus Christ. God is holy, he is righteous, he is mighty, and he is powerful. God is God all by himself.

Thy Kingdom Come

A kingdom is a territory ruled over or governed by a monarch or a ruler. That ruler exercises complete authority and dominion over his kingdom. As evident in the Synoptic Gospels, the Kingdom of God formed the central theme of the message that Jesus conveyed to the listeners. Repentance from sin followed in hot pursuit. Jesus began to preach repentance right after John the Baptist was imprisoned (Matthew 4:17).

In the Jewish apocalyptic writings, the terms "Kingdom of Heaven" and "Kingdom of God" are used interchangeably (Psalm 103:19, 145:11, 13; Daniel 4:3). Listening to Jesus' vernacular, one understands that this kingdom is in full and effective operation. Jesus Christ, the visible manifestation of God—the God man—exercised the sovereign power of his Father in every aspect of his ministry.

The evidence remains to this day: demons were exorcised, the lame walked, the blind saw, the dumb spoke, sicknesses was healed; the head of the serpent was wounded at the crucifixion; and then there was the resurrection (Matthew 4:23, 11:2–15; Luke 4:40–43; 8:1–3, 9:1–2, 11, 10:9; Luke 11:18–20).

The Kingdom of God is not made with hands; it is established by God. It expands and advances of its own accord. The Kingdom of God and the kingdom of darkness must coexist until Jesus comes again and separates the wheat from the tares.

Jesus sometimes used parabolic statements when referring to his kingdom (Mark 4:30–32; Luke 13:18–19). Using metaphors, Jesus was saying to the listeners: "You figure out my discourse." His presentation of the kingdom didn't always attract men to him; it irritated some so much that they sought to kill him before his time.

Feasts or elaborate meals played a large role in covenant relationships, which is one of the reasons the Pharisees were disgusted with Jesus. He ate and fellowshipped with Gentiles, publicans, tax collectors, and sinners. To eat with somebody meant that you were in covenant relationship with him (Matthew 9:10–12, 2:15–17). The scribes and Pharisees were self-righteous and stuck on salvation by works, but Jesus showed that the only way to be saved was through his death. Heaven rejoices when the lost children of the kingdom come home.

The believer needs to always remember that the Kingdom of God is under attack. The spiritual warfare being waged isn't just against an individual, but against the Kingdom of God. The angel of darkness wages war against the angel of light. There is warfare between good and evil, and between heaven and hell.

God gave our fore-parents the key to the kingdom. He gave them dominion over every created order. Their duty was to occupy, be fruitful, multiply, exercise dominion, and subdue. Alas! Adam and Eve surrendered dominion to the devil. They experimented with death, and thus it was pronounced upon mankind.

The Lord has made it known to man in this age that his priority is to take care of that which pertains to his kingdom and righteous living. God will supply us with material things as well as spiritual things (Matthew 6:33; Luke 17:20–21; Romans 6:12–14). Many today seek to build empires rather than the Kingdom of God. Many are seeking self-aggrandization rather than exalting the name of the LORD.

The Kingdom of God begins in the heart of the believer; therefore, wherever children of the kingdom venture, the Kingdom of God goes right along. The Kingdom of God is an advancing and productive kingdom (Matthew 13:3–9). This gospel must be preached in every corner of the earth before the second coming of the Lord.

Jesus gave the disciples the authority and power to bind and loose on earth. He also promised that what they bound or loosed on earth would be paralleled in heaven (Matthew 16:13–19). In rabbinical vernacular, the term "to bind" means "that which is forbidden." "Loose" means "that which is permitted." As an apostle, Peter, as well as the others, were empowered and sent forth into a violent atmosphere to bind and forbid false doctrine, and to permit, through teaching and preaching, that which is biblically authentic. The Holy Spirit teaches the believers; therefore, the believer knows what to bind and what to loosen.

Notice that a key is an instrument of authority. The person who has authority over anything carries the keys; he can open and he can shut. The keys signify entrance and exit. The door or the entrance is opened to those who should come in; the key can lock the door to disallow the intruder from entering.

Peter was one of those apostles privileged with winning souls for Christ. He showed them the way of salvation. Those who accepted the gospel repented and received water baptism. They were received into fellowship with the other believers in the church. Those who rejected the gospel and turned not from their wicked ways remained in bondage.

The apostles of the first century bound and loosed under the authority of the Holy Ghost, but we also see where the authority to bind and loose were misused. False teachers entered in and perverted the gospel of Jesus Christ. They taught the legalist concept, which dictated that the only way to enter the Kingdom of God was through circumcision (Galatians 1:6–9). The Word of God must not be overridden. Whatsoever the Christian loosed on earth is already paralleled in heaven. This promise is forever signed and sealed in the annals of heaven.

Paul stepped in and corrected the controversy. It was cited that the Christian was bound by the stipulations of the new covenant of grace, not to that of Law. Circumcision was mandatory under the Abrahamic covenant. Physical circumcision of the foreskin is not applicable to the born again believer. Under the new covenant, the requirement is "circumcision of the heart" (Deuteronomy 10:16–18, 30:6; Romans 2:25–29; 1 Corinthians 7:19; Colossians 2:11–14).

The Holy Spirit is still in operation in the church today. Jesus said that when he is come, he will lead us into all truth. Jesus is already reigning in our hearts. He also reigns from his throne on high.

The disciples asked Jesus a critical kingdom question just before his ascension. They wanted to know if Jesus' mission to earth included restoration of the rulership of the throne of David. I believe this was the implication in Acts 1:4–8. Jesus cleared the record. Their greatest concern at that moment were to be faithful witnesses. Spreading the gospel of Jesus Christ and his mission of mercy to save souls for the Kingdom of God was of utmost importance. He would send them the Holy Ghost. When the Holy Ghost came, they would receive power. That power would convict men of their sin and draw them to God. Winning souls for God is the priority of the age.

The phrase "the kingdom of God" is found some seventy times in the New Testament. This tells me that declaring that the Kingdom of God is come is of utmost importance. No matter what is happening around us, Jesus, the Lord our God, reigns omnipotent. God is not limited by circumstances or availability of resources. He reigns, and his kingdom exists in the life of the believers. God's kingdom is wherever he has taken up occupancy and rulership.

We Lift You Up

Lord, we lift your name on high. We lift you up, Lord, because your kingdom is an everlasting kingdom that does not fade away.

Father, we lift you up, because nobody elected or appointed you into office; therefore, nobody can vote you out or overthrow your rule. You are sovereign, and you are mighty; you are the victor and never the victim. You have power to promote and power to demote. When you speak, storms must calm.

Lord, I lift you up, because you do not need an invitation to enter any premises; you can enter and leave at will. Knowing this, Father, I want to keep my vessel in constant readiness, because the countdown for takeoff has begun. I bless your holy name, Father.

In the name of Jesus, I give you thanks. Amen.

Chapter 22
Dissecting the Lord's Prayer: Part C

Thy will be done in earth as it is in heaven

Earlier in chapter 13, we discussed praying according to God's will, his plans, and his purpose. This portion of the Lord's Prayer can be considered a sequel to chapter 13. While the perfect will of God is being carried out in heaven, we cannot say the same for earth. The person denying the existence of God will not execute his will. Why? "The fool hath said in his heart, There is no God" (Psalm 14:1). The atheist disclaimed God; therefore, the atheist will not perform the will of the God of heaven.

The evolutionist will not magnify the name of the Lord or do his will because he doesn't embrace the divine Creator who spoke all things into being and fashioned man in his own likeness. There are those spoken of in Romans 1:18–32 who will not do the will of God, because "[They] changed the truth of God into a lie, and worshipped and served the creature more than the Creator, who is blessed forever" (Romans 1:25).

Carnal desires have caused even the believer to sway from the will of God. The will of the flesh took precedence over the will of God in the case of Adam and Eve. Adam and Eve had good eyesight, but no vision. God placed destiny within their hands, and they gave it up and satisfied the "wants" of the flesh.

Adam and Eve succumbed to the will of the devil. They chose death over life. God had certainly warned that those who ate that fruit would die. Our will, our desires, must be in conformity with what God has in mind for us. Jesus is our great example of one who has performed the perfect will of the Father. Jesus was faced with various struggles and oppositions while trying to accomplish the will of his Father, but he did it (John 6:38–40).

The will of God is not arbitrary or negotiable. It must be implemented in the manner expected by God. Anything short of this is a detour to doom. When we pray, "Your will be done in earth as it is done in heaven," we are really admitting that, of ourselves, we are nothing and know nothing. God is the Master Designer, and we are marred lumps of clay. He has the power to make us, to break and reshape us into another vessel as he deems fit.

It's clear from the Garden of Eden that God has given man freedom of choice. Man must choose to do the will of God. Adam wasn't just given power—he was delegated the authority to exercise that power. God gave Adam dominion over every other created order under heaven. He had power over the tree of the knowledge of good and evil. He had the choice to eat or not to eat.

We become slaves to that/whom we give power. The precepts of God are clearly defined in scriptures. You will never go wrong when you consult, understand, and use scriptures in context.

Jeremiah was one of those prophets who was always aware of and sensed his inadequacies in fulfilling the will of God. As a matter of fact, he tried to get out of doing the will of God, but the Lord wouldn't allow it (Jeremiah 1:4–10, 20:7–9). Before God gives one an assignment, he'll also give the measure of anointing that is suited to the assignment.

As you seek to do the will of God, the Holy Spirit will give you the inner prompting that you need. This prompting leads you in the way that God wants you to go. Your spirit will bear witness with the Spirit of God.

Obedience Brought Me Peace

Doing the will of God demands that you make some tough decisions that will affect your life. Nevertheless, if you trust him and put your faith in him, he will guide you onto the right path (Proverbs 3:5–6). You will not enjoy peace until you have done the will of God.

When the Lord called me some years ago, I shrugged my shoulders and didn't take heed. I can testify that the years that I played "hard-to-get" with the Lord were the most miserable years of my life. I had no peace or contentment within.

At the age of eighteen, I went with my family, for the first time, to a house party. It was in the basement of family friend. The little church girl who was brought up in a pastor's house broke loose and shook her little booty on the dance floor. Like a bird set free from its cage, I danced, and it felt good for a moment. Each time I danced, I would hear a voice saying: "You were not brought up this way."

I told nobody of my experience. I desired to be like every other eighteen-year-old, but I wasn't. I tried to shut it out, but it kept coming back each time I went on the dance floor. I felt guilty, because my mother had said to me, "I want to hear good report." Dancing at a party was not good, even though it was a house party. I felt as if I was betraying my mother.

I was also offered my first glass of liquor at that party. I'd never drunk liquor before. It was a mixture of vodka and orange juice—they called it a screw driver. Well, it did to me exactly what the name implied. It rooted everything from my gut. From 11:00 p.m. I began to vomit. It didn't stop until 8:00 a.m. the next day. I never touched liquor again.

I went to another house party, and my countenance betrayed me. The disgust and lack of enthusiasm was so evident on my face that a guy wanted to dance with me but was afraid to ask, so he asked my sister if he could dance with me. The harsh answer was, "No!"

I was angry with myself for playing Jonah. The man of God had prophesied over my life when I was eight years old. He said that I was called to feed the flock of God. I was separated from the womb to go to the nations unto whom God would send me. I knew that I had to yield to God or die. I didn't yield for a few years, but after I did, peace came. It flowed like a rippling rill.

In this age of rebellion and compromise, we need to seek the will of the Father and do it. Time is running out. The will of God must be done in earth as it is in heaven. He who knows to do the will of God and does not do it has sinned against God.

Give us this day our daily bread

It cannot be overstated that our heavenly Father knows what we have need of (Psalm 34:10, 84:11, 103:5; Matthew 6:31–34; Luke 12:22–30; Romans 10:11; Philippians 4:19; 1Timothy 5:8). God is acquainted with his children's needs. Looking back on the children of Israel's journey from Egypt to the Promised Land, we see how they never lacked any good thing. The Lord provided manna, quail, and water from the rock.

God is our provider. One of the wonderful things about God is that he not only caters to our temporal or physical needs, but he also supplies our spiritual needs. He gives us Jesus, the bread of life, that our spiritual man might be nurtured (Matthew 4:4). Every believer needs a daily diet of the bread of life. The Word of God is the food of champions.

No child of God is a neglected child. As a Father, he is bound by his own words to supply the needs of those who walk upright, obey, and abide in his words (Psalm 34:10).

Chapter 23
Dissecting the Lord's Prayer: Part D

And forgive us our debts, as we forgive our debtors

Jesus, the sacrificial Lamb of God, died to take away the sins of the world (John 1:29). Earlier I mentioned that when Jesus cried, "It is finished," he was proclaiming to the world that the work of redemption past, present, and future was purchased in full.

Because of the sin factor, man was declared unworthy to enter the presence of God. The veil in the tabernacle of Moses attested to this fact. Man was separated from God, but Jesus changed this when he died (Romans 5:1–8).

The love of God outshone the sins of mankind. Sin brought death and the penalty of death; but the blood gave life and the hope of a more abundant life. The one who receives the gospel and confesses with his lips that Jesus is Lord is forgiven of his trespasses. This person now enjoys peace with God because of the redeeming blood of the Lamb.

The question is: Have we received the forgiveness that Christ has given us? We must forgive those who have offended us, because God has forgiven us (Romans 3:23; 1 John 1:8–10).

Since we sin daily, either by commission or omission, we need to ask God to forgive us. Because man is prone to sin, he must place himself under the subjection of the Holy Ghost (Galatians 5:24). Bear in mind the connection between God and yourself, and yourself and the world. The love of God descends to us vertically; now we must extend our love horizontally to the people around us (Mark 11:25–26).

Jesus paid an inconceivably high price to redeem us from everlasting damnation: he gave his life and he shed his blood. Thus, he taught: "And forgive us our debts as we forgive our debtors." Forgiveness of others is one of the greatest themes of the gospel of Jesus Christ.

And lead us not into temptation

Once again, we are faced with the reality that we are engaged in spiritual warfare (James 1:13–15; Ephesians 6:10–18). God does not lead his people into temptation; in fact, he has given us his word that he will show us how to escape when we are faced with temptation (1 Corinthians 10:13).

It's within the nature of man to give way to temptation, so when Jesus taught his disciples to pray, "Lead us not into temptation," it was just another way of saying, "Lead us away from the things that will cause us to stumble." Man made himself vulnerable to the wiles of the devil from the time he disobeyed God in the Garden of Eden. Sin runs through the ages like blood runs through the capillaries, veins, and arteries in our bodies (Genesis 3:6, 39:7).

Jesus faced temptation just as you are faced with it today. Jesus passed this way, and he overcame the devil by the power of the "Word." Joseph was a young man, and all of his faculties were intact. He could have yielded to the enticement and seduction of his master's wife, but he respectfully declined and ran. We escape yielding to temptation by application of the Word of God. How can I do this wickedness and sin against God? Jesus overcame sin, temptation, and the tempter (John 16:33).

We have within us the divine nature of the Father. We have the DNA of Jesus' blood running through our spiritual veins. Jesus was both man and God. He won the victory over sin and Satan; we have been delegated the power and authority to overcome them too.

Whenever you are tempted, take refuge in the Word of God. It will lead you and guide you away from temptation. He will also provide you with a way of escape when temptations come. Temptations, no matter how severe, are no match for the power of God (Psalm 108:12–13, 119:9–11; James 4:7–8).

When you pray, ask God to lead you away from temptation. Jesus was faced with temptation, yet he did not yield. He defeated the devil with the Word of God. Be encouraged! The dragon's head has already been crushed at Calvary. In a matter of time, he will be cast into the lake of fire that burns forever and ever.

One of these days, there will be no more devil and demons to encounter. Until that time, stand fast and stay the course (1 Corinthians 15:58).

Chapter 24
Dissecting the Lord's Prayer: Part E

But deliver us from evil

This world is in a state of spiritual darkness and moral declension. One would think that the heart of man would be closer drawn to God, since the rapture of the church is eminent. The answer, sadly, is no. The man of perdition is very much at work in the world. He manifests himself in the lives of those who have yielded their bodies to be used of him as instruments of sin (Genesis 3:1; 2 Thessalonians 2:7–17).

One of the reasons evil is so dangerous is that it's not always presented in its true colour.

The man of perdition entices mankind with things they cannot afford. He hangs the spider's web and waits in his corner. He traps the unsuspecting wanderer, and the rest is history.

Vision of the Man of Perdition

I recall the day the Lord pointed his index finger at me and gave me this warning: "If you do not serve me, I will strip you of everything." God brought me, like the prophet Ezekiel, into a valley and showed me this vision.

God passed a picturesque cinematographic scene before my eyes. In it I beheld a bottomless pit that was darker than midnight. Everything that was dear to me went down into the bottomless pit. Even the dogs in the yard and the furniture in the house were cast into the pit. The most horrifying moment came when my family members began to plunge headlong into this bottomless pit. I heard their shrill wails for help as they went down.

I was so tormented in my spirit that I couldn't hold my peace. I related it to somebody, who said to me, "Don't worry about it; it's nothing. Our good God will never do that"

I knew it wasn't a figment of my imagination. God was giving me warning. He had a plan for my life, and if I didn't yield to his imperative, I'd suffer the consequences. I had a life changing decision to make. I lived with this torment, every day, for the next six years.

One Sunday morning in February, I attended a Winter Revival Crusade. The visiting evangelist began to sing a song. I didn't need to hear the message, because the song did it.

In medical terminology, the word "lithotripsy" refers to the use of high-energy shock waves to fragment and disintegrate kidney stones. The shock waves shatter the stone into small fragments so it can be eliminated through the urinary system.

During the altar call, the evangelist stated, "He who hears this message and does not heed it will one day find himself in hell. This message will rise up against you as a testimony." I heard him loudly and clearly. I was convicted. God used holy lithotripsy to break apart the stones in my heart. The words of the song fully pulverized them. I knew that if I didn't make Jesus my choice that day, something bad would have happened. In the evening service, I surrendered my life to the Lord. The Lord ordained that I should be prayed for twice that evening. I left that sacred precinct with a double portion of God's blessings.

This is not the end of the story. As I matured gracefully, I began to understand the "but" Evangelist Graham spoke about years ago. He had said, "You are going to be … but." These "buts" must be destroyed by the power of the Almighty, who has called me out of darkness and into his marvellous light. Every "but" must be discovered and brought down by the power of God.

I thought I'd had trials before, but after my baptism and inception into the body of Christ, all hell broke loose. The devil was mad. He wanted me back. He laid stumbling blocks in my way trying to hinder me; but, God opened my eyes to his wiles, and I escaped them every time.

It was dawn one Sunday when I was brought back to that horrible, dark, bottomless pit that God had shown me six years earlier. This time the devil stood before me and, with enticing gibberish, tried to win me back to him and his employ. His words were as smooth as butter. I could sense the presence of the Lord above me. In yonder azure deep, the sun was blazing in resplendent beauty. The splendour of the sun was blinding, and I had to shield my eyes from the rays. Wonderfully, it didn't burn; it was just magnificent. O the glory of his presence, I thought to myself.

As if on wings, I mounted to the sky and began to fly towards the sun. Not surprisingly, the devil took on wings and began to pursue me like an avenging predator. He slackened his pace. I thought he'd stopped pursuing, but he hadn't. In his stead, he sent his minions ahead of him to destroy me. There were legions of demons coming after me. They looked like a great swarm of black locusts. They buzzed like bees. In the amidst the deafening buzzing, I heard the voice of God saying, "If you fly into the arms of the Son, daughter, the devil will not be able to harm you."

I kept on flying. Every time a demon came close to me, the Lord blasted it down with the radiance of the sun. Those demons were rendered ineffective by the power of the one and only Almighty God. I flew into the arms of the Son, as directed by my Father. The Lord spoke to me again, saying, "If you stay in the arms of the Son, daughter, the devil will not be able to pluck you out of my hands or destroy you."

I thought the devil had left, but he hadn't. He'd landed on the other side of the sun. In the pitch blackness, I sensed him over there, effortlessly reaching to see if, by any means, he could pluck me out of the Master's hands. The voice of the Father kept prompting: "Stay in the arms of the Son, daughter. If you stay there, the devil will not be able to destroy you."

This was no nightmare. Again, this story is not a figment of my vivid imagination. I had an encounter with the wicked one, but what a consolation—I also had an encounter with the Living God, the Son, and the Holy Spirit. God protected and preserved my life.

I'd had a divine revelation from God, but I had no understanding of it. I began to pray and weep before the Lord. The voice of the Lord said, "Turn in your Bible to 2 Thessalonians 2."

What I discovered in this passage was informative, inspiring, and awesome. The antichrist spirit is already in the world. Satan has been trying to imitate God or to excel above him.

In Daniel 2:31–35, God revealed a four-dimensional image: head of gold, breast and arms of silver, belly and thighs of brass, legs of iron, and feet of iron intermingled with clay. In Daniel 3, Nebuchadnezzar presented a gigantic image of pure gold and commanded that it be worshipped. The Babylonian monarch was trying to override God's dictate in Daniel 2:31–35.

According to Revelation 13:11, this beast is an offensive parody of the Lamb slain before the foundation of the world (Revelation 5:9, 12). The beast bears the tell-tale sign of one that has been slaughtered. God gave power and authority to the Lamb; the dragon gave power and authority to the beast. The Lamb is to the church as the beast is to the world.

Revelation 16:13–14 exposes the imitating trinity. The Father, Son, and Holy Spirit operate in juxtaposition to effectuate the good works in humanity. This malevolent, diabolical trinity—the dragon, the beast, and the false prophet—stand juxtaposed with each other to do evil and to make the Word of God of non-effect. The despotic devil has always opposed God, the people of God, and the things of God.

The world needs deliverance from evil. We need intercessory prayers more than ever. Jesus began his evangelistic ministry with the message of repentance. Surely Jesus is coming quickly; man will perish if he does not repent. (Matthew 24:4–13)

North America and the world need to cry out unto God: "Righteousness exalts a nation: but sin is a reproach to any people" (Proverbs 14:34).

We are in the last days. Seducing spirits are busy depositing their corrupt seeds in receptive minds. It's time for man to arise from his slumber and call upon God. When man drifted off into spiritual slumber, the enemy came and spread seeds of discord, division, malice, despair, hopelessness, and death. It's time to lift our heads and pray unto the God of heaven.

I just receive a revelation from God: Evil is just one letter short of devil. The letter is "D." Remove "D" from devil, and we're left with evil. Place "D" before evil, and you'll see who is before all evil—the devil. Evil is evident in every institution of life. It has found itself in the education system where there are impressionable and vulnerable minds. Evil shows up in every arena of life (2 Timothy 3:1–7).

Good and evil continue to contend with each other for the heart and mind of man. History has introduced us to many folks termed "geniuses," but their deeds testified against them (Romans 1:22).

This world has changed. Things are not as they used to be. The church that once scoffed at the spirit of compromise and conformity now turns her head away and allows everything, but the bride that Jesus will present to his Father will be a flawless bride (Romans 12:1–2).

Anybody whose mind has not undergone a total spiritual metamorphosis will yield quickly to the slightest of temptations to sin against God. This is why the devil is able to convince so many to sin against the holy standards of God.

Evil prevails because the devil still has the affinity to conceal the truth from man. He is still able to put a mask over man's face and plugs his ears so that he can neither see nor hear the truth. The devil has blindfolded many so that they cannot see the Light. But I know in my spirit that God will arise and vindicate his glory, because the glory belongs to him.

This iniquitous generation has little or no reverence for those in authority. This generation is disobedient to parents. Paul profiled the older woman who had proven herself to be a pattern of maternal excellence to teach the younger women (Titus 2:1–5). Today there seems to be no distinction between the elders of the church and the juniors. The kind of teaching Paul emphasized seems to be extinct.

In the Old Testament era, the high priest held supreme power over the people. He was acknowledged as God's vicegerent (a person exercising delegated power on behalf of a sovereign ruler, or a person appointed by a ruler or head of state to act as an administrative deputy). Today there are many priests and clergymen who walk in violation of the statutes of God. The stories you hear are so shameful, making it difficult to witness to the unsaved.

In these last days of idolatry and sacrilege, you need to know how to pray. When you pray, you need to say, "Lord, lead us away from evil. Deliver us from the wiles of the evil one. Not only me Lord, but deliver my brothers and my sisters also" (1 Chronicles 4:9–10; Matthew 24:12).

Iniquity still abounds, but God is supreme and has sovereign rule over the world. God still has power to preserve and protect that which you have committed unto him against the evil day. If you remain connected to the vine, you shall not go under.

Chapter 25
Dissecting the Lord's Prayer: Part F

For thine is the kingdom, and the power, and the glory, forever. Amen!

The Lord's Prayer begins by declaring the supremacy of God over all the earth, and it culminates with the same powerful revelation. The kingdom is still his, the power is still his in heaven and in earth, and all glory belongs unto him forever and ever (Psalm 24:1–2; Matthew 28:18). Amen!

The authenticity of the Bible remains the same from the time that God breathed it to holy men. It is still the infallible word of Jehovah. Scientists and other professionals have reviewed and revised their findings on certain subject matter, but the Bible remains unchanged (Luke 21:33). God never changes his words.

The devil masquerades as the king, but scripture declares that Jesus Christ is preeminently the all-powerful king of glory over all the earth. David was just a young lad when he invoked the name of the LORD and killed Goliath with only one small stone. From that time onwards, Saul tried to kill David, because he felt threatened.

Saul realized that his reign was about to expire, and he wasn't about to be taken out without a fight. David behaved himself wisely in the Lord and refused to fight with Saul or even kill him. Saul was warring against the wrong person. David wasn't trying to overthrow him; he overthrew himself when he disobeyed the commandments of God. Saul wanted the glory, but it had departed from him.

The devil likes prestige. He likes to be worshipped and praised. He behaves as if he has been declared, "the king," but to the contrary. Ephesians 2:2 states that the devil has been addressed as the "prince of the power of the air," not the king. As long as the king is alive, the prince can only be a secondary force. He cannot reign with the king.

Satan is the archon who rules over the world system. Not only does Satan control the territory where he rules, but his minions rule in those realms also. They have authority and power in these spheres as well. Because of his great influence, he is referred to as "prince." On some occasions, he is also hailed as Beelzebub, the prince of demons.

The devil has boundaries; therefore, his authority is not absolute. His kingdom is the kingdom of darkness, which stands in opposition to the Kingdom of God, the kingdom of light. The devil is prestigious in every region where the unregenerate is found.

Humans reproduce, but there is no reproduction in the realm of demons. The same old demons are still at work in the world today. They receive their assignments from the principalities and powers and are stationed all over the cosmos, but they are not omnipresent. They can only be in one place at one time.

God is omnipresent. He is everywhere. All power and glory belongs unto him.

Chapter 26
The Characteristics of Demons and the Error of Satanic Consultation

✢ Demons are evil spirits. They are malevolent and despotic.

✢ In scripture, they are described as evil spirits, unclean spirits, lying spirits, angels of Satan, or fallen angels (Matthew 10:1; 1 Kings 22:23; Mark 1:27; Revelation 12:9; Jude 1:6).

✢ Demons have no legal authority or power on earth. They are apprentices of Satan; therefore, they need the permission of receptive vessels in order to operate on earth. A person gives permission to the devil to work when he willfully sins, dabbles with the occult, makes unholy soul ties, associates with false religions, etc. (St. Matthew 8:31, 12:43; Mark 16:17–18). Before the devil could touch Job, he had to ask God's permission (Job 1:6–12).

✢ They have individual names, or they are named according to the group with which they associate (Mark 5:9).

- They are highly intellectual. They are theatrical and can put on a convincing act. They can speak in audible voices, and they perform the imperatives of their master—the devil (Acts 19:14–16).

- Demons know that God and Jesus have almighty power in heaven and in earth (Luke 4:31–36; James 2:19). They know that Jesus Christ is the Son of God, and they are also aware of their prophesied destiny. Some of them are territorial and want to remain in a certain locality (Matthew 8:16, 29; Mark 1:32–34; Acts 19:15).

- They are the promulgators behind every doctrine of devils. They work to shipwreck the faith of vulnerable believers whose ears are always itching (1Timothy 4:1–4; 2 Timothy 4:3–4).

- Demons can invade and reside in the bodies of humans and animals; they can be very combative and will even strive with the angels of God (Matthew 8:28–32; Revelation 12:7–9).

- They are wicked; therefore, they must not be toyed with or entertained, but must be discerned and exorcised in the name of Jesus and by the power of Almighty God (Matthew 12:45).

- They can differentiate between the authentic Christian and the imposter (Acts 16:16–18, 19:13–16).

- They have the capacity to physically, emotionally, and psychologically afflict the victim (Matthew 4:24; Luke 9:37–42; Acts 16:16).

✢ They are extremely strong and are very fierce; therefore, the person in whom they operate can exhibit extraordinary strength also (Matthew 8:28; Luke 8:28–33).

✢ They have the power to enter the receptive vessel, leave, and re-enter with many other spirits more wicked than itself (Matthew 12:43–45).

Satan can masquerade as the angel of light; therefore, his ministers can also be transformed or masquerade as the ministers of righteousness (2 Corinthians 11:14–16). Believers must stay close to the Lord and ask him to grant them the spirit of discernment. The people experimenting with the occult use demons as mediums to extract information from the surroundings and from others (Deuteronomy 18:9–13; 2 Kings 17:17).

Paul and Silas met a damsel who could speak deep, mysterious things, because she was controlled by a spirit of divination. She brought in much dividends to her masters by soothsaying (Acts 16:16–18). Under the Mosaic Law, idolatry, demonic practices, and consultation with the spirit of divination and sorcery were prohibited (Leviticus 19, 20; Deuteronomy 32:17; Psalm 106:36; 1 Corinthians 10:20). Anyone who was caught in any of these acts were either excommunicated or stoned (Deuteronomy 18:9–15).

After Samuel died, King Saul consulted with the witch of Endor. Saul indulged himself in the occult by visiting one with a familiar spirit who had been excommunicated from among the people of God (1 Chronicles 10:13). Demons can imitate the voices of people, dead or alive, as you'll recall from the story about Marva. King Saul engaged the witch of Endor to inquire of the dead. Saul contacted the witch because God would not speak to him by dreams, by Urim, or by prophets.

Some people seek to tell fortunes by means of bibliomancy. In bibliomancy, a specific question is asked by the enquirer. The diviner randomly opens a book, usually the Bible. The enquirer moves his finger over the page until he is stopped. The word or the verse on which he stops is considered the answer to the query.

The occultist manipulates the Word of God to cater to his own wicked thoughts. God sends enlightenment through his words, but his words are not to be used esoterically to satisfy whims and evil deeds. God condemns any affiliation or consultation with the devil and his angels—even if the Bible is used in the process.

Another New Age movement is channeling. In this paranormal encounter, a person is invited to contact "a spirit guide" from the spirit world. The spirit speaks to the outside world through the person—the channel—who is usually in a trance-like state. This is only a synopsis of what channeling entails.

Christians and non-believers need to know that mingling with evil spirits and demons will eventually have serious ramifications. You can become possessed with evil spirits. God has placed the Holy Spirit within every born again Christian; however, when the Spirit of God has gone from a person, what is next? Such a person will turn to mediums. God will leave them to their reprobate minds to do the unorthodox.

Satan, the god of this world, has blinded the eyes of those who have yielded themselves unto him. They remain in spiritual darkness, even though the Light has come (John 1:5-8, 12; 2 Corinthians 4:3–5). Demonic infestation and influence are not extinct. Magic, witchery, consultation with mediums, and Satanism are no longer practiced in a dark room in the back. They're right on the television screen. Many things might be lawful and permissible in society, but that doesn't mean they're edifying to the body of Christ.

Paul stated his determination not to be controlled by anything that was outside of the will of God (1 Corinthians 6:12, 10:21–23). The devil is subtle, and we are not ignorant of his evil devices; therefore, we should safeguard ourselves and the innocent so that he will not get the advantage over us (2 Corinthians 2:11).

The children of God should not prostitute themselves with those who claim to have connection with the dead, or those who are conjoined with mediums and familiar spirits, witches, and wizards. Your brain has more gigabytes than any computer system. One can only retrieve that which is programmed into the mind, and what is programmed into your mind and thoughts will either return to bless or torment you.

We need to pray and cover ourselves with the blood of Jesus Christ. Demonic interference can cause physical and mental maladies in man. They can cause blindness, dumbness, and epileptic attacks. They can send man into vagabondage (Matthew 8:28–34, 17:14–18; Luke 8:30).

Demonic forces can totally overpower a person in such a way that the person's entire personality, voice, and demeanor changes. The account in Luke 8 testifies to this. It also reveals that demons have specific names. According to The Free Dictionary, a legion in the Roman army may consist of 3,000 to 6,000 or more soldiers. What is happening here? I'm inclined to believe that even though there were many demons, there was a principal demon.

Every army must have a general who reserves authoritative rights to issue orders and ensure that delegated assignments are implemented according to protocol. I believe that it was the principal leader that spoke to Jesus. Be aware that what you see at first might not be the whole picture. The man in Luke 8 was possessed with more demonic spirits than first thought.

In Matthew 8:28, we encountered demons that infested tombs; they liked to mingle with the dead. Demons must have a body to indwell, or something to attach themselves to, in order to manifest their full powers. If they cannot find human bodies, then animals will suffice.

There were demons within this man with the personality of vagabonds. They drove the man into the wilderness and into the mountains, as Mark reported. He went home, but couldn't stay there, because the demons overcame the fetters and drove him back into the wilderness.

There were demons in this man who were fascinated with blood. I'm inclined to believe there were suicidal spirits present also. They compelled the man to cut himself with stones.

It's dangerous to have demons in your presence and not know it. They can impersonate worshippers. The spirit of divination in Acts 16:17 spoke as though it was promoting Paul and Silas, but to the contrary. They entered the presence of the Lord, as did the other worshippers. That was a cover-up to escape being exorcised.

The loud, expulsive cry of the demon-possessed man of Gadara was a telltale sign that what was happening in his life was far from normal. "I adjure you by God" is another way of saying, "I command you in the name of God," or "I charge you earnestly and solemnly not to torment me."

One demon spoke on the behalf of the rest of the legion. To escape impending judgement, the demon requested permission to enter into the swine. The swine discovered their plight and decided that they didn't want to live a life of demonic infestation, so They ran headlong into the waters and were drowned (Mark 5:1-13).

The believer who expects God to answer his prayer must remove himself from demonic influences and satanic consultation. One cannot serve two masters. Wherever your heart is, there will your treasures be also. God specifically told the children of Israel that they should have no other gods besides him (Exodus 20:3; Deuteronomy 5:7). The LORD, whose name is Jealous, is a jealous God (Exodus 34:14).

Demons can block your answers coming down from God (Daniel 10:12–13).

Let Us Pray

Father, we thank you for giving us the gift of the Holy Spirit. Because of the Holy Spirit, we can discern the secrets, even the deep, dark mysteries surrounding us. But every now and then, our spiritual eyes become blinded and our spiritual ears become deaf. I pray, Father, in the name of Jesus, that you will clear the fog that obscures our eyes and remove the plugs that stop our ears. Thank you for the continued protection of your subjects in this rebellious age. Help us to come up higher so that we can see farther in the spirit. We submit ourselves to your rule and to your will. We pray this prayer in the excellent name of Jesus Christ of Nazareth. Amen.

Chapter 27
Demonic Possession

How does one become demon possessed? Scripture provides insight into this question (Matthew 12:43–45; Luke 11:21–22). A demon considers the place where it dwells to be its property; therefore, it will protest and fight against anyone who tries to interfere or exorcise it.

A spiritually strong child of God clothes himself in the whole armour of God. The child of God who gives no place to the devil can never be demon possessed. However, the person who lives carelessly exposes himself to the devil to be used as an instrument of sin. One who indulges himself in the works of the flesh becomes a candidate for demon infestation (Galatians 5:19–21; Ephesians 4:25–32; Colossians 3:5–6). The devil can access a person's life through various mediums. Keep your spiritual armour intact and watch in the spirit. Pray that God will keep you from the snare of the tempter.

Prayer is power; therefore, no prayer means no power. Without prayer, the enemy will back you into a corner and pummel you until you give up and give in. Paul exhorted us in Ephesians 6:18 to make prayer and supplication unto God, in the Spirit, for every saint. Paul also pointed out in Galatians 6:7–8 that everyone who indulges in sin will reap the penalties reserved for sin if they don't repent, but those who repent will live with Christ forever.

Sin creates a flaw in the spiritual armour and leaves the door wide open for invasion by the devil and his demons. The laws of the Lord are written in the minds of the believer. God wants us to meditate upon his words daily.

If we fill our minds and hearts with a daily portion of the Word of God, we'll have no room for junk and the things that will bring damnation to our souls. No demon can possess the mind that is stayed upon Christ. God has granted us freedom of choice. He will not impose upon our privacy unless he must. The person who wants to see the devil run must resist him and submit himself to God (James 4:7).

If the devil must spoil the goods of the strong man, he must first bind the strong man. If the strong man remains strong, the devil has no power to bind him. If, however, the strong man is bound, and if his goods are spoiled, it becomes obvious that the strong man is suffering from some weakness (Mark 3:27).

God has not left us destitute. He has armoured us and deployed us to fight. We are told that the weapons of the Christian's warfare are not carnal, but they are mighty through God to the demolishing of strongholds. The sword of the Spirit, which is the Word of God, is a weapon of power and might (2 Corinthians 10:3–6).

We have the power to triumph over the reasoning of pagans and philosophies of the biased and the ignorant. The mind is the greatest battlefield; therefore, if we don our helmets of salvation, the fiery missiles of the devil will not be able to penetrate and infiltrate our being. Gird up the loins of your mind with the infallible, authentic Word of Jehovah.

Having prayed and feasted on the Word of God, the next thing to do is walk in the Spirit. The one who walks in the Spirit will not hasten to fulfill the demands or the lusts of the flesh, as Paul puts it (Galatians 5:16–17). The Spirit and the flesh are always at enmity with each other. Once you have yielded your body unto the Lord, you become his property. The devil cannot pluck you out of his hands. All you need to overcome the wicked one is already within you.

Demons should not be underestimated, toyed with, or entertained. They must be discerned, rebuked, and cast out. Jesus exposed all demonic activities that he encountered, and he is still Lord over all the earth. Not partial power, but all power, has been delegated unto him both in heaven and on earth. Both man and demons must bow at the sound of his name. He is forever Lord, and all glory and honour belong to him. In the name of Jesus, all other powers will be brought down. He laid his life down and took it up again. The grave had no power over him, because he is the resurrection and the life; though he was dead, yet he lives and will reign forevermore. Prayer is not an optional weapon but an essential one.

Chapter 28
Praying for a Revival Revolution

I stood by my living window and gazed with awesome wonder at the phenomenal transition from winter to spring. As if in a cinematographic scene, I watched as the snow banks melted to nothingness, and the trees, which seemed dead all winter long, began to bud, then blossom and then bloom. The fruit bearing trees produced fruits. Then it dawned on me that the harvest truly is ripe, but the labourers are few. It's time to put in the sickle. The rapture of the church is nearer than we think.

There's a quickening in my spirit, and I can sense that the stage of the last days has been set; there is coming a mighty global revival. My spirit beams with joy. I don't know about you, but I'm ready for takeoff. I'm ready to walk down the aisle with my Lord.

This coming revival is being precipitated not by shared human philosophy, not by the rhetoric of the famous rhetoricians, not by the loquacity of the linguists or the media, not by the brilliance of the geniuses, not by the convincing performance of the renowned thespians, and not even by the eloquence of the soft spoken or the thunderous preaching of the pulpiteers. This mighty revival is being stirred up by the continuous, fervent power of prayer.

All people, tongues, tribes, nations, nationalities, and cultures need to know that God has rent the heavens; he has descended like the dew of Hermon; he has opened heaven's flood gates and released the Spirit of revival, because saints everywhere have been praying.

The voices of the prayer warriors have outraced the blockers and ascended into the throne room of heaven. When upon the cross of Calvary, Jesus Christ tore down the middle wall of partition. The angel bearing the Spirit of propagation has released the viable seeds in the ambassadors of righteousness. They are going forth and sowing the seeds in fertile soils.

Prolificacy has been pronounced upon that which was once called barren. In the name of Jesus Christ of Nazareth, the barren in the body of Christ shall bear and bring forth.

Formerly, Christians were better prepared for pleasure than for prayer. They were more dressed for the supper room and the ballroom than for the prayer room. To them, the house of prayer had become unattractive and unfulfilling. They could do everything in abundance, but pray. But there has come a shift; people are being drawn to the prayer room again.

Behold, he comes! Will we, like the mercenaries at Gadara, bid him to leave this territory, or will we prostrate ourselves at his feet? Jesus Christ has made time for us; let us lay aside our set agendas and make time for him. The time has come to dispossess and repossess.

Let people arise everywhere and lift holy hands in prayer and praise to Jesus, our king. Prayer causes the blind to see, the dumb to speak, and the lame to walk and dance. Prayer can cause the weak to be strong and the barren to be prolific. Let the weak say, "I am strong." There is power in prayer. May God bless us richly as we gather at each session to pray.

Prayer is hard work. It demands that a person discipline himself and make sacrifices, especially when the answer does not come speedily. Prayer is difficult, because many people come as spectators rather than as participators. People seem to get distracted easily and thus quench the Holy Spirit.

A national departure from God is always preceded by a personal departure from God. Eve, the first lady of humanity, sinned and thus experienced a personal separation from God. She then gave the forbidden to her husband. He chose death over life. Eve didn't cause Adam to backslide. He had some help, but he made the decision to separate himself from God. After Adam sinned, there came a national separation from God.

Before there can be a national or global revival, there must first be personal repentance and confession of sins unto God. Like the prodigal son, man must come to his senses and admit that he has wasted his substance on lawless living. He has rebelled against God. He has attached himself to many things that are displeasing to God. He must break away from them by the power of the God of heaven.

In order to experience personal revival, one must acknowledge his impoverished condition. In order for there to be revival, we must understand that sin separates man from God, and that the only way to restore a right relationship with the Father is to receive the forgiveness that he has provided in the atoning blood of the Lamb of Calvary. Coming home to your Father is a personal choice that only you can make ((Luke 15:18–24).

Calling Upon the Name of the Lord

It must be understood that the prodigal son desired to be a hired servant. He wanted to assume the status of paid personnel. A hired servant, as opposed to a bondservant, didn't have to necessarily live under the master's roof. A hired servant can be compared to a contract worker. Service might be for a season only. A bondservant is obligated to live under his master's authority and serve without wages. The spiritual purport here is that this prodigal son was not ready to totally surrender his will to the will of his father.

The prodigal son seemed to be trying to restore his relationship with his father by the legal dictates of works. He knew that what he did was deserving of death. He placed the greatest priority on food and shelter. He had a need to satisfy a present hunger, but the father knew exactly what he needed. He released a son into the world; he did not release a slave. Therefore, he wanted reconciliation with a son, not a slave. The father, on his terms, re-established the covenant relationship with his son. The prodigal received a son's blessing, not a servant's.

In prayer for personal revival, we need to understand that it is God who will set forth the terms and the stipulations. What are you willing to sacrifice for revival? The prodigal son reached out to his father, and his father extended his arms towards him. As a matter of fact, he didn't have to walk alone. The father met him halfway. The father forgave him and received him, but he never granted his son's appeal. The father welcomed him home and revived him: "It was meet that we should make merry, and be glad: for this thy brother was dead, and is alive again; and was lost, and is found" (Luke 15:32).

In revival, the dead receive life, and that which has been lost is retrieved. You know when you're experiencing revival in your soul, because your walk with God is no longer legalistic or according to the works of the flesh, but according to the will of God. Righteousness has been restored. You identify fully with Christ, because the glory of the righteousness of God has returned to your temple. You now walk in resurrection power.

In a corporate prayer setting, everybody must seek God for himself. Everyone must pour out himself before God. When man comes to the end of himself, God will step in.

Jacob came to the place of total surrender and to the end of himself at a place called Jabbok, a ford or tributary of the Jordan River. He received a change of identity and his blessings only after he crossed over from a life of deception and trickery. He could only take full possession of the covenantal promises of God after he crossed over Jabbok.

Under Moses, God brought the children of Israel through the Red Sea as one company. They wandered in the wilderness alone. God brought the entire entourage of his people, under Joshua, across the Jordan River and into the Promised Land. But notice that when Jacob would be revived, he stood before God as one in solitary confinement.

God deals with our personhood and sends us personal and then corporate revival when we come to that place of separation.

Jacob had to separate himself from his Leah, his Rachel, his Bilhah, his Zilpah, and from his children. He had to disconnect himself from some things in order to reconnect with God. Jacob prayed and called unto the Lord (Genesis 32:9–12). He had compromised his walk with God when he deceived his father and received the birthright unlawfully, but God was about to restore order to his life. During the night of wrestling, Jacob had to confess that he was a heel catcher and a supplanter. "My name is Jacob." God changed his identity.

Revival will come when we admit, before God, who we really are and repent. Revival will come to me when I submit myself totally to the God of all creation. Stop being hypocritical and tell it like it really is: I am a liar, a cheater, a heel grabber, and a deceiver. I put on a disguise in order to get what I want. In the light of the Word of God, your true self will be exposed. What is your name? Say it like it is and then revival will come.

There is power in obedience. Is the old man hindering revival? Let us call unto God and crucify the flesh now. Jacob prevailed when the old man was put to death in the place of separation. After the night of wrestling at Jabbok, he won the victory over sin; the light of God dawned upon him at Peniel. It always seems to take a crisis to get man to bow before his Maker in prayer and intercession.

The Gift of Influential Leadership

Every personal, local, and international revival revolution begins when man acknowledges his errors, turns from his wicked ways, and seeks God in prayer and fasting. Revival will come when man is driven to his knees because the putrefactive odour of sin is irritating the spiritual nostrils. God will hear and answer prayers when we begin to pray and call upon him on the behalf of the metropolis, municipalities, countries, monarchies, kings, kingdoms, and nations (2 Chronicles 7:14–15).

In Jonah chapter 1:1-2, we are told that the people of the great city of Nineveh were very wicked. In chapter 3:1-4, God sent the prophet Jonah to deliver a very pertinent message to the Ninevites. Disobedience is a cyclic offense that goes around and around like a revolving door. The salvation of the people of Nineveh was contingent upon their obedience to the imperative of God. The Ninevites needed to turn from their wicked ways in order to be spared the wrath of God.

First, notice that Nineveh's revival began because of the obedience of the prophet. Jonah, having repented of his error, delivered the message from God without compromise and without wrath. He added not; neither did he take away. Jonah put aside his own personal biases, prejudices, and anger towards Nineveh and delivered the message exactly as God said. "In forty days, Nineveh will be overthrown." The number forty is indicative of probation. Nineveh was given forty days to repent and turn from sinning against God.

Living a holy life and abiding in the calling wherewith we are called is essential. The unsaved might be walking outside of the precepts of God; nevertheless, they are still looking and waiting with eager anticipation and hope for the life-changing word from the prophet of God. The righteous person is the catalyst that God uses to create a shift in this hostile environment.

Next, we see that the Ninevites heard and received the Word of God. They believed the Word of God and also acted upon it. The inhabitants of Nineveh became proactive because they realized that God was not a joker. He said what he meant, and he meant what he said. God is forgiving, but he will scatter the unrepentant and vindicate his glory. God does not play games with the mind of man. God does not lie. His words were clear: If the inhabitants of Nineveh did not repent, they would be cut off from the face of the earth. God gave them forty days.

What happened next? The people related the word of the prophet to the king of Nineveh, and the entire nation believed God. The king commanded that Nineveh should enter a season of national fast. Also, he sent forth a decree and a declaration that even the livestock should be on a fast. In other words, none should have an excuse not to be involved whole-heartedly in what was decreed. In addition, none should be preoccupied with or encumbered with anything that would hinder the full success of this fast.

Leadership is everything, and every leader is appointed to reach specific peoples. The apostle Paul was God's gift to the Gentiles. Every leader, strong or weak, will reproduce himself. No movement or organization will rise above its leader. The strength and success of your movement will be as successful as the leader you enlist.

Exceptional results are achieved when the conscientious leader builds relationship with his subjects. The sum of the whole is always greater than the sum of the individual parts. This is the doctrine of synergy. A wise leader will focus his attention on team building. More importantly, he will boost the spirits of those working below him so that they will be highly motivated to do the work. Few people will follow or support a leader who fails to influence and inspire them. Nobody can follow a parked truck.

A powerful and influential leader has the affinity to attract, employ, and recruit others to run with his vision. They engage others and also give them the support that is needed to succeed and become influential leaders themselves. Whatsoever the leader is interested in and wherever his heart is, there will the heart of the people be also. Whatever the leader places emphasis on, promotes, and become involved in, is what or where the people will gravitate towards. Show me a weak ministry or minister, and I'll show you a ministry or minister with little or no leadership support. Whatever or whoever the head supports, the people will support also.

Consider the human body. If the head is missing, the rest of the body is dead. No movement, no organization, no business will function optimally without a significant head. The lack of significant headship will eventually evolve into a monster, because everybody will do his own thing.

Two of the greatest assets an influential leader can possess are engagement and availability. Involve your people and be there for them as much as humanly possible. A good doctor makes rounds regularly to see how his patients are faring. He doesn't just pop in when there's a crisis or impending crisis to scold them for not following their treatment regimen. He visits his patients regularly so that he can assess their progress. He reads their progress notes to see if the therapeutic measures are working. He doesn't behave like a dictator and just give orders; he hears and listens also.

A leader visits with his protégés as often as possible. He cheers them on and gives constructive criticism and feedback. If the leader can infect his subjects with his vision, they will embrace it and run with it. Likewise, if the leader is laid back about prayer, the people or nation will have the same attitude towards prayer. It's not enough for a great leader to just equip followers—he must produce leaders. Revival comes when the leader gets excited and motivates his followers.

Nobody in Nineveh had an excuse for not participating when the king spoke and gave an impartial command. The king was in favour of revival; he was bodily involved in the edict he gave. The nobles were involved, as were the men, women, children, suckling, and the livestock. Neither man nor beast wore fancy garb. They were all covered in sackcloth and ashes. When the men and women looked at each other, they saw sackcloth and ashes. The survival of their city depended upon their obedience and compliance with the Word of God.

The king removed his royal vestures and laid down his crown. He put his sceptre aside and stepped down from his throne. Before God, everybody was equal; there was profound unity of minds, soul, and spirit. There was no distinction between king or queen, prince or pauper. What a sight that must have been. That atmosphere was conducive to revival.

Does this not sound like what Jesus did? He laid down his crown, his sceptre, and his royal vestures and stepped down from his throne in heaven in order that he might die for us. In my own spirit, I feel the electrical charge of the Holy Spirit in my surroundings. I cannot keep myself from shouting "hallelujah." Jesus did this all for you and me.

The decisive ingredient came next. All the Ninevites were commanded to cry mightily unto God. In other words, they were to pray aloud unto God from the bottom of their being.

The king was specific about what he wanted the people to do. He needed them to cry aloud, not just make noise. Loud noises don't necessarily come from a penitent heart. The King of Nineveh sensed that, so in his proclamation he ordered everyone to repent.

Some of us use our positions of authority to victimize, lord over, bully, and gain control over our protégés. We use our great influence to overpower those whom we can; those whom we cannot overpower, we intimidate and excommunicate. If there is iniquity in our hearts, God will not hear our cries.

The King of Nineveh did what he asked his people to do. He was a part of the prevailing problems; therefore, he must be a part of the solution. If the head of the stream is dirty, the body of the stream will be dirty. We can't correct the problem by chopping off the branches. Many times the branches aren't the major problem—the roots are. The King of Nineveh practiced what he preached (Matthew 23:1–4).

The Evidence of Revival

Because of that spirit of humility and repentance before God, the entire nation experienced revival. Every revival revolution that man has ever seen began when the repentant sought the face of God, turned from their wicked ways, and prayed. The king and the people of Nineveh discovered that the only way to health, wealth, and happiness was to undergo a complete metamorphosis of mind, heart, and spirit towards God.

We know that revival has come when vile sinners open their mouths like the Ninevites, cry mightily, and confess that Jesus Christ is Lord. We know that revival has come when man, with his depraved mind, begins to cry for mercy and acknowledges that Christ is the door to heaven. Anyone who tries to get in through any other door is a thief and a robber.

Revival is here when the head of the household takes the initiative to proclaim the gospel that Jesus Christ died for the sins of humanity. Revival is here when man doesn't have to be pumped and pushed like an old jalopy to worship God, but from the introduction of the worship service to the benediction he prostrates his heart and mind before God in worship and adoration.

Revival is here when men, unprompted by stringed and percussion instruments, melodiously break out in sacred songs and solos in the sacred precincts. Revival is here when scrutinizing spectators become contributing participators in the presence of the Lord. Revival is here when every man, woman, boy, and girl shines with the radiance of the Holy Ghost and blazes like the sacred fire on the sacrificial altar in the tabernacle of Moses.

Revival is never quiet. It comes with a shout, exuberant worship, the clapping of hands, and stomping of feet. Revival doesn't stop here; like the river that Ezekiel envisioned, it will flow to the next city, and the next, and so on.

In the quest for popularity, many churches have become lukewarm. They boast enormous cathedrals and a multiplicity of followers. In the quest for achievement, they have lowered the moral precepts and holy standards of God. They have watered down the gospel and compromised sanctity. They have desecrated the house of God with unlawful conduct and indecent acts. They scoff not at sin, neither do they rebuke that which is abominable or brings damnation to the soul. They have become friends with the world. Anyone who delivers the truth of God will not be friends with the world.

The world system hates truth in the same manner that they hate light. They will not make prayer a priority. Jesus lost most of his audience because folks couldn't accommodate his kind of teaching. After he delivered his discourse in John 6:66–71, many of his followers defected.

In John 6:69, Peter took the liberty of speaking on the behalf of everybody. "We believe and are sure that thou art that Christ, the Son of the living God." Peter probably should have spoken for himself because he didn't know the hearts of the other disciples.

Man looks on the outward appearances, but only God can see what is hidden in the deep recesses of the heart. Peter wasn't even aware of his own deceitful heart, because later he denied Christ. Amongst those twelve there was a doubter, the proud and puffed up, and a deceiver. What a bunch! But the Lord kept them.

We are likely to see a place of worship on many street corners. We have a lot of apostles, prophets, evangelists, teachers, pastors, missionaries, and ambassadors all over the globe. We all agree that the world is in rebellion, but God is faithful. He is about to send forth a revival revolution all over the globe. Whosoever will may come and experience a refreshing. Stop halting between two opinions. There is an abundance of spiritual rain in the forecast.

In the days of Elijah, God gave a sign to indicate that the rain was coming. A little cloud resembling a man's hand arose from the sea. If God be God, serve him and get soaked with the latter rain. A revived people will praise and worship the Father. A revived people will forsake sin and uphold righteousness. Revived people are contagious people. They will spread the good news abroad, and others will join in and rejoice. When revival rain begins to fall, you won't just walk with the good news … you'll run with it.

Many people probably didn't believe Elijah when he made the announcement that a great downpour was coming. Many who believed might have doubted when it didn't happen right away. Six times Elijah's servant went forth and looked towards the sea and beheld nothing. The encouraging words were: Keep on seeking and looking for seven times. If God said that he is going to do it, he will do it.

After the seventh time, the servant came back with promising news. "I perceive a little cloud resembling a man's hand arising from the sea." When God rained, he rained even upon the wicked. Ahab behaved less than graciously towards the living God; however, he was a recipient of the blessings of God when it manifested.

Ahab had to prepare for the rain, which tells us that even though God makes a promise, we could miss it if we're not prepared. When the promises of God manifest, we must be in the right place at the right time. When the Holy Ghost came on the Day of Pentecost, the believers were in the same place, at the same time, waiting for the same thing—the promise of the Father. They all received the Holy Spirit and the gifts he brought.

That little cloud, seen from the heights of Mount Carmel, grew into bigger clouds, and the winds came. Next there was a downpour. God rained a great rain upon the land; even the wicked were watered.

Because of the righteous, God has not consumed us. Had it not been for the righteous men and women of God, the wicked and the nations that forget God would be turned into hell (Psalm 9:17). If it weren't for the praying and interceding people of the world, who knows what God would do to the rebellious? But he spares us according to his loving kindness and tender mercies.

The Word of God is not arbitrary or negotiable. Nothing that God has spoken will return unto him void. It will accomplish that which it sets out to do. The king and the inhabitants of Nineveh heeded the Word of God and thus were spared. The king's decree applied to humans and animals. This was a very conscientious king. God promised to spare the city if the people repented. He wanted no man to have an excuse not to be involved in a time of fasting and repenting before him.

Every man submitted to the authority of the king and was spared. Thank God that there are still a few in Sardis who have not defiled their garments. They are still holding the torch of righteousness high. By these, God is going to bring about revival in this age of grace. God will not punish the righteous with the wicked. Keep on praying and seeking the face of the Almighty. He is coming with power and with glory.

Leave a Legacy

The King of Nineveh had great influence upon the Ninevites, and I believe that it began with relationship. He was authoritative, influential, and obedient. Influential leaders have the affinity to draw ideas from the proclivity of their own spirit. They take visions and dreams and formulate them into tangible legacies, and then impart them into the spirit and hands of their faithful protégés. Their protégés take those visional mandates to the next dimension. Out of the opulence of their own reservoirs of ideas, dreams, and visions, these recruits become influential leaders—an unbroken cycle of greatness. This is how empires or legacies are formed. A conscientious leader leaves a legacy behind.

There's a major difference between a dictatorial manager and an influential leader. A dictatorial manager issues orders but hardly ever becomes involved. An influential leader delegates and at the same time becomes involved as much as possible. Influential leaders motivate others by mastering and then modelling skills such as effective listening, communication, and accepting feedback and constructive criticisms. Influential leaders transform lives. They equip followers and then transform them into leaders. You can follow the leader who is following God. The ministry, the business, the work that you have begun will not end in a vacuum but will be carried through to the next generations.

Keep on praying. I hear the sound of an abundance of revival rain. The land is thirsting for a refreshing. Before the fire came down, Elijah prayed unto God (1 Kings 18:36–39). Before the rain came down, Elijah prayed (1 Kings 18:36–39; James 5:17–18). Samson's last and greatest victory over the Philistines came after he prayed unto God. He slew more Philistines on the day that he died than he ever did before in his life (Judges 16:30).

Chapter 29
An Eternal Perspective in a Temporal World

Victory over Sin and Satan

Nobody can experience victory over sin and Satan without prayer. Prayer for the saints is not an optional weapon, but a very necessary weapon. Adam and Eve lived in a temporal world; however, they forgot that they were not living for themselves. They were given the gift of reproduction. In turn, Adam was supposed to pass on the precepts of God to his offspring.

From the commandment "to multiply," we learn that their placement on earth was not mainly for a temporal purpose. They needed to keep the eternal perspective of their calling and commission in mind—they were God's first ambassadors to humanity. Adam and Eve missed the vision. They yielded to the devil's wiles and corrupted their faculties. Sin came in. In Genesis 5:26, we see man begin to call upon the name of the Lord. God answers and gives victory.

Sin is not a developmental deviation that occurred during organogenesis. It is a carefully orchestrated plan of the devil to separate man from God. The entire creation, from the fall, groans as a woman in travail: man, beast, and plant life inclusive. It groans because of the impact, futility, and bondage that it is subjected to because of sin. But amidst the groaning, God gives us hope for a better future in Christ—the second Adam. Receive him today and have a new experience. Even the Holy Spirit groans while he intercedes for us.

After the agony of birth pangs will come the joy of the new birth. Man was subjected to death so that he would learn to appreciate life ... not only life, but a more abundant life. In Romans 8:22–23, God gives us a complex simile involving birth pangs, adoption, and the redemption of the body. Jesus Christ came to earth on a rescue mission to ensure that we have a more abundant life (1 Corinthians 15:57–58). He exposed the corruption of sin, but he didn't stop there. He also showed us the glorious future of the believer (1 Corinthians 15:19; 2 Timothy 4:6–8).

A Vision of the Rapture of the Church

When I was nineteen years old, the Lord showed me a vision that I'll never forget. He brought me in the spirit back to my old homestead. As I sat on the front porch, the trumpeting call came that Jesus was on his way—the rapture of the church had come. Everyone ran towards the intersection where three streets met.

I couldn't see Jesus because of the brilliance of the light above, but in my spirit, I knew he was there. I looked towards the cemetery on the grounds of the Presbyterian Church on the slope. The earth shook, tombs began to open, and people dressed in white began coming out. I saw the risen dead rising, as if on wings, into the air.

I held tightly to my mother's hand, but suddenly she separated from me and was rising to the sky with her older cousin, whom we respectfully called Mum.

There was great wailing everywhere as the people who were left behind tried desperately to rise into the sky but couldn't. The feet of the lost stampeded the ground like elephants on the plains. My cries rang out in the night for Mama, but she was leaving me behind. She, along with other people, were going up to meet Jesus. Suddenly, a voice said to everyone, "Return to earth. The rapture is not for a while yet." Those who had risen into midair returned to the earth. I did not see the person who spoke. A voice spoke to me saying, "Go read Psalm 37 and then pray." The scene before me suddenly disappeared. I snapped out of the vision immediately. My body was trembling like a leaf caught in a hurricane.

I wasn't saved at that time. If that had been the real snatching away of the church, I would have been left behind. I began to pray and intercede. My life, my sanity, depended upon prayer. For the next while, even to this day, I meditated on Psalm 37. It is an awe-inspiring passage of scripture. These verses have left an indelible mark upon my mind:

Delight thyself also in the LORD: and he shall give thee the desires of thine heart. Commit thy way unto the LORD; trust also in him; and he shall bring it to pass. And he shall bring forth thy righteousness as the light, and thy judgment as the noonday. (Psalm 37:4–6)

My soul could not rest in peace until I placed my life into the hands of the Lord. I learned how to pray; now I'm not fearful that I'll be left behind when Jesus comes to snatch his bride away.

As I've said times and time before, I have made prayer a priority in my life. Through prayer and intercession, I have experienced many personal breakthroughs over life's challenges.

I join with the Apostle Paul in saying, "Now thanks be unto God, which always causeth us to triumph in Christ, and maketh manifest the savour of his knowledge by us in every place" (2 Corinthians 2:14). Jesus paid the price that we could not afford because we were in bondage to the slave master—sin.

Pressing Forward

Today we can move forward in the victory that was purchased for us through Christ at Calvary. We don't have to gaze back, nostalgically, at that which was lost at the fall; we can look towards that which has been restored and gained through the crucifixion.

Through Christ's meritorious work on the cross, we can walk in total victory. Christ's righteous DNA has been transferred to us. We have no excuse to live lives of defeat. Every child of God who does not learn to use the weapons of defense and offense that God has given him will be miserably defeated by the devil and his minions.

We are pilgrims and sojourners. We are seeking, like Abraham, that city having foundations, whose builder and maker is God (John 14:1-3; Hebrews 11:10). Only those who are transformed by the precious blood of Jesus Christ will enter that city (Luke 21:36).

The devil knows that his head was crushed at Calvary. When Jesus went to the cross, he didn't just win the victory over a mitigation of sin; he won an everlasting, extensive victory over sin. Jesus Christ conquered sin; he slam-dunked sin and trampled it under his feet. The blood of Jesus is still efficacious to cleanse man from the corruption and defilement of sin. No one needs to die in his sin (Romans 8:1–3).

Jesus has already conquered and vanquished Satan and sin, our most ferocious enemies. You and I are guaranteed victory through Christ Jesus. Consider the biblical examples of those who won the victory over sin and Satan.

Satan, sin, and the world system were personified in Pharaoh, Egypt, and bitter servitude. But look what the LORD did. He sent forth his Son, Jesus, personified in the man Moses. God saved Moses from premature death; he emancipated the children of Israel from the land of Egypt on eagle's wings (Exodus 2:23–25, 19:4). The children of Israel cried unto God. They placed an S.O.S call to Jehovah, the covenant God. God heard and delivered them from Egypt. He brought them out with a strong and mighty hand (Psalm 34:15; 1 Peter 3:12). God hears and answer those who call upon him in prayer and supplication.

God took the children of Israel through the Red Sea on dry ground (Exodus 12–15). When they went through the clouds and the mist, they experienced something that was synonymous with the ordinance of water baptism (1 Corinthians 10:1–4). But the pursuing Egyptians perished in the midst of the sea. In this we see an epitome of the crushing of the serpent's head. We get the picture of the fate of the unsaved, and a clear understanding of what it means to be lost and undone without God and his Son.

Another example in which the children of God won a great victory over Satan can be seen in the showdown between David and Goliath. Christ, personified in David, went up against Satan, personified in the giant, Goliath of Gath. Goliath was armed with his sophisticated weapons of warfare; David had only a sling. David gathered five stones, but he needed only one to bring the giant down.

Jesus was destined to be crucified only once. He would strike the devil only once in the head. Likewise, David needed to release only one stone, because he was a personification of Jesus and what he would do to the monstrosity of sin (1 Samuel 17:44–51). Jesus would die, but only once.

When the giant went down with a thunderous crash, David hastened to the place and pounced upon him. He decapitated the giant and brought the head back to the king. David brought back the evidence of what had been accomplished. Jesus won a major victory over sin and Satan. He aimed for the head of the devil and bruised it, as the first messianic prophecy said (Genesis 3:15). Man's redemption was purchased. Jesus brought the blood evidence to the holy of holies in heaven and performed the duties of the high priest.

Early in the morning, the third day after the crucifixion and burial of Jesus, pious women came to the tomb seeking Jesus, only to find him alive again. Jesus forbade Mary to touch him, because he had not yet ascended into heaven (John 20:17, 19).

Jesus entered the holy of holies of the temple in heaven. Like the high priest, he sprinkled his own blood on the mercy seat as an everlasting atonement for man's sins. His blood declared that once and for all man has been reconciled to God, his Maker. The blood of goats and beasts was no longer necessary (Hebrews 9:11–12, 24–28).

Jesus Christ now sits at the right hand of His Majesty as our intercessor. He has an unchangeable, everlasting priesthood. Jesus travelled the road before us; therefore, he is acquainted with our infirmities. He lives, so we can live also. We have a divine connection with him through prayer. We couple fasting with prayer to heighten our intimacy with him.

Jesus spoiled principalities and powers. He disarmed the host of hell at Calvary. Jesus stated that he would be three days and three nights in the heart of the earth (Matthew 12:40).

When Jesus arose from the dead, he dealt the devil and all those who defied the holy ordinances of God a severe blow—just like he did Pharaoh and all those who defied God's holy ordinances.

On resurrection morning, Jesus stunned the hosts of hell and left them defeated and confounded. Jesus is alive!

"Fear not, Brother John, but listen to my testimony. I am not he who was alive and now dead; but I am he that was dead and now I am alive. I am alive and will be forevermore. Not only this, John, but I hold in my hands the keys of hell and of death. What I open no man can shut, and what I shut no man can open. I and only I have the keys" (Revelation 1, 3, paraphrased).

The saints have the keys to the kingdom, but Christ has the keys of hell and death. We have full access to the kingdom; therefore, we have the power to bind and loose. You have the power, in the name of Jesus. Jesus has already crippled all the obstacles that would try to hinder or impede his work of mercy to the generations. The dispensation of the gospel is now at its peak, because Jesus will soon be putting in his appearance.

Prophetic disclosures attest to the fact that we are now in the period of grace. If you have keen eyes and a spiritual sense, you'll notice that the spread of the gospel is greatly accelerating around the globe. The heralds of mercy are positioned in the waste and desolate places of the earth. The ambassadors of the gospel are taking the Great Commission over the great panoramic expanse of the universe. The empowered ambassadors of the gospel are not limited by present or visible territorial limits or limitations. We are equipped with television, radio, Internet, and satellite. Jesus gave us authority to take the gospel universally. We can do all things through him who strengthens us (Acts 1:8; Philippians 4:13). Prophetic declarations and prophetic decrees are now breaking forth in full manifestation and fulfillment. When you see these things happening, look up, because redemption is at hand.

Yes, he who opposes righteousness is behaving as if he is wearing the crown and carrying the sceptre. The devil behaves as if he is the one who is seated on the throne of glory, but soon we shall see the King of heaven emerge in all his splendour and glory. He will wage the last war against the dragon, which is called the old serpent and Satan. Jesus will wrest the sceptre from the hands of the impersonator.

Satan never had the privilege of wearing the crown, because God never called him king. God calls Satan the prince of the air. A prince only bears the title of prince, but he never wears the crown until he is crowned king. Jesus is still the king. The devil was never given everlasting dominion; his reign has always been temporary and his power limited. Let the devil huff, and let the devil puff. But never let him blow your house down.

In this modern world, we deal with the monster of effeminacy. Sometimes it's hard to identify the real man. A real man is a man with moral decency. A real man is a man who will not inveigle the innocent to surrender her chastity. A real man is a man who will stand up and take responsibility for his actions. A real man will stand up and be the foundational stone God has created him to be. He will not behave like a basement sissy, but like the strong leader he is called to be.

The heralds of God must continue to let man know, without apology, that his only terminus is God. God made him from the dust, and to the dust God will bring him again. The religionist needs to know that no man can come to God except through Christ Jesus.

Jesus has the power to save to the utmost. The work which the Master began continues in perpetuity. He also said that greater works shall the apostles, and subsequently us, do. I don't know what God saved you from, but I'm thankful for the day that he saved me.

Today my soul is nourished by the draughts of good things that I am drinking from the spiritual fountain. Today my soul magnifies God, and with my spirit and my mouth I give him praise. I enter his presence lifting holy hands—we are still covenant partners.

There is a five-fold coming together of the governmental office of Jehovah—not as some reckon it to be, but as God intended for it to be (Ephesians 4:7–13). Prayer is the glue that holds everything in Christendom together. Prayer is the source that gives the engine of a ministry or a movement power. No prayer, no power. We are advancing towards perfection and towards the finish line.

Back in the days of antiquity, Abraham, the first international evangelist, built an altar of worship unto God and for the glory of God. That altar typified one of the purposes of the church. She is called to be a worshipper of Jehovah. The church was called so that she might be a living witness to the rest of humanity and that she should present herself before God as a living sacrifice, holy and acceptable unto God. It is her reasonable service.

As the kingdom of God advanced, we see that Moses was charged with the building of the tabernacle in the wilderness, which was a type and shadow of the person, work, and office of Christ. The brazen altar was a picture of Calvary and the work of redemption. The laver and the water depicted a washing by the water of the Word. As man came to the laver, he stared at a picture of his depravity. He saw himself as he really is.

The candlestick was emblematic of Jesus Christ, the light of the world.

The table with the loaves was symbolic of the body of Jesus that would be broken for all, and of fellowship and the holy ordinance of communion.

The golden altar of incense was a portrayal of prayer and intercession. The incense carried with it a double witness.

Firstly, it witnessed that prayer should enter the nostrils of God as a sweet smelling savour. Secondly, the smoke shielded the face of the high priest so that he would not see the brilliance of God's face and die.

A veil separated the holy place from the holy of holies. It was bedecked with figures of embroidered Cherubim. The veil served as a barrier that shielded the face of His Holiness from sinful man. It also testified that because of sin, man was separated, eternally, from God. No man can look upon the face of God and live (Leviticus 16:2).

The ordinary man had no access to the throne of grace then, only the high priest. Once yearly, on the Day of Atonement, the high priest entered the mercy seat in the holy of holies. Before he entered, he meticulously prepared himself. He had to wash himself and then attire himself appropriately. He couldn't enter the presence of Jehovah half naked, as that would be irreverent and disrespectful.

The high priest had different sets of garments that he wore on the Day of Atonement: one in the morning and one in the evening (Leviticus 16:4). He couldn't even wear the same clothes that he wore outside when he entered the presence of God. Neither could he wear outside the same garment that we wore when he made atonement before the Father.

Once the high priest finished his work, he discarded, in a designated place, the garment he wore when officiating in the holy of holies. He would never wear them again. He would then wash himself with water in the holy place and put on other garments (Leviticus 16:23–24).

The Old Testament taught us that only the high priest was authorized to burn incense before God. The high priest couldn't enter the presence of the holy God except he first infiltrated the atmosphere with sweet smelling incense. He could then pass through the veil. As he entered the holy of holies, he came face to face with the mercy seat and the Cherubim. God would speak to him from between the Cherubim.

After all things were made manifest in Christ Jesus, the veil was rent and man could come boldly to the throne of grace and find mercy and pardon for his soul.

God allowed Solomon instead of David to build the temple. This temple superseded the tabernacle in the wilderness. It was constructed from the same blueprint that God gave Moses. Both the tabernacle and the temple were places of worship, prayer, and intercession.

We see the destruction and reconstruction of the temple of Jerusalem. We see the contribution of people such as Ezra, Zerubbabel, and Haggai. We read how Nehemiah, by divine revelation, learned of the shame that was being experienced by the people of God. Prophetic declaration was about to be fulfilled. Nehemiah considered the dismal situation and set out on a venture to rebuild the walls and gate of Jerusalem.

Later in time, we see the erection of the synagogue, and today we enjoy the luxury of majestic cathedrals of worship.

What do the tabernacle, the temple, and the church have in common? These monuments were, and are, places where sacrifices, prayers, and intercessions were made regularly. Does the church make sacrifices today? Yes, she does. She brings the sacrifice of praise into the house of the Lord. She offers up to God the sacrifices of thanksgiving.

Every aspect of the tabernacle—its structure, furniture, and the priesthood are described in awesome particularity. Everything was perfectly detailed. These things weren't recorded solely because they were markers of Jewish customs and etiquette. The recording is also for our information and learning.

A. The tabernacle offers us a sneak preview of heaven—the dwelling place of God. (Hebrews 9:24; 1 Kings 8:27, 49–50). David envisioned heaven and shared his thoughts with us in Psalm 24:3–4.

B. The tabernacle presented us with a picture of the Saviour and his earthly ministry. Christ was personified in the tabernacle and its furnishings. He is our sovereign king, our Saviour, our Redeemer, and our healer.

C. The tabernacle teaches us about relationship. Without relationship, no man could stand before God. God is envisioned traversing his way from the mercy seat in the holy of holies towards man. The personal sacrifice of Jesus at the brazen altar made it possible for man to find his way to the mercy seat and to the Father. God has given us his word that he is with us. Emmanuel means, God with us. Because of Jesus, we can have a close and intimate relationship with the Father and receive answers to our prayers. Man left God, but God has not left man. There was an eternal perspective to Jesus' mission to earth. God will be with his people forever (Matthew 28, 20; Revelation 21:3).

D. The brevity of Christ's life as a human, and his ministry, were also seen in the tabernacle. The tabernacle was temporary. Jesus would be here, in the flesh, temporarily. The tabernacle was broken down and carried from place to place when the children of Israel were in transition. Jesus never tarried in one place for long when he was here. He was always moving. Jesus' body was broken for all, just as the tabernacle was broken down when in transition.

E. Moses placed within the Ark of the Covenant the rod of Aaron that blossomed, a golden pot of manna, and the Decalogue (Exodus 16:33–34; Numbers 17:10; Hebrews 9:3–4). Just as a rod is a symbol of authority, Jesus is the ultimate authority in heaven and in earth. Manna was the food that was given to the Israelites as they travelled to the Promised Land. The manna was prototypical of Jesus Christ, the bread of life, broken for all. The Decalogue is the Law, which was fulfilled in Jesus (Matthew 5:17).

F. A very intriguing thing about the tabernacle is that it had but one entrance. It was evident that anyone who would gain entry to the tabernacle must enter through the one door. Jesus presented himself as "The way, the Truth and the Life." Nobody, man or woman, can access the Father except through him. Anyone who tries to enter by any other route is a thief and a robber (John 10:9–18).

In their encampment in the wilderness, the tribe of Judah was stationed, on the east side, close to the entrance of the tabernacle. This meant that one must enter through the tribe of Judah, because the entrance to the tabernacle was on the east side (Numbers 2:3). One does not need a rocket scientist to interpret this. Jesus came from the tribe of Judah. He is the lion and the Lamb. The sceptre blessing was also prophesied upon the tribe of Judah (Genesis 49:8–10; Revelation 5:5).

G. The tabernacle was the gathering place of the children of Israel. It was the place where they assembled to worship Jehovah. The church gathers today to worship the king in spirit and in truth. We speak as the oracles of God. We pray and submit our will to him. God is a Spirit, and those who worship him must do so in spirit and in truth (John 4:23–24).

H. Both women and men played a phenomenal role in the building and furnishing of the tabernacle. God gave the blueprint of the tabernacle and instructions to build to Moses. He anointed Aaron, from the tribe of Levi, to stand in the office of high priest. God called and equipped Bezaleel and Aholiab with wisdom and cunningness to build the tabernacle.

He enlisted the women in the work of the kingdom (Exodus 38:8). They donated their looking glasses to build the brass laver in the outer court of the tabernacle. The act of the women taught us a lesson of submitting and surrendering unto Jesus, who is the author and finisher of our faith. The women willingly submitted what they could not keep unto God in order to gain what they could not lose—redemption through

Christ. It was at this laver that the servant of God would wash himself. This symbolized the washing of water by the Word (Ephesians 5:26).

Not only did the women gave their looking glasses, but the wisehearted spun with their hands. They donated to the building the fine blue, scarlet, and purple linen they had spun. Also, when their hearts were stirred in wisdom, they donated the goat's hair they had spun (Exodus 35:25–26).

These acts of benevolence certainly typified the men and the women who were active in the life of Jesus (Luke 7:37–38; 8:2–3; John 12:3, 18:10). How chivalrous was the deed of the lad who gave his five loaves and two fishes to Jesus! Jesus wrought a great miracle from these (John 6:1–13).

God will never run out of stewards. All he needs to fulfill his purpose are lumps of clay. He is the Master Potter. He can mold those pieces of clay until they become grand, beautiful vessels with carrying capacities. He can fortify them with varying degrees of admirable designs.

God needs vessels that will withstand the fire of testing and that will come out as pure gold after the trial. A broken vessel, a cracked vessel, a marred vessel ... Whatever state your vessel is in, come to Jesus in prayer. He can mend broken vessels (2 Corinthians 4:7).

When we understand the consequences of the fall and how sin has corrupted every aspect of man's being, we can appreciate the goodness of God. God has placed the life-giving gospel of Jesus Christ within us. Paul declares that the ministers of God are stewards of the mysteries of God (1 Corinthians 4:1). He reveals his secrets to his servants, the prophets (Amos 3:7).

Despite all that man has done unto Jesus Christ, God still has mercy upon him, and still imparts unto him the golden nuggets of his Word. The angels in heaven were not privileged to be the recipients of the stupendous truths—his infallible Word. Because of Christ, the mortal man now preaches not only the crucifixion, but also the resurrection from the dead. Those who are crucified with him are also resurrected with him; therefore, they are destined to reign with him in glory. The words expostulated to the unrepentant sinner can be found in Luke 13:3. The words dispensed to the regenerate are found in Job 27:5 and Revelation 2:10, 3:11. Although made of clay, we the ambassadors of God have the treasure of his Word within us (2 Corinthians 4:7).

The Word of God remains as authentic today as the day God inspired the holy men and women to pen them. It is what it is, and so shall it be forever (Matthew 7:24–29; Luke 10:16–20). A sheep fallen into a ditch will struggle to escape; it will never settle until the shepherd comes and frees it. Likewise, the true child of God who falls because of sin will struggle to get out of it. He will not be contented in a life of sin. The person who hears the Word of God and takes heed will be likened unto the person who builds upon the rock and overcomes the storm, but the one who rejects the Word of God is compared to one who builds on the sand and perishes in the storm.

If we endure the pangs of the moment, we will reap the blessed joy of tomorrow. The pleasures of the day are so enticing; therefore, it is extremely difficult, but not impossible, to resist the temptation to indulge. Today's pleasures are nothing to be compared to the joys that we will share with our Lord and Saviour Jesus Christ tomorrow.

Time is swiftly gliding by. I have learned many valuable lessons over many years, and one of them is: no enemy can defeat me in public except he has defeated me in solitude. If the enemy can get into my mind, he can change my perspective on life. He can change the way I view the Lord and the people whom he has appointed me to shepherd. If I must triumph over the enemy of my soul, I need to be able to see beyond the natural realm into the spiritual realm (2 Corinthians 4:18).

Don't lose heart; instead, guard your heart. You might be suffering today, but God will restore unto us all that the enemy has robbed us of (2 Corinthians 4:16). Suffering for the sake of Christ is unique to every believer. It produces much-needed self-control. It cuts us down to size so that God can use us even more. (Psalm 119:67–68). The penalty for disobedience came after our progenitor, Adam, went astray. Suffering debases the human inflated ego so that God can bring him up.

Before Jesus could bring us up, he had to come down (Hebrew 12:1–2). Jesus came to earth with the knowledge that his earthly mission had an eternal perspective. He stuck to it, even in the presence of severe temptations and sufferings. He fought, he finished, and he won. As the adopted son of Pharaoh's daughter, Moses was destined to be the next crown prince of Egypt. Pharaoh's daughter saw him as a gift from the god of the River Nile. But while man had a plan, God had a better plan. While man saw the small picture, God saw the bigger picture. Moses would not become the next Pharaoh, but the next deliverer of the children of Israel from the land of Egypt and bitter bondage. The Bible says that he refused to be named the grandson of Pharaoh. He forsook Egypt (Hebrews 11:24–29).

Daily we witness the sufferings of this present world.

Physical maladies: These rob and restrict us so that we cannot enjoy the pleasures of life. The pain that comes with the maladies is sometimes excruciating. I have lost track of the many times I have prayed over people with cancer, diabetes, CVA, MI, hypertension, brain aneurysm, eye diseases, and other conditions.

Laborious employment: We now know what the Lord meant when he said unto Adam: "In the sweat of thy face shalt thou eat bread, till thou return unto the ground; for out of it was thou taken: for dust thou art, and unto dust shall thou return" (Genesis 3:19). Man must work hard for his living.

God gave Adam carte blanche over the earth and every other created order. Man was privileged to be fruitful, to multiply, to replenish the earth, and to subdue. He was to dress the garden and keep it. Adam was the watchman and security guard over the Garden of Eden. The word "subdue," in both Greek and Hebrew, means to conquer and to bring into subjection.

It also carries with it military connotations. Adam did not subdue as he should; therefore, he lost his job and his home. Not only this, but today the entire creation groans. If we do not subdue the enemy, the enemy will subdue us.

Mental and psychological illnesses: Many people cannot function normally in society; therefore, they must be institutionalized. My work in the psychiatric or mental institution has brought me face-to-face with suicidal clients who have leapt over bridges, slashed their wrists, cut off the private parts of their bodies, mutilated themselves, and swallow pills or other substances in an attempt to find relief from their distresses.

I've worked with people suffering from dissociative identity disorder, schizophrenia, and depression. I've been acquainted with those suffering from delusions of persecution and delusions of grandeur. Betrayal, abandonment, failure, sickness, or a lack of zest for life are but a few of the things that drove them to these extremes.

These things illustrate that people need Jesus. God wants you and me to be catalysts of change in the lives of desperate people.

Undoubtedly, we will suffer for the sake of Jesus Christ. As the apostle says, all who live for Christ will suffer persecution (2 Timothy 3:12). Jesus foretold that we would be persecuted for righteousness (Matthew 5:11, 10:18).

Jesus Christ is the fulfillment of the law. The penitent can now come boldly into the presence of Almighty God and cry out for forgiveness (Hebrews 6:19–20, 10:19–25). Jesus still sits as mediator between man and the Father (John 17:20–22). He prayed that the disciples would be one. We should be praying for each other that we would be one in Christ Jesus. It cannot be overstated that unity gives strength.

Pray without ceasing. I know what prayer can do. It's impossible to be a servant of God without prayer, because our adversary, the devil, is always standing by to harass and challenge us. The goal of the saint's prayer should always be for the glory of God. The challenges of the time call not just for prayer, but intercessory prayer.

Fatal Distractions

The efficacious blood of Jesus Christ still stands as the continuous bond that unites the believer with the Father. Jesus arose from the grave with resurrection power, and he ascended on high in a blaze of resplendent glory.

The greatest bond that exists between people is the blood bond. The devil continues to wage war against the saints, but he will never be successful. He can never break asunder the blood bond between God and his subjects. Nothing shall be able to separate us from God the Father and our Lord Jesus Christ (Romans 8:31–39).

We must live in this temporal world, and we will suffer many things at the hands of the adversaries as we undertake and carry out the work of the kingdom. Booby traps and obstacles surround us, carefully orchestrated and set to distract us from our main focus. We must discern them in the spirit and leap over them. We must pray that God will give us discerning eyes so that we can see ahead that which is set to entangle our feet and cause us to stumble and trip. We can choose from among many variables, but we have chosen the better part: to carry out the mandate of the kingdom.

Many of our good intentions can be the very hindrances that stop us from executing the mandate God entrusted unto us. In John 11:21–22, Martha says to Jesus: "Lord, if thou hadst been here, my brother had not died. But I know, that even now, whatsoever thou wilt ask of God, God will give it thee." We can assume that she believed in the power of Jesus Christ to deliver.

Martha confessed that Jesus was the anointed Christ, the Son of God. Based on her expressed words, she also believed that Jesus shared exceptional intimacy with God. The Father in heaven always answered the prayer of Jesus. She had the right dogma or lingo, but when challenged to put her faith into action, she went silent. When Jesus arrived, she commented that if he would pray, God would answer his prayer. The supernatural was now ready to be manifested.

Martha was one of the vital links in the recovery of Lazarus. She needed to believe; however, she still expressed concerns: "Lord, by this time he stinketh: for he hath been dead four days." (John 11:39). She had faith in the future, but was lacking in the "now faith." Martha had all the right words. She didn't fail to express them; but she failed to act on them.

Jesus went to the home of Lazarus, Mary, and Martha. Not everyone had the privilege of entertaining Jesus while he was in his physical form, but this family did. Martha's mind, however, was preoccupied with many things. Having too many things on her mind robbed her of the most essential thing—the indispensable Word of God and fellowship with the Saviour. In the presence of the Lord, everything must fade away (Psalm 16:11). There is nothing more beneficial than basking in the presence of the Lord.

In this hour of grace, we need to know the Lord Jesus Christ and have a right relationship with him. Jesus never implied that the physical needs of man were unimportant, but he did say that feeding the soul was critical (Matthew 4:4).

We need to feed the belly nutrients, but at times bowing down before him in worship, adoration, and prayer is all we need to do. Worship from the heart, mind, soul, and body is of utmost importance to God. Jesus Christ will meet you right where you are.

Don't make the fatal mistake of spending your life accomplishing all that you can, but leaving your soul unfed and unattended. One day everyone must stand before the Maker and give an account of how they spent their time on earth. You are either saved or lost. You are either with Christ or against him. If you miss heaven, you cannot miss hell (Galatians 6:6–10).

What time is it? It's time to pray and intercede for people everywhere. Let us not be worldly wise. Let us not become encumbered with everything and leave our soul neglected and famished. It's time to seek the Lord. It's time to pray. Jesus will meet you at the point of your need. Cry unto God from where you are. Jonah did from the belly of the whale.

Delivered from the Gunman

Some time ago in a night vision, I beheld a gunman about to attack one of my brothers and his family. I stood upon my feet and interceded for the safety of my brother and his family. I brought my entire family before the Lord. This was on a Wednesday night. On Saturday afternoon, my brother and his family contacted me. They related an event that sent me back to my knees in worship and thanksgiving unto God.

Thursday night had been very warm, so he fell asleep with the bedroom window partly opened. His wife awoke just in time to see a gunman trying to gain entrance to their home through the open window. She shouted at the man, and he moved a few feet away. As the man walked away, he looked back and they could hear him saying: "You are all so lucky; you are all so lucky."

God saved my brother and his family from being massacred by that gunman. Somebody's life is dependent upon your prayer.

Ten Year Mystery Solved

Once I ministered in a local church. The church clerk spoke to me after the service about her concern for a son she had not heard from in ten years. This son had disappeared without a trace.

I promised to go to her home on Wednesday, when we would fast and intercede unto the Lord concerning her son, which we did.

"Father," I prayed, "if this son is alive, send us word about him and his whereabouts. If he is dead, we are prepared to receive this news also. We need a word from you quickly."

We waited. By week's end, she'd received a call from England from her son's wife—a wife she didn't know about. Her son had left the country for the land of his birth without telling anyone. Not only was he married, but he had two little girls. The wife had called because she and the grandchildren wanted to visit at Christmas. Her son was alive, but he was in and out of the mental hospital. The family was reunited that Christmas—after ten years. The son is in treatment and doing much better. I know what prayer can do. Distance and time do not limit God.

Don't become engrossed in things that will not satisfy or be of benefit to the spiritual man. Jesus waits to fill the empty void in your life (Isaiah 55:1–3). We are indeed in a temporal world, but our perspectives are eternal. Pray! Intercede until God answers.

Chapter 30
Wait with Joyful Hope and Expectation

You have fasted. You have prayed. You have interceded. Now, wait upon God with expectancy. Look for the results. Continue to pray without ceasing (1 Thessalonians 5:17).

Expectant couples live each day waiting for the baby to arrive during the ninth month after conception. While they wait, they prepare the homestead to accommodate the coming baby.

The mother-to-be goes for routine check-ups, she sticks to a healthy diet, and she avoid anything that will harm or jeopardize herself and the child. As the day of delivery approaches, the mother can feel in her body and spirit that the birth is eminent. When labor pangs begin, she knows the day has arrived: "I will stand upon my watch, and set me upon the tower, and will watch to see what he will say unto me, and what I shall answer when I am reproved" (Habakkuk 2:1).

According to The Free Dictionary, the word "wait" means to abide until something happens; to remain or rest in expectation; or to serve as a waiter or waitress. "Wait" bears the connotation of expectation. We look with eager hope and anticipation for the answer to our prayers. I kept on looking, because I expected something to happen. Wait also means that one should keep busy while waiting. We don't mope about while we wait upon God; we continue to do service in the kingdom.

Car, Come Forth!

In an earlier chapter, I told you how my car engine failed. Well, let me tell you how I received my car. In December 2008, the regional overseer was speaking at my church on a Sunday night. He informed us that he was going to ask us to do something that might look "stupid" to the natural thinker, but not to those looking through the eyes of the Spirit. He continued, "Walk out of your seats, come to the altar, and turn around seven times while repeating: 'This coming year will be the year of my turn-around.'" The Lord had told me before that he was going to give me a car.

It took a rebuke from the Lord to get me to walk out of my seat to the altar that evening, but I did. I turned around seven times while repeating, "2008 will be my year of a turn around." The first thing on my heart was the car I desperately needed. God said that he was going to give me a car; therefore, I kept on looking for a car. Every chance I got, I claimed that car. I began to speak into the atmosphere: "Car, come forth! Car, come forth! God promised me a car. Car, come forth!"

January, February, March, April, and then May came ... and there was no car. The Lord promised me a car, and I kept looking for it and speaking the Word of God into the atmosphere. "In the name of Jesus, car, come forth!" I interceded for that car. June came, and God gave me a car—free of costs.

The next hurdle to overcome was the high insurance rate I'd have to pay. I began to pray and ask God for reasonable insurance coverage. I called several brokers, but was discouraged by the steep prices. I decided not to call any more companies; instead, I revisited two of the ones I'd previously called. These two promised me coverage at a low price. Terms and conditions made this price available only to people who'd had insurance coverage within the past five years, but I had no previous coverage.

The first company took my driver's license number a second time and returned to me with shocking news. "Cordell, you have insurance coverage, and it is within the time limit specified for this cheaper insurance coverage. You are covered under the insurance of Mr. and Mrs. J. B."

In 2003, this couple had placed me on their insurance plan, because they were going out of town for an extended period. When they returned, they didn't remove my name; I was still covered.

I received insurance coverage according to the terms and conditions listed under the special offer. I already had comprehensive coverage and didn't even know that I had it. I waited patiently for God, and he delivered as he promised. I kept on praying and interceding while looking with great expectation and ardent hope for the fulfillment of the promise. It came in God's appointed time. God always deliver, in season.

I know what prayer can do. I am blessed of God and highly favoured. Even if God hadn't give me a car, I would still worship him, pray, and intercede as I ought to.

And because he saw it pleased the Jews, he proceeded further to take Peter also. (Then were the days of unleavened bread.) And when he had apprehended him, he put him in prison, and delivered him to four quaternions of soldiers to keep him; intending after Easter to bring him forth to the people. Peter therefore was kept in prison: but prayer was made without ceasing of the church unto God for him … And when Peter was come to himself, he said, Now I know of a surety, that the Lord hath sent his angel, and hath delivered me out of the hand of Herod, and from all the expectation of the people of the Jews. (Acts 12:3-5, 11)

Peter kept his cool, even in the wake of a crisis. God gave him such peaceful composure that he could fall asleep between two soldiers. He was bound with chains and naked, but he slept. The church kept on praying and waiting. God answered their prayers and delivered Peter (Psalm 37:7, 40:1–4, 62:5–6).

God always speaks to his people. Wait upon the Lord and be of good courage, and he will strengthen your heart (Psalm 27:14).

Comprehensive Coverage and Protection for the Journey

The Lord gave me a word for a sister. He said to tell her that she would be going on a journey and must fill up, because she was going to need the power of the Holy Ghost to help her. Then the Lord spoke to me saying, "You will be going on a similar, but longer, journey. Your mother is going to be sick, and the lot will fall on you to take care of her. When you get there, I will be sending you through the churches. You are going to encounter demonic forces, but I will be with you and I will protect you." It was Wednesday morning. I passed on the word to the sister and we went into a time of intercessory prayer.

On Friday evening, the sister called to say that her journey had begun. Her mother had passed away, and she had to leave for the funeral. We prayed again. The next Wednesday evening, eight days from the revelation, my journey began. My mother suffered a cerebrovascular accident (stroke). I went overseas to my ailing mother's side. As the Holy Spirit revealed, the lot fell upon me to remain and care for my mother, who was also blinded in both eyes by glaucoma.

I cared for my mother from July to September. I never had time to go through any church, because I was exhaustingly busy. My return flight to Canada was booked for Wednesday, September 14. My mother was doing better, so I decided to return to Canada on the date planned.

The day prior to my departure, the Holy Spirit spoke to me: "Do not return to Canada tomorrow, because your work here is not finished."

"I'm going back tomorrow," I told the Lord.

I packed my luggage and began my journey to the Sangster International Airport, Montego Bay, Jamaica W.I., the next morning. All along the way, the Holy Spirit kept saying to me, "Do not get on that plane today. Go back home. Your work here is not finished." I insisted on returning to Canada that day.

At the airport, I collected my luggage and wended my way towards check-in. The Holy Spirit spoke to me again: "Have I not told you that you are not returning to Canada today because your work here is not finished?"

The Air Canada Boeing 747 jumbo jet was at the hangar getting ready for its flight back to Canada. I was in trouble with the Lord. I prayed and repented. I picked up my luggage again and turned my face towards my native home. God had told me to turn back, because my work was not finished.

That Friday, the Lord said to me, "Go to that church on yonder hill on Sunday. There is work there for you to do."

I went, and for the next four years I worked with the churches as the Lord directed. I did useful and effective work amongst the people, especially the youth. In four years, God brought me through a total of seventeen churches. Many people came to know the Lord as Saviour, were baptized, and brought into fellowship with the churches. I beheld as the Lord filled many people with the Holy Ghost and with fire. He also bestowed upon them the gifts of the Spirit. I watched with a thankful heart as God healed their diseases and delivered them from satanic oppression.

As the Lord had said, I did encounter demonic opposition, some of which I told you about earlier. But God was true to his words. He delivered me from them all. Fasting, prayer, and intercession became the major entities of my daily routine.

The Weapon Was Formed, but It Did Not Prosper

I was conducting a week of crusade in one of the churches—Sunday to Friday. Instantaneously, a few people decided that they did not like me—the girl from Canada. They persecuted me and tried to sabotage the meetings by not coming and encouraging others not to come. Attendance was very scant Monday to Wednesday; however, I dedicated a part of my time to intercessory prayers unto God.

On the Wednesday night as I stood in the pulpit preaching, everything suddenly went ghastly black before me. I couldn't move from where I was, because I could hardly see a step ahead. Although the electric lights were burning brightly, there was such a black-out in the spiritual realm insomuch that only silhouettes of the people could be seen. They could hear me, but I couldn't hear them. The devil had released a host of demons to attack me. They surrounded the sanctuary. There were two-headed demons coming at me. I began to pray warfare prayer, and the congregation joined me.

As we prayed, the darkness dispelled and the demonic forces disappeared. Church was dismissed. I went home very tired. I lay across the bed on my back and closed my eyes.

Suddenly, I heard a noise like the buzz of many bees. The demons left the church, but they did not leave the territory. They loitered in the vicinity with plans to attack me at home.

I saw demons gathering at the junction where three streets met. They held a conference, and I was the subject of interest. They planned to engage themselves in a race to see which one would get to me first. I was physically tired, because I'd been preaching since Sunday. I was also very concerned about my sick mother and the housekeeper.

I called upon the name of the Lord Jesus Christ as I rebuked, bound, and turned them back. They were persistent and kept on coming. Suddenly, a tall, slim, dark messenger came into my room. He wrapped his arms around my shoulders and said, "Don't worry, daughter, you are well protected." He disappeared.

As soon as he said this to me, the demons scattered in every direction away from my home. God protected me and the members of the household. I remembered the Word of God, which says, "When the enemy shall come in like a flood, the Spirit of the LORD shall lift up a standard against him" (Isaiah 59:19b); "… they shall come out against thee one way, and flee before thee seven ways" (Deuteronomy 28:7).

That night, demons wreaked havoc on the streets, I was told. People couldn't sleep because they were terrorized by menacing demons. I and my household slept like babies. God granted me comprehensive covering and protection. He sent his messenger to deliver me out of the hands of the enemies.

For the eyes of the Lord are over the righteous, and his ears are open unto their prayers: but the face of the Lord is against them that do evil. And who is he that will harm you, if ye be followers of that which is good? (1 Peter 3:12–13)

The eyes of the Lord are upon his people. God has even the hairs of your head numbered (Matthew 10:30).

God has set a seven twenty-four APB (All-Points Bulletin) on every enemy of your soul. Your guardian angel is aware of them and their modus operandi. Wherever they are, God will find them. Those who wait for the Lord will never be ashamed (Psalm 25:3; Romans 10:11). God has you on the top-most line of his agenda. He will answer you in due season, even now.

That man at the pool of Bethesda suffered with impotency for thirty-eight years. The rule of thumb was that anyone who was first to step into the water when it was troubled would be healed of his infirmities. Jesus knew that he was impotent; therefore, he met him where he was.

God can meet you right where you are. Jesus healed this man by his strong and mighty power. You need to bring yourself to that place in the spirit where you can press past people.

Press past the critical; press past the doubtful and unbelieving; press past those who are still walking in the flesh; press past gender barriers; press past social categorization; press past political correctness; press past religious bigotry; press past the hypocritical; and press past physical, mental, and emotional limitations.

You need to press past negativity and unbelief and reach up to Jesus as he reaches down to you.

You need to press into the sphere of the spirit where you can see Jesus. Jesus already knows that you are coming. He will avail himself to meet you by the way.

Did he not do it for Zacchaeus? (Luke 19:1–10)

Did he not do it for the woman with the issue of blood? (Mark 5:25–34)

Did he not do it for the woman by Sychar's well in Samaria? (John 4:1–42)

Did he not do it for Jairus? (Mark 5:22–24)

Did he not do it for the widow of Nain? (Luke 7:11–17)

Did Jesus not do it for the Syrophenician woman's daughter who was possessed with devils? (Mark 7:24–30)

Did he not bring back Lazarus who was dead and buried in the grave for four days? (John 11:43–44)

God saw Meshach, Shadrach, and Abednego in the burning fiery furnace; he saw Daniel in the den of lions; he saw Joseph in the pit and in the prison; he saw baby Moses as he drifted on the crocodile infested River Nile. God is alive and kicking. His eyes are watching you. If God says wait, do not choose the alternative. Wait! God is never a minute too early or a minute too late. He comes in season. When your season comes, nobody can stop it. He is coming. Wait for him. Keep on praying and watching.

The Power of God over Witchcraft

I was the keynote speaker during a week of evangelistic crusade in a certain place. A warlock lived within proximity of the church. He feared neither man nor God.

Crusade continued from Sunday through Friday. On the Thursday night, as I began to minister, I perceived him, in the spirit realm, about to touch the buttons on his boom box. He had said to himself, I am going to turn the volume up very high and drown out the message she is preaching. Nobody will hear her tonight.

I stopped preaching, turned my face towards the house, and cried with a loud voice, "Thou man, if you touch that dial, you will die. The Father rebuke you; the Lord rebuke you; the Holy Spirit rebuke you." Thus says the Lord, "If you and your witchcraft partner do not repent and turn from your wicked ways, God is going to wipe you out."

I saw him as he touched the dial but could not turn it because God gave him a holy shock. His body jolted. He retreated and curled himself, like a fetus, through the rest of the services.

That Saturday morning, the wizard went from his house to three different churches asking to be baptized, because God said that he was going to kill him. The pastor of one of the churches obliged and baptized him that Saturday morning.

I met the warlock face to face the coming Sunday morning. He came to me in the middle of the street, and I braced myself for what was about to happen. He looked at me then shook my hands. "I got baptized," he said, "so I'm a brother now. I am a friend of the church."

The next week I received the report that his partner in iniquity died suddenly in a motor vehicle accident. Upon receiving the news, the warlock barricaded himself inside his house and refused to venture outside. He was afraid because he thought God was going to kill him.

Anyone who messes with Zion must answer to the Father. God has power over lions. God has power over fire. God has power over the works of witchcraft. No witch or warlock has power to hex you, because you are under blood protection. The blood of Jesus Christ, and the seal of the Holy Ghost, are upon you.

Are you under the spell of a witch? Don't worry anymore. God can remove every spell and break every chain. Want to be loosed from that bondage? Seek God wholeheartedly.

It Is a Setup, but No Weapon Formed Shall Prevail, and Judgmental Tongues Shall Be Condemned

A while back I was invited to speak in a certain place. As soon as the invitation was voiced, the Lord spoke to me: "Beware! Haman has hung the gallows. Accept the invitation and watch me destroy the plans of the adversaries." I automatically knew that this was an invitation staged to judge and then persecute me. I accepted the invitation and was booked for the 7:00 p.m. to 9:00 p.m. session. I began, like Esther and Mordecai, to fast and intercede. "Lord, I am in your hands. Let not the wickedness of the wicked prevail against me" (Esther 3–9).

The plot against me was precipitated by the spirits of envy and jealousy, but God saw the "setup" and planned to discomfit the enemy. Knowing what was about to happen, I fasted and prayed from Wednesday to Saturday. I prayed the promises of God:

- God promised to preserve those who walk in his precepts (Psalm 121:7–8).

- God promised that I would not be smitten either by the evil forces of the day or the evil forces that lurk in the darkness of the night (Psalm 91:1–3).

- God promised to protect me from the onslaught of the wicked one (2 Thessalonians 3:3).

- God promised that he would be with me always (Matthew 28:20).

- God promised that hell will not be victorious over me (Matthew 16:18).

✢ God promised to deliver me out of the hands of those enemies who might come masquerading as friends (Luke 22:47–49).

✢ God said that the weapons would be formed, but they would not be prosperous (Isaiah 54:17).

I began to praise God and pray, because not only is he famous for correcting adverse situations, but he is also famous for stopping present orders as well as pending orders.

At the time of the invitation, I was told that three busloads of people were also invited to attend from elsewhere. The Holy Spirit revealed that they were especially invited to critique and condemn me for the Word and the work of God.

I called upon the name of the Lord, who is worthy to be praised. I prayed and then gave God the praise and thanks, because I knew he was about to do something unusual, something supernatural, to deliver me out of the hand of my persecutors.

How did God deliver? He sent down torrential rain on the day in question from 3:00 p.m. until 9:30 p.m. The highways and byways flooded with water. Those persecutors missed death by the skin of their teeth when God washed away the bridge they had barely crossed. They were the only ones in attendance that night. Their sin was exposed. Jehovah, my covenant God, rained out the gathering so that the plot couldn't materialize. God made this declaration in Isaiah 54:15:

"All who maliciously gather against you shall be confounded and fall" (paraphrased). This is one of the blessings of the righteous. God dissolved the plot against me.

The Word of God is profitable unto us. It suffices us in varying capacities. The heavenly Father has recorded in his registry every aspect of our being. Even the very hairs of our heads he has numbered.

There is power in prevailing prayer. Prayer is a potent weapon. Learn how to wield it and then leave the rest to God. You have been praying and fasting about certain conditions. You have gone before God in intercession and supplication. In supplication, we make our requests known to God. All you need to do now is give God thanks and wait on him (Psalm 125:1–5; Proverbs 16:7; Romans 10:11).

The kingdom principle regarding sowing and reaping dictates: "Be not deceived; God is not mocked: for whatsoever a man soweth, that same shall he also reap" (Galatians 6:7). Keep on praying and fasting. God will not let you down. He will not leave the desolate to perish. God has a contingent of angels who encamp about those who fear God and delivers them. He is attentive to the supplications of his people. I know what prayer can do.

Chapter 31
Desperate Situations Call for Desperate Actions

My father was a truck driver, but he loved to ride his bicycle when he wasn't around the wheels. It was close to Easter when the Holy Spirit revealed to me that the devil was about to kill my dad. I asked the Lord how the devil planned to do it, and he told me by traffic accident.

I immediately called a prayer warrior and asked her to fast and intercede with me concerning this accident that was about to happen to my father. We fasted and interceded together on the behalf of my father. We earnestly sought God to reverse that order from hell. I sent forth an edict into the atmosphere commanding all satanic activities against my father to be shut down, in the name of Jesus. After prayer, I sent my dad this message: "Be careful, because the adversary wants your life. But I have prayed for you and asked God to keep you safe."

Three weeks passed, and my father sent me this reply: "Daughter, thank you for praying. On the same day that I received your letter, I was riding my bicycle from the post office. Up came a car from behind and knocked me clear of the bicycle. I was thrown to the one side and the bicycle to the other. The bicycle suffered much damage, but I was spared. I bless the Lord."

Imagine my joy. I called my partner in prayer and together we rejoiced and gave God the glory. "Great is the LORD, and greatly to be praised in the city of our God, in the mountain of his holiness" (Psalm 48:1). Prayer stopped the funeral.

The Pain Is Gone

A few years had elapsed since the accident that should have killed my father, and the devil was still pregnant with the grudge and hatred. Whatever the reasons, the devil was determined to take my father out by an accident. I had visited with my father five months earlier. The last conversation I had with him concerned his soul. He assured me that he had accepted the Lord as his Saviour. I hugged him, prayed for him, and left.

It was a Wednesday night in March, and I was asleep in bed. Suddenly, I began to have a most painful experience. My entire body was in excruciating pain. I groaned loudly. I was happy to awaken from that frightful nightmare, but I sensed that somebody was groaning in severe pain. I did not know who. My body remained in great pain, yet not in pain. The person kept groaning.

Everybody at my home was sleeping peacefully in their beds. My pain wasn't occurring in the natural, but somewhere in the spirit realm. I was picking up somebody's pain.

The groaning became louder, and the pain increased in intensity. I fell on my knees and began to cry and travail in prayer. The more I prayed, the more the person groaned. I asked my heavenly father who was groaning; he kept silent. It dawned on me that the person who was in such great pain wouldn't recover. The Lord was going to, or had already, delivered him/her, but not to life.

Even with this revelation, I kept praying for God to spare the person. Suddenly, after almost three hours, the pain left my body, and the groaning in the spirit realm stopped. Up to this point, I didn't know who was in this great pain, but in my spirit, I knew the person was now gone.

I was troubled, so I continued to pray. No phone calls came Wednesday night, Thursday, or Friday morning. Friday evening came, and the phone rang. "Hello!" It was my brother. He was calling to inform me that our father had passed.

"Excuse me?" I questioned.

"Our father has passed," he repeated.

He had been killed in a traffic accident on Wednesday, but he hadn't passed instantly. Now I understood the groaning and the great pain that I'd sensed in the spirit realm on Wednesday night. I prayed. Why God chose not to bring him back, I do not know.

I didn't see this one coming, because the Lord chose not to show me. I don't know why God brought me through the ordeal with my dad before he passed, but my duty isn't to know the how, why, what, or when. My duty is to give God praise despite the storm. My heavenly Father didn't instruct me to give thanks for everything. He said to give him thanks in every situation (1 Thessalonians 5:18).

Is God still a good God? Yes, he is. Is prayer still a powerful weapon? Yes, it is (Job 1:20–22, 13:15). The captivity of Job turned around when he prayed for his friends. The Lord is still a great God whether he answers with a request granted, request denied, or wait. He is still a great, mighty, loving God, even when he seems silent. Prayer can still change things. Death is deliverance in many instances.

My nightmare was over. My father passed, and I didn't lose my praise.

"I will bless the Lord at all times. His praise shall continually be in my mouth. My soul shall make her boast in the LORD" (Psalm 34:1-2).

I will still make my boast about the goodness of God and the potentiality of prayer. The God of heaven is still God.

Again, No Weapon Formed Shall Prosper

It was on a Tuesday when the Lord spoke to me saying, "The devil is planning to kill you."

"How, Lord?" I asked.

"By an accident. He has issued an edict that you will die, like your father died, by traffic accident. He has sent his juggernauts to execute his summons against you. When you enter a vehicle, remember to buckle your seat belt and do not lean against the doors."

My prayer partner joined with me in intercessory prayer and fasting. "The devil's decree concerning me will not happen. I declare that the Lord is covering me from every angle. I will not be afraid; neither will I be affected by the elements that surround me. The God of heaven is my rock, my shield and my hiding place. God has been known to stop funerals. I shall not die prematurely. God decides when I die. The Lord of my life is mighty in battle. He shall conquer and discomfit the enemy of my soul. He shall vanquish the enemy of my life."

On a Sunday afternoon, I tarried with some youth in prayer. At the end of the prayer time, one young lady asked me to bless and pray through the apartment she'd just rented. We turned south on the one street and then east on another. As she was turning east, the passenger door flew open and swung back and forth. I cried out, "The door! The door!" She panicked and accelerated instead of slowing down. She cleared the intersection and then stopped about a hundred metres later. I reached over, grabbed the swinging door, and slammed it shut. The devil lost again.

The God of heaven who sees ahead and knows ahead saved again. The sword might be drawn, the fiery missile might be released; but they will never accomplish what they set out to do. I place a "return to sender" order on them, in the name of Jesus. I condemn every lying tongue that revolts against me in judgement. And so shall this be for all who trust God and serve him.

I Have Brought You over by Another Way

One of the most trying times of my Christian walk occurred in the years 1989 through 1998. I endured nine long years of hardships, rejection, and mental torture. It was most difficult for me, because I wasn't as mature in the spirit as I am now. I told myself that if I overcame those years, I could overcome anything.

There are some things that happen in life that should not be shared, because they will not edify anyone. It's better to pray and leave them at the foot of Calvary. I quoted before that there is a kingdom principle concerning sowing and reaping. Make no mistake, we will reap the crop from what we have planted (Galatians 6:7).

The program coordinator said something to us interns on the day we entered the School of Ministry internship program. He said: "Welcome to suffering." I wished he was joking, but he wasn't. The furnace will be turned up seven times hotter once you embark upon the mission for God. I had this rude awakening from the very day I received ministerial credentials, until now.

Not only will the "wicked one" try to kill you, but he will also try to kill that which you have given birth to. It's therefore imperative that you erect a wall of prayer around that which you have pushed forth from your spiritual womb. Predators are always on the loose. Anyone who is following Christ or desires to follow him needs to know that the way of the cross is the way of suffering and even death (2 Timothy 2:12).

It was always fascinating to watch the boy and girl cadets at my school practice. Anyone entering the military will tell you that it's not easy, because he or she has to undergo a season of basic training. They must learn how to use weapons of warfare, and they must develop combatant and other skills. A soldier doesn't receive credentials to sit back in a La-Z-Boy chair or a recliner. He is trained, armoured, and deployed to fight in hot battles. You have been divinely selected to serve on the front lines. Not only are we trained to wield weapons, but we must learn how to dodge weapons.

The era in which Timothy ministered was one of distorted morals. A Christian then was not a religious fop who walked around in sartorial elegance, but neither was he a stuff shirt and glutton who sat in the seat of the higher echelons of the religious world, sponging what he could from the hard-working people of society. Christians in the days of Timothy did not repose in four poster beds with satin sheets and down-filled pillows. Christians at that time were men of war and POSW (prisoners of spiritual warfare). Some were always on the run. They were stoned, beaten, burned, crucified, or thrown to ravenous beasts.

In those days, the bigwigs of the Roman Empire opened the arena for sport, and often the "sport" was the Christians. The Christians came face to face with the host of hell and the steamrollers of Satan. The prophet Isaiah wrote that God was pleased to bruise the Lord. It was because of us that this happened.

It was under these often gruesome and trying conditions that Paul exhorted his young protégé, Timothy, to endure hardness as a good soldier of Jesus Christ. (2 Timothy 2:3) In every age, Christians will suffer the same kind of pangs—some more than others.

King David was one of the soldiers in the army of God. There came a time when David— the lion, bear, and giant killer—found himself in a bind in Adullam. The Philistines had garrisoned Bethlehem. David longed for a drink of water from the well of Bethlehem. Three of his valiant men broke through the host of the Philistines and brought him water from the well of his desire. When he received the water, he could not drink it, but instead poured it upon the ground as an offering unto the Lord (2 Samuel 23:15–17). David had his share of suffering, but in his last words to the people of God, he said:

"NOW these be the last words of David, David the son of Jesse said, and the man who was raised up on high, the anointed of the God of Jacob, and the sweet psalmist of Israel, said, The Spirit of the LORD spake by me, and his word was in my tongue. The God of Israel said, the Rock of Israel spake to me, He that ruleth over men must be just, ruling in the fear of God." (2 Samuel 23:1–3, emphasis added)

He who rules over men must be just; he must rule in the fear of God, because whatever goes around will eventually come around. Whatever we do is cyclic. It comes back to us in full measures, pressed down, shaken together, and running over. David wasn't perfect, but he was a man after God's heart. He had on his mind the things that God had on his mind.

The children of God today suffer no fewer pangs than those of God's people of yesterday. Their trials and prisons come in different forms—but they are prisons nevertheless. We have been scourged with rods, even rods of iron. Jesus' last prayer over the disciples is striking (John 17:14–16).

If you are a child of God, you will be involved in warfare. Christianity begins with Christ, and the devil has waged war against Christ from his birth. The war is on against Christ's subjects.

Jesus carried the cross because of you and me. Crucifixion was the most degrading way anyone could die in those days, but Jesus carried it all the way to Golgotha's hill, and there he laid down his life for us. He laid down his life, but he took it up again in victory. The grave could not hold him captive—he had power over the dark domain of death and the grave.

The war is not our greatest problem, because we know of the conflict that existed between light and darkness. Our greatest problem can be our attitude towards the war and in the war.

Endurance in the battle will determine whether you finish and receive a medal and a prize, or only a certificate for participation … or nothing at all.

Wherefore seeing we also are compassed about with so great a cloud of witnesses, let us lay aside every weight, and the sin which doth so easily beset us, and let us run with patience the race that is set before us, Looking unto Jesus the author and finisher of our faith: who for the joy that was set before him endured the cross, despising the shame, and is set down at the right hand of the throne of God. (Hebrews 12:1–2)

In this age of compromise and apostasy, the clarion call is still to endure hardness as a good soldier of Jesus Christ. Nobody can actualize his full potential until he realizes that he has potential. All that you need to overcome is already within you. The children of God have spiritual strength, power, might, and bravery, but if we stay trapped in that place of cowardice, we will never discover what we have and are capable of. We are charged to endure, not to give up and run. Take your stand as one having authority.

As I began to tell you earlier, I endured some of the hardest years of my Christian walk from 1989 through 1998. I endured nine long years of shame and pain. Being young in the spirit, I struggled to handle those years. They were the years when I complained the most to God rather than praying, rejoicing, and being exceedingly glad. When you detect an ill cycle, you need to have it destroyed by the power of Almighty God.

Sarah was barren until the time of God's visitation. She became pregnant and brought forth Isaac. But the cycle, if it was a cycle indeed, was not destroyed. Rebecca was barren. Isaac interceded for her, and God gave her twins. Rachel was barren until God visited her and gave her Joseph and Benjamin. Then we see Mrs. Manoah, a daughter of the Danites. She was barren until the time of God's visitation. She gave birth to Samson. Later in the New Testament, we find Elizabeth, a daughter of Aaron, barren. This means that she was of the tribe of Levi, a son of Jacob, a son of Abraham. She was barren until the time of God's visitation. She gave birth to John the Baptist.

I don't know if this barrenness was a part of a cycle, but I know that God broke them individually. God will allow some things to happen for his glory. On the other hand, some cycles are Satanic. These must be discerned and destroyed. If they aren't destroyed, they will become a recurring cycle.

I often use the term "break the cycle," but the Holy Spirit just dropped something into my spirit. He said that there is a vast difference between breaking a cycle and destroying a cycle. I never thought of this before. The Greek derivatives from which the English word "break" comes mean to loose, to dissolve, to set at naught, or to loose that which is compacted together. The Greek words from which the English "destroy" comes is translated as to utterly destroy; to bring death to; or to ruin.

Anything that is merely broken can be repaired and salvaged, but that which is utterly destroyed cannot return. Therefore, anything in our lives that is not for the glory of God should be destroyed.

Many of the things I suffered for the sake of Christ during this period could only be destroyed by the power of the Word of God, the authority of the name and blood of Jesus Christ, the leading of the Holy Spirit, and prevailing prayer and fasting. I sought God in tears over certain situations. I needed to learn how to leap over obstacles and chop down interferences that wanted to blind my spiritual eyesight. I felt as if I was drying up and dying.

One Sunday night I was seated in a crusade. The evangelist pointed over towards the side where I sat and said, "Somebody seated over on my left side is drying up. The pain and hurts are taking a toll on you, and you are getting weak."

I didn't know who else on that side of the auditorium fit into that category, but I knew that hurts, disappointments, discouragements, and the pain from them were beating me down. I was drying up. I went to an altar of prayer.

One day in June, the Lord spoke to me saying, "I notice that you are getting dry and about to die; I am sending you on a journey. I know you do not have any money, but I will supply your needs. Your sister will accompany you."

God is not a man that he should lie. Out of the blue, several family members said to me, "You have done a lot for us. We are sending you on an all-expense paid vacation to the place of your choice." What a mighty, caring God we serve! In July one of my sisters accompanied me on my vacation. She stayed for two weeks, and I remained for four weeks. During this time, we sought the Lord together. The matriarchs and patriarchs of Zion surrounded me and prayed me through. The Lord rejuvenated me. He sent the fire of the Holy Ghost through my entire being. I did not shrivel up and die. I found comfort in Psalm 40:1–3. God showed me a better way of handling adversities. I returned to the place I now call home.

One morning I was in the spirit when the Lord said, "Follow me." I followed him, in the spirit, to an intersection. Many people were there, but five stood out from the rest. They were dressed, from head to toe, in full suits of yellow rain coats. I couldn't see the faces behind the disguise. It was meal time. As I went to the counter to pick up my food, the five people mounted five motorbikes and rode away up the winding street.

The Lord said to me, "You are on a journey, but if you follow the instructions that I give you, you will not be lost. Your journey will be uphill, but follow the path that I instruct you to take. Observe the special markers." The markers along the way were as follows:

An old two-room house stood on the hill. The elderly lady in the house would feed me and give me further instructions. Along the way there would be fruit-bearing lemon and lime trees, and there would be a significant bifurcation in the track at the top of the hill. I should make a right turn at the bifurcation. This would bring me back to the main street. I went uphill following God's instructions and found everything as God had said.

The Lord showed up at the end of the journey on the other side. I looked down the road, because I knew that the bikers dressed in yellow had ridden that way. They were nowhere to be seen. The Lord said unto me, "Do not worry about them. They are enemies. They went ahead of you to stop you, but I have brought you over by another way."

Are you tested and tried? Are you feeling dried up and possibly ready to die? Are you disappointed, discouraged, berated, and rejected? Are you feeling oppressed, depressed, used, and abused? Have you been shamed and ridiculed and left alone? Do not quit. The Master overcame all the above and much more. The believers in every age overcame all the above. The same God who brought me over by another way is still available to bring you over also.

Chapter 32
The Unfailing, Unlimited Power of Prayer

How is your prayer life? In these closing notes, I'd like to reflect on the great miracles God has wrought in my life. I have discovered the efficaciousness of prayer.

My mother told me that before my second birthday, I became very ill, and I didn't respond to any medical intervention. The medical team gave the prognosis, and it was anything but favourable. "Take her home," the doctors said. "If she lives, she lives. If she dies, come back tomorrow and I'll write you the death certificate."

A travailing mother of Zion came to the rescue. She travailed for my life. God heard her prayers, and today I'm alive and well. I'm here because somebody saw what the doctors could not see and interceded for my life.

Losing your ability to pray is like losing your ability to inhale and exhale. Everybody can pray, but not everybody can pray a strategic, intercessory, prevailing, or warfare prayer. God would have us to be intimately and powerfully connected to him. This intimate union can only be achieved through the blood of the Lamb, through a consistent prayer life, and by adherence to the precepts outlined in the Word of God. Having said this, let me hastily inject here that I thank God that it's not by man's might or by his power, but by the Spirit of God (Zechariah 4:6).

The circumstances of life can be horrible and frightening at times. Peter experienced this when he challenged Jesus to allow him to walk on water. He became afraid when he saw the boisterous winds. He began to sink, but he cried out to Jesus, who delivered him (Matthew 14:30–31).

Many folks believe that Peter began to sink when he looked at the boisterous waves. I believe that Peter began to sink when he focused his attention on the power of the waves to drown him rather than steadfastly focusing his belief on the power of Christ to save him.

In whom do you put your trust? Is it in God, or your present circumstances? Fear and faith cannot coexist. When fear knocks at your heart's door, you need to allow faith to answer it. Fear is dispelled when faith puts in its appearance. Fear shrivels up and dies when faith arises.

Fear flees when faith disembarks. Fear crumbles when faith stands up. When fear says no, faith says yes.

I have learned that God will never send you in the valley to do battle with the devil and his minions unless he equips you first on the mountain top. God would never send you to do warfare in the realm where the war between the powers of darkness and the power of light rages without anointing you with the Holy Ghost and fire.

Prayer has the capacity to break bondages, to set the captives free, to deliver the oppressed, and to set the stage and atmosphere for miracles and supernatural occurrences. God takes care of his children holistically.

God Showed Up on Mother's Day

I was ministering on Mother's Day when I saw a mother weeping bitterly. She had rejected her son because he'd had a child out of wedlock.

"Mother," I said, "you need to accept your grandchild. He might be the only one you ever have. Do you want a relationship with your son and your grandchild?" The answer was yes. "I'm going to pray," I continued, "and ask God to restore the relationship between you and your son so that you can meet your grandchild before the day is through." We called upon God and asked him to bring that wandering boy home.

After praying with her, I went to pray for another person who was desperately weeping for a backslidden child. Another woman sought prayer because of an imminent deportation. One of the criteria for her remaining in the country was employment. If she could produce proof of employment, or an offer of employment, she might be given a chance to remain. Her next visit to the immigration centre was that very Tuesday. The requests in the prayer line varied, but the presence of the Lord was very strong.

The Holy Spirit moved as we interceded for the requests. We called upon the name of the Lord to bring the backslider back to the fold. We asked God to provide employment for this woman and to stop the deportation order. While we were praying, a young man came through the front door with a baby and sat in the back pew. The first prayer was answered even before we finished praying. That mother's joy was full. She embraced her son and her grandchild. We glorified God for that instantaneous answer.

The immigration problem was solved that Tuesday. Not only did God stop the deportation order, but he gave her two job offers. She didn't have to worry about deportation. God fixed her papers.

The backslidden son returned to the fold a few months later. I know what prayer can do.

We gave God the glory. He chose to deliver three people on Mother's Day. God is worthy of our worship. We need to give him praise and glory. God is not Santa Clause and he doesn't always come when we want him to, but I guarantee that he will never be late. There are numerous times when God didn't answer my prayers instantaneously; however, even if God doesn't answer my prayers, I'm still going to give him glory, honour, and praise.

And the Rain Came Down

I vividly recalled the day I went to the shopping plaza. A thunderstorm was ready to happen. While I was shopping, the rain came down in heavy torrents. The wind blew violently, the thunder boomed, and the lightning flashed.

Wow! My brand-new car is getting a good shower, I said to myself. I didn't have to go to the car wash. Nature was washing it clean.

Outside, puddles of water settled on the ground. In other places, water flowed in streamlets towards the drain. I returned to my car, and to my utter horror discovered that the front passenger side window was opened all the way down. I couldn't remember touching that button. The only window that should have been down was the driver's side, but it was closed.

Water was running all over. The car should have been soaking wet on the inside, but thanks be unto God, not one drop of water went on the inside of that car. If the water went on the inside, it would have soaked into the electrical gadgets. I, along with three other people, had prayed over that car.

God didn't stop the rain. He rained upon every other aspect of the car, but he sent his ministering angel to cover the opened window. God prevented the car from getting damaged. It would have cost a pretty penny to clean up the car and fix the water damage inside. God protected my property, even when I didn't know that my car was in jeopardy. The eyes of the Lord are always over his children. God protects that which is important to his people.

Yea, even if death and hell assail me I will not fear, because God is with me. Sometimes I cannot feel him but I know that he is never far away. God deserves the glory. Hallelujah! My God reigns and is mighty.

Discharged with a Sentence of Death

It was a Wednesday evening when the phone rang. "Hello!" The caller was Sister Rubina. Her husband, Brother Heggy, had been sent home from the hospital to die. The doctors had given up. It was a matter of time before the death angel knocked—so the doctors said. Her husband had been asking her to call me for days, but she told him not to bother me, thinking I was tired. She changed her mind and summoned me to the home as the husband grew worse.

I showed up on Saturday afternoon. Brother Heggy was curled up in bed and burning with fever. His skin had turned to midnight black. Parts of his body were covered with scabbed pustules. He was in severe pain, especially on the left side of his body. His family did not join me at the bedside. They resorted to another section of the house.

"Brother Heggy," I said, "why did you choose to call me to pray with you and not your own pastor? I don't want any conflict."

He insisted that his pastor visited with him often, but God told him to call me because he was going to use me mightily in his miracle. I wasn't there to argue, but to execute the will of the Father. I began intercessory prayer, after which I sang healing songs. I also expounded from a healing scripture (Isaiah 53:5).

"Do you believe you're going to receive your miracle this afternoon, Brother Heggy?" I asked.

"Yes," he returned.

"Get up and sit on the edge of the bed," I instructed.

He did this despite the pain.

"Begin to give God thanks for your healing, Brother Heggy."

He did.

"Now stand upon your feet, brother, and walk."

It was a painful process, but he complied with the regime that God had set for his liberation. He walked the room.

"Now, Brother Heggy lift your hands in the air and wave them in praise and thanksgiving unto God."

He made one attempt but stopped, because the pain was excruciating.

"You can do it, my brother," I cheered him on. "In the name of Jesus Christ of Nazareth, you can do it."

Suddenly, Brother Heggy lifted his hands high in the air and began to wave them. He began to dance and shout and give God the glory, because the pain was gone. I'd never seen a grown man cried like that before. How can anyone who has received such favour from God not give him the praise, honour, and glory? It would be a sin if I took the glory that belonged to God.

Brother Heggy was healed. God removed from him the sentence of premature death. Surely, he has borne our griefs and carried our sorrows. Jesus was despised and rejected of men; a man of sorrows, and acquainted with grief. But with the stripes he received, we are healed. (Isaiah 53:3-5 paraphrased) When they finished with Jesus on the day of his crucifixion, his visage was marred beyond recognition. Jesus came and did it all for us.

I left Brother Heggy that afternoon, totally healed by the hands of our loving Father above. Even though his wife was skeptical about me coming, I went in obedience and God delivered his son.

The next Tuesday I heard a rat-a-tat-tat at my door. It was Brother Heggy. He had come to say thank you.

"Look at my skin—the scabs and the sores are gone. I am healed."

"Let's continue to give God the glory," I said. He left rejoicing and giving God thanks.

The shadow of death encompassed him, and the scavenging demons sharpened their teeth in readiness to devour him. They couldn't wait for him to die, but God extended his love towards this brother. Brother Heggy was one of the people Christ died for. There is always healing in the atonement.

Christ didn't die for this brother only, but for us all. God looked upon the importunate state of Brother Heggy and delivered him. Oh, the possibilities of prayer!

Satan, The Blood of Jesus Is Against You. I Am Coming out Alive

This next testimony is up close and very, very personal. I entered menarche (puberty), and almost immediately there was trouble. The monthly cycle became very irregular. The worst thing about the situation was that, except for the Mittelschmerz, I had no clue when the next cycle would be.

Mittelschmerz refers to the lower abdominal and pelvic pain a woman feels at the time of ovulation, or midway through the menstrual cycle. During ovulation, the mature ovum shoots from the ovary and lands in the fimbria of the fallopian tube. It is then propelled, by peristaltic motion, towards the womb, where it awaits fertilization. If there is no fertilization, the egg dies. The uterus will then shed the lining, and the result is a monthly flow. Mittelschmerz pain, or cramping, is a normal process.

I feared embarrassing accidents. By the grace of God, it happened just once in high school and once in college. Imagine a teenager having to walk every day with a bag of protection. I endured those adolescence years and then entered young adulthood. The situation grew worse. It would show up the one month, and then for the next three to five months ... nothing. Then when it did show up, it was with vengeance.

Like the woman with the issue of blood in the synoptic gospel according to Mark, I suffered many things at the hands of the physicians. The probing, the invasive procedures, came one after the other. The worst procedure ever was what they call the "transvaginal ultrasound."

I refused to subject myself to that. I stopped the technician, because I am a single Christian woman. "Satan, the blood of Jesus is against you. You are already defeated by the blood of the Lamb. I have been praying and waiting on God for total victory over the situation."

I went from one gynecologist to the other, and they all found nothing. The conclusion was that I was suffering from hormonal imbalances.

They suggested no therapy besides day surgery, so I found myself for the sixth time on the surgical bed undergoing another D & C. I despised the invasions with a passion. One day I asked the gynecologist if all the invasive procedures could cause damage.

"They aren't good," he said, "and they might cause a rupture or scarring of the uterus, but right now we have no other choice."

I became very resentful of doctors and didn't want to visit them anymore. I hated the invasion of the aspect of my being that is supposed to be private and very personal. There had to be another way. I changed doctors.

The life is in the blood, and I was losing life. The first comment that the next doctor made was: "I'm appalled that nobody suggested hormone replacement therapy." He also concluded that my problem was a hormone imbalance.

By this time, I was so anemic that when I filled out my medical records for college, the doctor refused to put my hemoglobin count on my forms. He said it would hinder me in school. He decided to give me iron injections for seven weeks to build my blood before filling out my forms. He also gave me iron pills for maintenance.

Those iron injections were painful, but I endured them. My hemoglobin was normal again, and I felt good. But the iron caused another problem. I had bouts of severe constipation that sent me weekly to the hospital for emergency enemas. Every week I saw a different doctor.

Too embarrassed to tell anyone, I suffered silently. Only my family knew what I was going through.

One Friday I went into the emergency room at 11:00 p.m. Having seen another doctor, I received an enema, with good results. The doctor promised to speak with me afterwards, but she never did. I must have fallen asleep, because when I looked at the time, it was 6:00 a.m. on Saturday. I hurried to the triage station and enquired why the doctor never came back to see me.

"We called for you," they said, "but we didn't hear you. We thought you'd left. The doctor is gone, but she left a prescription for you."

That was scary. I was in the emergency room and didn't respond to calls, but nobody bothered to check to see if I was in distress or dead. I filled the prescription—ten pills. I learned the hard way that those pills were not for constipation but for people who were experiencing premature menopause. I was prescribed the wrong pills. You can use your imagination and guess what happened. I was hospitalized immediately and had to endure an unnecessary D & C. Seven days I was in the hospital calling, "Jesus, where are you? I need your help." This episode passed, and I was placed on mineral oil to regulate the bowels. When it was regulated, I weaned myself from it.

Next, I was placed on hormones to correct the other problem.

"The pills will regulate your flow," the doctor told me. "When you're finished nursing school, come in and I'll give you a hysterectomy. If you prefer, I'll keep you on hormones until you're forty years old." He then added while tapping his pen on the desk, "I don't want to remove your womb, because you're not even thirty-five years old."

Well, the pills regulated the cycle, but they caused a greater problem. They left me with a voracious appetite. I was eating food like it was going out of style. The weight began to come. I was pushing close to two hundred pounds in body weight. This was not good. "Satan, the blood of Jesus is against you. You are defeated by the blood of the Lamb." I cried unto the Lord, because I needed to triumph over that death sentence. Again, the life is in the blood. I was losing my life in a slow, tormenting way.

By divine inspiration, I did a urine test on myself and discovered that my blood glucose level was at the high side of normal. I immediately consulted with my family doctor. He tested and made the same discovery.

"By golly," he said. "You have a tendency towards diabetes. You've gained too much weight, but if I take the pills away, the problem will return. I need to get you into a weight loss program."

The suggested program began with a charge of $350.00. I refused, because I didn't have that kind of money. I went on my own weight loss program. The weight began to fall, and so did the blood glucose levels. Everything tapered off to normal; however, I was ever conscious of the long-range effects of the pills. I spoke with my doctor, and his suggestion remained the same: a hysterectomy. That was the verdict for my future.

As I said earlier, the enemy had learned of my prophetic destiny. He wanted me dead. God had revealed emerging realities unto me, and I delivered them with compelling clarity to many people. Prophetic declarations informed me many times that I was a threat to the kingdom of darkness, which was why the enemy wanted me dead. I kept declaring: "I shall not die, but live and declare the works of Jehovah."

I was busy preaching healing through prayer and faith in God, but mine was delayed. I have seen many people received their victory over their situations. It was now twenty-two years since that menacing condition began in my own body. The doctors called it hormonal imbalance, but I called it a death sentence from hell.

As you've learned in this book, I had a multiplicity of victories over many things that should have killed me, but God destroyed the works the wicked one had against me. Twenty-two years is too long to suffer from the same condition. I told myself, "I am coming out of this one alive."

As already stated, there is a difference between deliverance and freedom. The hormone pills offered me deliverance, for a season. They remedied the situation, but only temporarily. In time, I would have to forsake the pills and be back at square one. I was a preacher preaching healing, deliverance, and freedom, but I was not free. While I was engaged in the loosing of others, I was still bound by a prevailing condition.

God had granted me victory and freedom from innumerable obstacles, but there I stood with the one that was draining my system of the substance of life—the blood. I was not going to tolerate it any longer. It had to stop. I had been in bondage for twenty-two years, but I was coming out.

One Tuesday morning I opened a new container and was about to pop a pill when the Holy Spirit began to minister to me. God said, "Put your trust in me and see what I will do."

I lifted the pills towards heaven and said, "Father, this morning I'm looking unto thee for freedom from this condition. I'm going to dispose of these pills, and by faith I'm going to believe that I will never have to take them again. You are going to free me from this health condition right now. Arise upon me now with healing in your wings. Regulate what needs to be regulated in my body. Bring those hormones under the subjection of the Holy Spirit. Bring equilibrium and bring alignment to every body member that is out of order. Thank you in advance, Father. I will never take another pill again. Thanks, Father, for performing your good words toward your humble servant."

Instantaneously, I discarded those pills. The Holy Spirit came upon me, and God gave me a brand-new endocrine and reproductive system. From that day until today, I never had that problem again. God cancelled the hysterectomy, D & C, and the pills to this day. Praise God, hallelujah! I am forever free. Not only did God grant me deliverance through medical treatment regimens, but he broke the chains of hormonal imbalance and the repercussions and set me free.

Some of you have great potential, but you're trapped by constraining illnesses that will not let you go. Some of you are fortuitous and are high achievers, but those debilitating conditions are holding you hostage. Some of you have administrative abilities, political abilities, and pastoral abilities. God has given some of you maternal and paternal excellence. You are the harbingers who will lay the foundations so that the next generation will have the nuggets that will help them become excellent achievers. We need healthy bodies and minds so that we can teach the next generation how to survive the coming night. It is almost midnight.

Some sicknesses are caused by lifestyle choices, and some by normal wear and tear of the body. But others are brought on by the works of the wicked one. The devil held a conference with his most wicked satraps. Your name is at the top of the list.

But I met the man called Jesus. I have proven that he is not only a deliverer, but a liberator. Jesus Christ set us free from the bondage of sickness. I know what prayer can do. Jesus will set you free. He set me free one day. Jesus did exactly what he said he would do—he opened the prison of those who are bound. I know what prayer can do. God delivered me from a hysterectomy and cured that hormonal imbalance that should have caused me to continue to lose life's blood.

Glory to God in the highest! He set me free. Prayer unto God is the principal thing.

Workers Compensation Case Overruled

Two years had elapsed since they closed the Workers Compensation Insurance case of this dear sister. She'd been severely injured on the job, and they refused to compensate her for her damages. She fought the case. They would only consider giving her benefits if they received new records from her doctors. All hopes seemed to be lost when the doctors failed to present records. The case was a closed deal. It was heartrending. It remained dormant for the next two years.

When I learned of the case, I began to fast and pray with her. At her request, I wrote a letter to the Workers Compensation Board. Before I released it into her hands, I asked her to hold one end of the letter while I held onto the other end. I prayed over that letter and asked God to remove every obstacle that was standing in the way of her receiving her overdue benefits. We prayed the prayer of faith, believing that God would allow the same old records to be brought back from dormancy and work in her favour. We believed God for removing every stronghold that was erected against his daughter. We claimed, in the name of Jesus, her outstanding, overdue benefits. We pursued, we overtook, and we were determined to recover all, by the power of Almighty God.

The letter was sent to the board. What do you know? The reply: We are reopening your case, and no new medical records are required. Not only was her case settled, but she received her retroactive benefits from the past two years. God came through and delivered this lady. Our God is mighty and can deliver in every aspect of our lives.

God Destroyed the July Thing

It was July. I'd been invited to be one of the speakers at an eight-day convention overseas. My sister and brother-in-law were already there on vacation. I made plans to spend some time with them after the convention. My heart was filled with elation.

I would never see my brother-in-law alive again, because just days prior to my arrival, on July 20, he became gravely ill. I prayed long and hard, but he never recovered. He died and was laid to rest. It was devastating, because I couldn't even attend the funeral service. This death was hard to handle. It was only by the grace of God that I preached without breaking down.

Strange things followed. Eight months later, another family member was discovered dead in his home. A massive cardiac arrest was the verdict. He was also laid to rest. During his funeral service, my oldest living brother made this statement in a tribute: "I will see you soon, my brother." My spirit grew angry as I listened to the tape recording of the funeral service. This was March.

Four months later in July, I marked the one-year anniversary of my brother-in-law's passing. His memorial service was set in order. Two weeks before the date, one of my cousins died. That funeral service would be held in the morning, and the memorial service would be in the evening. During the funeral service, my oldest brother, Uriah, affectionately called John, had just finished singing in the choir. He was the same brother who three months earlier at the younger brother's funeral service said, "I will see you soon, my brother." Brother John suffered a massive heart attack and died right there in the funeral service of our cousin. One set of undertakers took one family member to the grave, and another set took the other family member to the morgue.

Once again, I went into a season of prayer. It hadn't yet dawned on me that this was a carefully orchestrated plan from the dark world to bring trouble upon me every July. All my money was going towards burying the dead.

I was in the middle of a two-day conference when I learned of my brother's death. I had two more sessions: Sunday morning and Sunday night. I contemplated whether to cancel or not, but the Lord told me not to cancel. Sunday morning came. As I drove myself to the second day of this symposium, I heard a voice saying, "Accident! Accident! Accident!"

I drove exceptionally carefully that Sunday morning. I prayed and bound up the forces of darkness and averted at least one traffic accident along the way. "Thank God," I muttered when I arrived at the meeting place. No accident along the way. But before I could park, I found myself in the wake of a minor accident.

Imagine yourself going to preach while burdened with the death of a loved one. This happened at almost the same time the previous year. God granted me supernatural favour. I preached like I'd never preached before. July! I buried my brother.

There was something about July, and I had to find out what it was. I sought the Father. "Father, what is going on?" I asked. "I'm losing my substance to death and destruction. This must stop. Father, what is going on?"

The Father replied, "What is happening to you is called the 'July Thing.' The 'thing' is come to destroy you and to deplete your mental, physical, and financial resources."

"'July Thing,' you must go," I uttered authoritatively. I kept on interceding, but only months later, and before the next July, another family member perished in a fire.

I Know What Prayer Can Do

It was now July again, two years after the first offense. I was coming towards an intersection, and the traffic lights began to turn from green to amber. I pressed on my brakes attempting to stop behind the other car, and a most dangerous thing happened. My shoe fell from my foot and became lodged between the brake pedal and the gas pedal. It was as if the shoe was holding the gas pedal down. I was headed right into the car in front of me. I pressed on the brakes, but the shoe, like an iron column, held it up. The car kept moving. I cried out unto the Lord, and my car stopped right at the tip of the car in front of me bumper. I switched on the hazards light and then placed the car in park. I bent down and yanked the shoe away.

To say I was mad is an understatement. I was raging mad at whatever was set to happen. I pulled over into a parking lot and shut down the car. I called upon the name of the Lord in intercessory prayer and supplication.

"July Thing," I thundered, "be thou destroyed not tomorrow, not next year, but be thou destroyed now, in the name of Jesus. Satan, the blood of Jesus is against you. You have already been defeated by the blood of the Lamb. From this day forward, you shall have no more power or dominion over me, my belongings, anybody or anything that is related to or connected to me, whether directly or indirectly. Devil, I destroy your cyclic torment, intimidation, and destruction, not only in July, but in every other month of the year, in the name of Jesus. Do not ever come back again."

Six years has passed. God liberated me from the "July Thing." I have not stopped praying. I didn't understand it, but God knew and understood. The July curse had to be stopped and destroyed. Only God could do it, because he saw ahead and knew ahead. I needed to stay in tune with God so that I could learn the devil's next move. The stalker will sit around and wait for your unguarded hour. Watch and pray.

I prayed, and God delivered me from the avenging onslaught of the wicked one. Sisters and brothers, prayer unto God remains the noblest communication that his children could ever have with him. Prayer is the life-line connecting us to the Father. Do not cease to pray.

Not Qualified, but the Job Is Yours

Prayer and the power of God can bring you an employment position even if you're not deemed qualified. Just a few years ago, I was interviewed for a position. During the interview, I learned that I wasn't qualified for the job because I needed to have two years of experience in the field. It was disappointing; however, I was offered another job for which I met the criteria.

I began to work at the second job and kept on praying, because I knew that the will of God must be accomplished in my life. Two years prior, God had brought me, in the spirit, and showed me the place and told me that it would be my next place of employment.

It was a one-year contract position. At the end of the probationary year, I would be evaluated. I prayed and asked God for exceptional favour. I must have meaningful employment in order to meet the financial demands of my life. I had no doubt that God would open heaven's storehouse and send down covenantal blessings.

God promised not to withhold any good thing from those who walk according to his plan and his purpose. I arose early and prayed through that place every day. Every now and then, I teamed with another co-worker and prayed through the place. Not only did I see miracles wrought in that place, but I also saw God stop contemplations of suicide and murder.

Three months into the probationary period, I was called upon to do the job for which I wasn't qualified. This stunned a few people, because they knew I was turned down due to my lack of experience in the field. God moved marvellously and showed everyone that if he wanted me to do the job, he would make it possible for me to do the job. Here I was (the one who was not qualified) doing two different jobs—and let me add, I was doing them excellently.

Six months later I was offered not only a full-time position with all the benefits, but also the lead position in the second job. God is mightier than the mighty. He is stronger than the strong. If God says you can, you can. God promotes and demotes. God can move any obstacle and turn things around so that you will be granted favor.

The Lord allowed me to do both jobs. The king is responsible for his children. When he speaks, his words are accomplished. God will allow you to have even that for which you have no credentials.

I know what prayer can do.

Beyond the Veil in Prayer

Prayer works. When a life goes off course and out of alignment with the Word of God, prayer can recalibrate that life and lead the person away from the paths of destruction and back to the path of life ... that is, if you believe and pray.

Prayer can rejuvenate the life that is spiritually cold, dry, and dead. Prayer can shut down all territorial demonic activities. Prayer can mend broken relationships. Prayer can radically eradicate those cancer formations in your system, and every other sickness that is prevailing against you. The prevailing prayer can intercept the messengers of Satan who are sent to torment and disturb your peace. The prevailing prayer will crash the devil's delivery vehicles.

Prayer confuses the enemies in such a way that they lose their sense of direction, hearing, and their power of speech. God will push the mute button on the enemies so that they will lose their sense of communication. When prayer goes up, God will demolish the devil's headquarters and his plans. God will cause his glory to shine forth in the dark places.

God knows how to rectify the spiritual deformities occurring in the body of Christ. God knows how to correct every spiritual developmental deviation found in our personal lives and in the ecclesia (Isaiah 1:5–6; Luke 10:33–34).

God Is Able—Believe with Me

A change is coming! A phenomenal change is about to erupt in your life, in your ministry, in your relationships with God and man, in your finances, in your marriage, and in your health. You are about to experience a miracle that will affect your entire life.

By faith, those who despised and rejected you must confess with their tongues and repent. In the name of Jesus, every weapon that is formed against you shall be rendered powerless. By the power of the Holy Ghost, every standing order, every lie, every vendetta, and every scheme of the devil and his agents will be dissolved into nothingness.

Prayer will flush out and bring to light every secret thing that the devil is devising. Prayer will expose the gallows and the gins that the spirits like Haman have hung or set. The devil's head is already bruised. You are anointed and appointed to stampede upon what is left of his head. God will drive out the devil and his compatriots from before you.

You are blessed, not just with the dunamis power of God, but with the exousia power of God. This means that you have demonstrative power as well as authoritative power, in the name of Jesus. You have a right to homologeo (to speak the same) as God.

I have laid my life down at the foot of the cross. I have washed myself in the laver of the Word of God. I have fed my soul with the food of champions. I have offered up intercessory prayer. Now I will wait on the Lord for the answer.

I pray that personal, local, and international revival will come shortly as you continue to lift him up. Be touched by the presence of the Lord. Give him the glory, give him the praise, and give him the honour as you nestle in his embrace.

Prayer is not just a weapon, but one of the principal weapons that God has placed in the spiritual arsenal of his people. Use prayer to the honour and glory of God. If you have a weapon that you've never tested, you'll never know if it will work.

A person who can pray a prevailing prayer will have power, because prayer is power. If prayer has no power, God would never encourage us to pray without ceasing. Pray without ceasing simply means that you should continue, even when the answer isn't obvious.

According to Mordecai, if Esther did not bring his petition to the attention of the king, the Jews would have to seek enlargement and deliverance elsewhere. They didn't realize that God was about to add another chapter in the history of humanity. Esther's willingness to approach the king uninvited was the epitome of what Jesus would do at his crucifixion. When Jesus was crucified, the veil of the temple was rent from top to bottom. The ordinary Christian can now enter the presence of the king to make prayer and intercession. I am coming to the king, and if I am chastised, then so be it—but I am coming. Now is the time to stand boldly and execute the jurisdictional authority God has granted you.

Why pray in the outer court when the Lord has given us access to the holy of holies? It is time to press into the next dimension of prayer. God is still at the mercy seat in heaven. His ears are still open to the cries of his people. Jesus stripped the devil of his power. As the scripture says, Jesus made a public spectacle of Satan and his minions. I know what prayer can do.

Dedication

I dedicate this book unto the blessed Lord Jesus Christ, the anointed Son of God, who has brought me a mighty long way and has done great things for me whereof I am glad. Thank you, mighty Father, for not casting me away when I became marred, warped, and twisted out of shape by sin. You have broken me, sifted me, and allowed me to pass through the refiner's fire of affliction. You have remodelled me into a vessel of your likeness.

Fiery trials have made a golden Christian out of me. I praise you, I honour you, and I glorify your name. I appreciate you, Lord. Thank you, Father; thank you, Jesus; and thank you, blessed Holy Spirit. I avail myself to be used mightily of you.

Acknowledgements

The memory of my mother, Miss Jane, can never be blotted out, because she taught me to pray. Mama is gone, but I will never forget her. I will love and cherish her memory forever. O that she had lived to see this day. I thank God for Ma Jane.

Unto my family, I extend my gratitude. You are all inclusive, whether you are a part of the bloodline or whether you came through the bond of matrimony. I love you all and would not trade any of you for another. Thank you, family, for your supportive shoulders over the ages (Mable, Shirley, Winston, Fredrick, Angela, Bentley, Barry, Suzette, and all your children). A special thanks to Sister Nissa and Brother James, who brought me to Canada. I cannot repay you for all the things you did and are still doing. I pray that we will have more beautiful years together. Love you, my family. Thanks, all.

Words are not enough to express my thanks to Sister Sally. You are a great friend. Thanks to Sister Maud and Brother Sterling for your kindness towards a single lady. Thanks to Rev. Sharlene Level-Smith, my batch mate in ministry. There are blessings in good relationships. Thanks to all my spiritual sons and daughters.

As a member of a covenant community of believers, I would be amiss if I did not thank God for the members of the clerical order of my home church. I ascribe my deepest veneration unto you all. Very special thanks to the people of prayer and intercession who never ceased to make mention of my name unto the Lord.

When I was a babe in Christ, a brother approached me and, without hesitation, said, "Sister Cordell, if you continue to preach like this, you are going to be a great evangelist someday." Thanks, Brother Beresford, for that prophetic declaration. God never failed. Thanks, Sister Sybil, for that Psalm over thirty years ago. It still blesses me.

Thanks to everyone who has contributed to my Christian growth and spiritual grooming.

Thanks to all those who lay hold of the spiritual spoon and stir me. You viewed me as a fruit bottom yogurt. You knew that somewhere deep inside my being there were good things that needed to surface. Thanks for stirring up the gift that is in me. Like Moab, I had settled on my lees, but you stirred me so that I would pour out from vessel to vessel. I could not have done it without you all. Thanks.

Thanks to all who call me "Mom." Thanks for authenticating my maternal gifting. I would like to say especially to the younger generation that it satisfies my motherly heart to have you under my tutelage. I am blessed to be one of your tutors. As a matriarch of prayer, it gives me great pleasure to be among those investors who have deposited viable nuggets into your lives. I love you all and I bless you, in the name of Jesus. My prayer is that you will all become a part of that great body of revolutionaries who God is lifting up in this end-time season. You will be the next pastors, evangelists, missionaries, teachers, lawyers, doctors, and businessmen. You will be the next ladies and gentlemen who will sit in the highest seats of government. You will be the next set of trailblazers who will turn the apostate nations back to God.

I decree and I declare that you will lift the sword of the Spirit, which is the Word of God, without shame or cowardice. You will be like spiritual gladiators. You will use the power of the Word of God to chase the devil and his emissaries out of your territories. You will valiantly pursue the enemy; you will overtake, and you will recover all.

I decree and I declare that you will possess and repossess every territory that the enemy has stolen, in Jesus name. You will be more than conquerors. I endeavour to be unto you, "one of the fighter escorts." You will never enter the battle alone. Be tyrants for God, young people. Do not back up; do not back down; do not back out. Do not give up; do not give in. As Ephesians 6:12 says, "You wrestle not against flesh and blood, but against principalities and powers, against the rulers of the darkness of this world, against spiritual wickedness in high place."

God has given unto you the skills of valiant wrestlers. I impart unto you the spiritual moves and maneuvres of a skillful wrestler. In the arena of spiritual conflict there are fights, battles, and wars, but you have the skills of motion, stance, back arch, back step, penetration, level change, and lift. You shall be victors and not victims. When your names appear on the billboards of time, they will not be for something criminal, but for something noble.

Do not stop to inquire about every little thing that demands attention, but seek for those things that are congenial to who you are and who God has called you to be. I decree and I declare that you will be men and women of purpose. You are children of destiny with promising prospects. You have sharpness of minds and the affinity for creativity.

I pray that the spirit of dedication and commitment will be upon you. I reverse every order of diffidence and pray that you will be diligent in application and pursuit. I pray that you will not be procrastinators, but that you will be sedulous and persistent in your undertakings, according to the will of God. I pray that you will be people of good character and moral decency. You will flee youthful lusts and sexual perversions. I pray that you will be endowed with the obedience of Abraham, the chastity of Ruth and Joseph, the tenacity of Moses and Joshua, the cunningness of Bezaleel and Aholiab, the patience of Hannah and Job, the boldness of David and Gideon, the wisdom of Solomon, the courage of Daniel, the endurance of Meshach, Shadrach and Abednego, the persistence of Peter, the intellect of Paul, and the insight of Issachar. May the excellent spirit of Jesus Christ be upon you all, and may the indwelling presence of the Holy Spirit be within you. May you live for God and not die.

I pray that our youth will have the visual acuity of the eagle. You will be able to see into the deep things of God. You will be endued with the gifts of revelators. I pray that our progeny will be like efficacious salt. They will go into the world and change the putrefactive decay caused by sin. They will be changers of the atmosphere like the woman who broke her alabaster box and anointed Jesus. I pray that our youth everywhere will be like light and shine like Jesus shines in the dark recesses of the world, exposing sin and claiming sinners for God. Young people, be that light that attracts people to Christ.

I declare that this generation is the "cross-over" generation. You will go in, dispossess the rebel spirits, and possess that which the former generation failed to possess.

Finally, young people, you are potentials. Aim high to achieve success and excellence. Do not become liabilities in society, but become assets. When the day is done, you will sit as diadems upon the crowns of those who love you.

I speak this word to young people everywhere, especially my own. God bless you all abundantly.

In His Majesty's Service: Rev. Cordell May Thorpe

Disclaimer

While every testimony is authentic, some names have been changed to maintain privacy. Therefore, I cannot be held responsible for breach of confidentiality by anyone who might have similar name or situations as the ones mentioned in this book. —Author

About the Author

Reverend Cordell May Thorpe is one of those people who had the strength to make a comeback after every setback in her life. If God had not been with her, she would have given up and died many decades ago. Those lying words from hell that she was told continuously from the tender age of four years old and up kept revisiting as she advanced in age and in life: **"A child like you will never amount to anything in life. You will only go this far and turn back."**

Reverend Thorpe recalls a time in secondary school when she was voted the top student of the year and was selected for first prize at graduation. Some folks argued that she should not get the prizes even though she qualified; nevertheless, she received the prizes.

One of her greatest assets in her life is that she is a warfare prayer warrior. She has learned how to touch heaven and then believe God to reverse standing orders, to block upcoming orders, and to destroy generational curses. Cordell says, "God is a bondage breaker, and he is also a way- maker." Whenever the kingdom of darkness rises against her to bring her mind into captivity, she finds solace in the Word of God and in prayer.

After high school, Cordell attended Medical Administrative & Business Schools and received her credentials. She was turned down for every job she applied for. The words kept coming back to taunt her: "A

child like you will never amount to anything in life. You will only go this far and turn back." She just kept on trying. She will not be defeated.

Oppositions did not stop her from accomplishing her childhood dream—registered nurse. She was nominated for the award of excellence at graduation. Once again, she was rejected and the award given to a person who, made medication errors and slept on the job.

Her greatest achievements came when she answered the call to ministry. She became an ordained minister of Jesus Christ. She now operates as an itinerant evangelist, blazing trails and winning souls for the Kingdom of God. She also busied herself doing conferences, crusades, seminars and retreats. Hell cannot prevail against anyone who trusts God completely.

The Lord opened another new and effectual door unto her in the educational system. Reverend Thorpe is presently a professor/instructor equipping students in healthcare, student success strategies and professional skills. She is an excellent teacher of theology.

Like Jesus, she overcame some vicious, demonic beasts in the wilderness. God delivers her every time. This great woman of God advises: "Stand your ground. Failure does not have to be final. Never let yesterday's setbacks bankrupt today's efforts or block tomorrow's visions."

Cordell looks at herself and declares, "The devil was a liar then, and he is still the most notorious liar from hell." The circumstances of life staggered her, but they have not stopped her. This gracious, highly favoured woman of God keeps going from strength to strength. (By: N.T.)

"And [she] shall be like a tree planted by the rivers of water, that bringeth forth [her] fruit in her season; [her] leaf also shall not wither; and whatsoever [she] doeth shall prosper." (Psalm 1:3)